P9-DDP-498

OTTAWA

Ottawa's Enterprises by Beverly Goldfarb,
Marcus Davies, and Hugh Nangle

Produced in cooperation with the
Ottawa-Carleton Board of Trade

Windsor Publications, Ltd.
Burlington, Ontario

OTTAWA

MORE THAN A CAPITAL CITY

A Contemporary Portrait by Jane Wilson

Windsor Publications, Ltd.—History Books Division
Managing Editor: Karen Story
Design Director: Alexander d'Anca

Staff for *Ottawa: More Than a Capital City*
Manuscript Editor: Amy Adelstein
Photo Editor: Larry Molmud
Senior Production Editor, Corporate Profiles: Phyllis Gray
Assistant Production Editor, Corporate Profiles: Albert Polito
Editor, Corporate Profiles: Judith L. Hunter
Editorial Assistants: Phyllis Feldman Schroeder, Kim Kievman, Michael Nugwynne, Kathy B. Peyser, Priscilla Solis, Theresa J. Solis
Publisher's Representative, Corporate Profiles: John Bryant
Layout Artist, Corporate Profiles: Bonnie Felt

Design and Layout: Christina L. Rosepapa

ISBN: 0-89781-303-0

Published 1989
Printed in Canada
First Edition

Windsor Publications, Ltd.
Elliot Martin, Chairman of the Board
James L. Fish III, Chief Operating Officer
Michele Sylvestro, Vice President/Sales-Marketing

PREVIOUS PAGE: Heralding another year in Ottawa, a fireworks display lights up Parliament Hill on New Year's Eve. Photo by Greg Locke/ First Light

RIGHT: The Parliament Buildings are in silhouette at day's end. Photo by Dykstra Photos/ The Stock-Market

CONTENTS

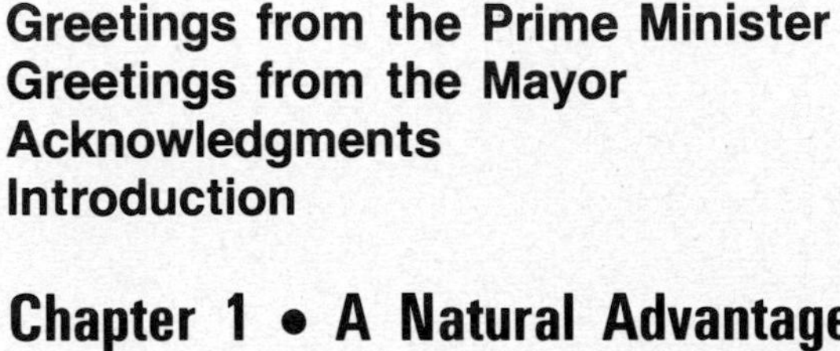

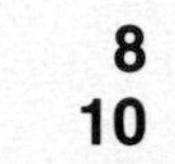

PRIME MINISTER · PREMIER MINISTRE

I am pleased to have been asked to convey my greetings and best wishes to the readers of **Ottawa: More Than a Capital City** by Jane Wilson in cooperation with the Ottawa-Carleton Board of Trade.

To my mind, the attraction of Ottawa is its symmetry of parkland and urban space, historic architecture complemented by new edifices, small businesses interacting with government, and the merging of Canada's two principal cultures within the city.

Both visitors to Ottawa and residents of the city acclaim its elegance and express pride in the Nation's Capital. They speak of the facilities and activities that reflect every season and every interest.

I trust that you will find this publication informative and a welcome addition to your library.

Brian Mulroney

OTTAWA

CITY OF OTTAWA
CITY HALL
111 SUSSEX DRIVE
K1N 5A1
(613) 564-1342

VILLE D'OTTAWA
HOTEL DE VILLE
111, PROMENADE SUSSEX
K1N 5A1
(613) 564-1342

JAMES A. DURRELL

MAYOR MAIRE

To use the title of the book, Ottawa is really much more than a capital city. It is a vibrant, prosperous and developing community striving towards a position of leadership in the 21st century. It gives me great pleasure to have this opportunity to extend official City of Ottawa greetings to all those who will be enjoying Ottawa: More Than a Capital City.

This cooperative effort between author Jane Wilson, Windsor Publications and the Ottawa-Carleton Board of Trade is a timely essay on the most beautiful capital city in the world. It is an in-depth look at a community which manages to successfully combine the new and the old; a city which manages to cope with the development of the 1980's whilst not losing the quality of life.

I congratulate everyone associated with this venture. I am pleased to see this type of literature on a city which means a great deal to all of us.

Yours sincerely,

James A. Durrell,
Mayor.

The face of the Peace Tower Clock is seen through the corner structures of the East Block. Photo by Devries Mikkelsen/ First Light

ACKNOWLEDGMENTS

We have a little routine in our family: whenever we are returning home after a trip away, a weekend in Toronto where I was born, or an evening with friends in the Gatineaus, there is always a point in the journey where we round a turn or come over a hill, and "There it is!" . . . home. Whether we see it as glittering city lights and the splendour of the Peace Tower and Library of Parliament, reflected in the calm of the Ottawa River, or as a metropolis that spans the river valley, its buildings reaching upward against the blue backdrop of the Gatineau Hills, Ottawa is home, now.

It has been a pleasure to write about the city I have come to love, but I couldn't have done it alone, not without the help of the many people who cheerfully volunteered information about the city, or who told me charming tales about the way it used to be. I met countless marvellous people who work for museums, government departments, institutions, and private companies, who all went out of their way to help.

In particular I should thank Louis Valenzuela, who recommended me for this book, and Anne Besharah, Frank Soriano, and Rhonda Birenbaum for their support.

Thanks also to the following: Howard Bloom, Brian Card, Patrick Mikhail, Mary Ann Smythe, Sharleen Bannon, Stan Seymour, and Maria Chiarelli.

Last, to my husband Norrie and to Jeremy and Madeleine for indulging me and "the book," my love and thanks.

INTRODUCTION

Most people in Canada—and probably throughout North America—can easily identify one particular image associated with Ottawa. It is, after all, what we see on the postcards, in the coffee table books of photographs of Canada, on the nightly TV news: that majestic view of the Peace Tower on Parliament Hill which is a symbol of Canada and its government.

There are other familiar images of Ottawa: tulips bending gracefully to the tourists who pass along the Queen Elizabeth Drive in spring; skaters gliding happily on the Rideau Canal in winter; the porte cochère at Rideau Hall, through which queens, princes, and heads of state have passed; and, of course, the Parliament Buildings themselves, the solid gray stone and green copper roofs accented by the red coats of the Mounties and the Governor General's Foot Guard in dress uniform.

This is the Ottawa that is known and loved by people across Canada, our capital city, and the embodiment of what we believe Canada to be.

But there is another Ottawa, beyond the imposing stone buildings of government, and the pomp and circumstance of summer rituals. There is a lively, eager, and vital city that surrounds the heart of Ottawa, a city that is perhaps unseen by the usual onlooker. It is difficult to miss the Parliament Buildings in which the House of Commons conducts the country's business, but outside the iron gates on The Hill, another business community

Left: A parade makes its way down an avenue in Parliament Hill. Photo by Wayne Eardley/Burke Communications Photography

Facing page: This spectacular vista is from Champlain Lookout. Photo by Wayne Eardley/Burke Communications Photography

Facing page: A jogger passes a familar landmark at Remic Lookout. Photo by Wayne Eardley/ Burke Communications Photography

thrives in splendid modern buildings of steel and glass, or in reverently renovated heritage sites.

Our national festivals of the arts are well publicized, but those who have not walked through the city know nothing of Ottawa's street singers and blues bands, or of the charming outdoor cafés in the Byward Market and along Elgin Street, or of the city-sponsored outdoor concerts and plays for children.

Our climate might seem to be severe if one looked simply at the temperatures listed in the newspaper each day, but the truth is our summers are a delight, with days as warm and sunny as any in California, and nights that are refreshingly cool. And winter? The average Ottawan laughs at snow and ice—Old Man Winter brings us a different kind of fun! Skiing is just minutes away in the Gatineau Hills, and in the city's centre is the world's longest maintained skating rink, the Rideau Canal.

The world has come to Ottawa, with embassies and high commissions from most countries located in the city and the resulting social and diplomatic circle of international figures, but less well known, perhaps, is the fact that Ottawa's population is itself a representation of the world. The Italians, Chinese, Lebanese, and Vietnamese are just a few of the cultural groups who have chosen Ottawa as home, and who have given the city a new and vibrant flavour.

The National Arts Centre is the showcase of Canadian culture in Ottawa, the capital city, but Ottawa is also a centre for culture in Eastern Ontario, showing off a vigorous theatre community, dance groups, music of all kinds, and a prestigious school of art.

What else is this city? It is a historic settlement whose story parallels the story of Canada itself. It is a city of incredible beauty, set amongst forest and farmland between two rivers. It is the scene of Canada's burgeoning high technology industry, and a centre of learning and research.

Most of all, though, Ottawa is people: more than three-quarters of a million people call the capital region "home." The people of Ottawa are literally the salt of the earth—we work hard, we play hard, and we care about other people. It's a city that welcomes visitors and newcomers with a smile and a helping hand.

It's a capital place.

A local radio station recently provided this fun-filled promotional bus tour. Photo by Wayne Eardley/Burke Communications Photography

This luminous image of a canoe manned by voyageurs was painted by Mrs. F.W. Hopkins. Courtesy, National Archives of Canada

1

A NATURAL ADVANTAGE

Bytown and its environs astonishes me; I have walked ten miles to view the river scenery and, though much fatigued, am highly gratified. This place has a large trade and will increase with the prosperity of the country around it; nature seems to have destined it for the site of a great city.

—William Lyon Mackenzie
October 11, 1851

As civilized and refined a city as Ottawa is now, the land upon which it sits was, before the nineteenth century, a place of savage beauty. The area around the meeting place of the Rideau and Ottawa rivers was dense forest through which ran a network of smaller rivers and creeks. In the wide valley that embraced the powerful waters of the Ottawa, deer, bear, and beavers coexisted with the Algonquin and the Outaouais, tribes of Indians who lived by hunting and fishing, and by growing crops of corn and beans on the fertile land.

The Ottawa River was first travelled by Europeans in the year 1610, and afterward was used by explorers, missionaries, fur traders, soldiers, and the *coureurs de bois* as the route inland from Montreal. Many now famous men travelled on the Ottawa: Samuel de Champlain, Pierre Esprit Radisson and Médard Chouart des Groseilliers, the Jesuits Father Jean de Brébeuf and Le Moyne Sieur d'Iberville, as well as explorers Sir Martin Frobisher, Sir Alexander Mackenzie, and the Earl of Selkirk.

The French developed an alliance

Three chiefs of the Huron Nation pose in their native dress in an English painting from 1825. Courtesy, National Archives of Canada

1

A NATURAL ADVANTAGE

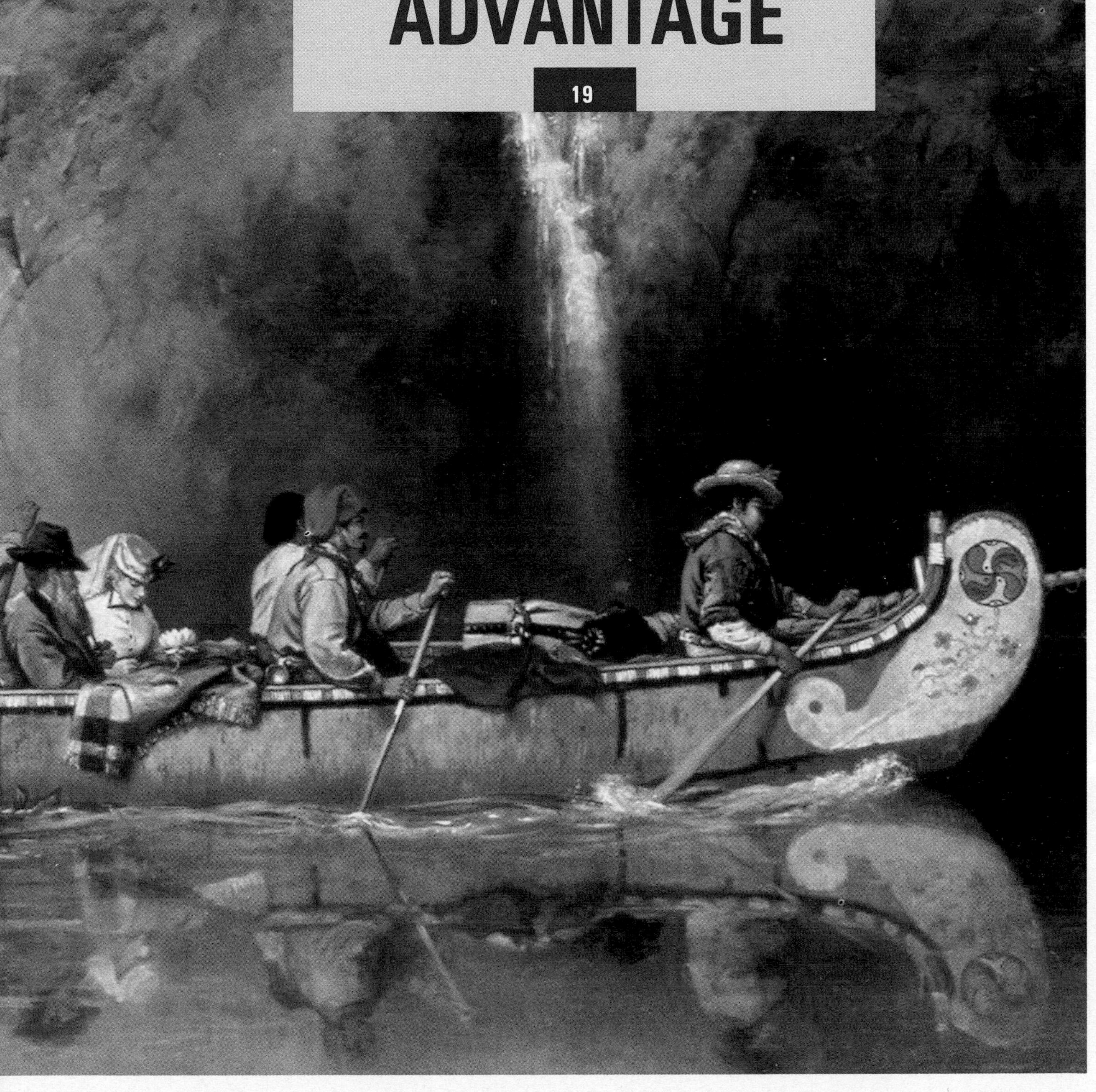

Bytown and its environs astonishes me; I have walked ten miles to view the river scenery and, though much fatigued, am highly gratified. This place has a large trade and will increase with the prosperity of the country around it; nature seems to have destined it for the site of a great city.

—William Lyon Mackenzie
October 11, 1851

As civilized and refined a city as Ottawa is now, the land upon which it sits was, before the nineteenth century, a place of savage beauty. The area around the meeting place of the Rideau and Ottawa rivers was dense forest through which ran a network of smaller rivers and creeks. In the wide valley that embraced the powerful waters of the Ottawa, deer, bear, and beavers coexisted with the Algonquin and the Outaouais, tribes of Indians who lived by hunting and fishing, and by growing crops of corn and beans on the fertile land.

The Ottawa River was first travelled by Europeans in the year 1610, and afterward was used by explorers, missionaries, fur traders, soldiers, and the *coureurs de bois* as the route inland from Montreal. Many now famous men travelled on the Ottawa: Samuel de Champlain, Pierre Esprit Radisson and Médard Chouart des Groseilliers, the Jesuits Father Jean de Brébeuf and Le Moyne Sieur d'Iberville, as well as explorers Sir Martin Frobisher, Sir Alexander Mackenzie, and the Earl of Selkirk.

The French developed an alliance

Three chiefs of the Huron Nation pose in their native dress in an English painting from 1825. Courtesy, National Archives of Canada

A Dutch print from 1665 shows Jesuit missionaries Jean De Brébeouf and Gabriel L'allemant rather stoically receiving martyrdom at the hands of their Indian captors. The tranquil background was used to offset the graphic details of the action, as it was felt that refined European sensibilities were not completely comfortable with the realities of the new world. Courtesy, National Archives of Canada

Three Ottawa Indians pose in an illustration from an 1801 French publication on British possessions in North America. Courtesy, National Archives of Canada

the Algonquin, even so far as helping them to fight off the marauding Iroquois who travelled up the Rideau River periodically to raid Algonquin villages. At the same time, the Algonquin had friendly relations with the Huron, a tribe that lived on Lake Huron, and acted as intermediaries, trading the Huron's furs for European goods.

In later years, after the British conquest of the French, they too recognized the Ottawa River's potential as the centre of development. In fact, the British government commissioned two expeditions to explore the regions that bordered the Ottawa and Rideau rivers. At this point, both river valleys were largely untouched and unexplored; the only people who knew them at all were Indians and fur traders, and no one knew what lay beyond the valleys. The result of the expeditions was a recommendation that this part of British North America be developed and settled.

The American Revolution was another crucial factor in the eventual settlement of the Ottawa-Rideau River area; when the

Americans declared themselves independent of Britain in 1776, thousands of the Empire Loyalists who had supported Britain in the conflict decided to move north to make a new home in Canada. Other settlers came because they had heard of the rich, undeveloped land. Because hostilities continued between Britain and the United States and because Canada was then a British colony, traffic on the St. Lawrence River was believed to be vulnerable to attack by the Americans. The British began to look for other routes inland, and for a time considered the Rideau River as a possible route, thereby enhancing interest in settlement near the river.

By the end of the century, many people had guessed at the tremendous potential for development near the Ottawa River, the most significant being Philemon Wright. An American from Massachusetts, he visited the valley in 1797 and

Communities like Perth, Richmond, Hull and the March Colony, shown in this Bartlett print, were well established before Bytown. Courtesy, Public Archives of Canada

LEFT: Philemon Wright sent the first timber rafts down the Ottawa River. In this 1930 painting, Charles Williams Jeffreys links the two early uses of the great river, as Wright is passed by fur traders. Courtesy, Public Archives of Canada

BELOW: Philemon Wright settled at the Chaudière Falls in the area of the City of Hull, Quebec, 25 years before the founding of Bytown. Wright is noted for his great river drives of lumber downstream to Montreal at the beginning of the nineteenth century. Courtesy, Historical Society of Ottawa

FACING PAGE: Early French settlers, led by the church, were successful in dealing with the native tribes in Canada. This stylized painting by A.S. Scott depicts Champlain's wife teaching Indian children from a "Book of Hours" around 1620. Courtesy, National Archives of Canada

recognized the immenseness of the timber resource. In the year 1800, Wright moved his family and a team of labourers to Hull township, on what is now the Quebec side of the Ottawa River. Wright brought people with many skills along with him so that the settlement he founded, known for many years as Wrightville, quickly became a village. It was Wright's dream to make a fortune on the lumber trade, but wisely, he determined that the community should be able to sustain itself and ordered that land be cleared for agriculture too.

Wright is an important figure in the history of Ottawa because it was he who began the great river drives of lumber downstream to Montreal in 1806. His determination to harvest the forest resources was the beginning of the lumber trade in the Ottawa Valley, and his early success doubtless encouraged others to settle the area. Many of them were descendants of American families, such as Braddish Billings, whose house still stands today on a hill in Ottawa South.

The steamer *Ottawa* passes the peaceful *Junction of the Gatineau with the Ottawa River* in a lithograph from Hunter's *Ottawa Scenery*, published in 1855. Courtesy, Public Archives of Canada

THE RIDEAU CANAL

The British continued to worry about the safety of ships travelling the St. Lawrence between Montreal and Kingston, a situation made worse by the War of 1812. Suggestions had been made on a number of occasions to the British government about the need for a strategic military naval route that would link Upper and Lower Canada, connecting the Ottawa and St. Lawrence rivers, but little was done about the idea until 1824. Finally, in 1826, Lieutenant-Colonel John By of the Royal Engineers arrived in Quebec from England with orders to design and construct the Rideau Canal.

The year 1826 was a turning point in Ottawa's history: what is now Wellington Street, a principal artery in the city and the location of the Parliament Buildings, was then just a scrubby plot of land covered in stumps and boulders, scarred by piles of earth left from excavations by settlers. The people who had settled in the area, many of them officers in the British forces who had been given plots of land after the War of 1812, inhabited simple log cabins and lived off the land, collecting their water from the many springs in the area that is now Bank Street. But soon this backwoods settlement was transformed into a construction site and the home for many professionals and military men and their families.

Lieutenant-Colonel By arrived in Hull township in the early autumn of 1826, after the arrival of the then governor-in-chief, the Earl of Dalhousie. Together they laid out a plan for the town around the construction site and plotted the canal route. Winter was not a good time to begin such an undertaking, however, and By left to return again the following spring.

This famous watercolour of Lieutenant-Colonel By watching the building of the Rideau Canal was painted for the Chateau Laurier by C.W. Jeffreys. By stands with Thomas MacKay, his masonry builder. Courtesy, Public Archives of Canada

In March of 1827, historians tell us, the Earl of Dalhousie also returned to visit the settlement at the canal site, and at a celebration dinner all in attendance decided that the community, which formerly had been called Richmond Landing or Chaudière Falls, would from then on be known as Bytown, after the chief engineer.

One of the settlers who had already come to the town from England to work with Philemon Wright was Nicholas Sparks, who, in 1821, bought a 200-acre tract of land from another man without seeing it. It is said that when Sparks first viewed the swampy land he'd bought, he sat down and cried; he couldn't know then that this property would later comprise downtown Ottawa, but he must at least have been cheered by the knowledge that the canal was to cut through his land, and the government had offered to buy a portion of it. Actually, the government representatives, eager to save money on the project, thought the price Sparks wanted for the land was too high and they simply expropriated it, taking more than they needed. The land not used was returned to Nicholas Sparks, but not until 1847, when the village was a very different place.

Bytown began to grow rapidly: workers were brought to the site from Britain, many of them poor labourers from Ireland. A number of French Canadian workers were also attracted by the prospect of steady work. The population of the village reached nearly 1,000 in the first years of the canal construction.

The canal served to divide Bytown in two, but the division was not merely a geographic one. Upper Town, the area west of the canal, was settled by senior officers of the Royal Engineers, contractors, and

RIGHT: *The Big Kettle,* reprinted from Wm. S. Hunter, Jr.'s *Ottawa Scenery,* shows Chaudière Falls in its early, pristine state; in another two decades, the artist would probably not recognize the place. Courtesy, National Archives of Canada

BELOW RIGHT: When Nicholas Sparks first set eyes on the 200 acres of swampy land he'd bought sight unseen, it is said he sat down and cried: he couldn't have known his property would one day comprise the metropolitan core of Ottawa. Courtesy, National Archives of Canada

RIGHT: The original municipal building of Bytown could trace its odd architecture to its beginnings as a market in 1848. It became the town hall in 1865. Courtesy, National Archives of Canada

Edwin Whitefield's color lithograph of Lower Town in 1855 looks down the Rideau River from Parliament Hill, as it flows toward the locks of the Rideau Canal. Courtesy, National Archives of Canada

FACING PAGE: Ottawa entered the modern steam age in 1854 when a track was built connecting the city to the Grand Trunk Railway at Prescott on the St. Lawrence River. This advertisement was printed in the *City Directory* of Ottawa in 1864. Courtesy, City of Ottawa Archives

professional men and their families, who were generally from England or Scotland. Lower Town, on the other hand, was where hundreds of labourers lived in poorly built cabins or shanties. Theirs was a very different Bytown, where violent fights broke out regularly between the French and Irish workers, many of whom itinerated throughout the settlement.

Colonel By was literally in charge of the town. He took some criticism for the way in which he organized—or didn't organize—the workers. It was by his design that the military and professionals lived in Upper Town on higher ground, while the desperately poor workers lived on the swampy lower ground, a situation that aided outbreaks of disease and discontent that in turn fostered violence.

The people of early Bytown got their provisions from government stores, which delivered the goods by barge from Montreal; within two years after construction of the canal began, many private businesses started up, such as Sparrows' butcher shop, and the post office and general store owned by Matthew Connell. By 1830 there were stores in both sections of the city but mainly in Lower Town, including shops owned by watchmakers, milliners, and confectioners. At that time the corner of Rideau and Sussex streets, very near the end of the canal, was the centre of commerce, with shops located outwardly along Sussex and on Cumberland, Clarence, and George streets. (This area is now the historic Byward Market area of the city, a marketplace more active than ever.)

The labourers and engineers who lived in Bytown because of the canal were not the only consumers in those years, however; the lumber trade was flourishing, and twice a year Bytown was visited by migrant workers. In the spring when the winter's cutting was finished, the lumbermen came to town with money in their pockets and headed straight for the hotels and taverns. In the fall the loggers and raftsmen returned to Bytown to wait for the team bosses to hire workers for the next season.

In 1831 the Rideau Canal was officially opened, but it wasn't really ready for navigation until the spring of 1832. Today, pleasure boats blissfully ply the waterway that 150 years ago was an engineering marvel; the Rideau Canal was 123.5 miles long and contained 33 locks, which overcame many heights of land. Dams had had to be built in order to maintain water levels throughout the canal, and many existing waterways were improved and made navigable.

The total cost of the canal construction was £822,804, a sum that was £300,000 over budget. In the beginning the British Government had offered to lend Canada the money to pay for the canal construction, but when Canadian officials pointed out that the whole idea of the canal was to provide a military route that would be a safe alternative to the St. Lawrence, the British agreed at least to share construction costs.

When the project was completed, Lieutenant-Colonel By returned home to England, but he did not receive the honours there that he had in Canada. A disgruntled former employee, one Howard Burgess,

Richard William Scott was Bytown's sixth mayor, serving in 1852, and is famous for his 1875 drafting of the Canada Temperance Act, popularly called the "Scott Act." King Edward VII conferred knighthood on him in 1908. Courtesy, Public Archives of Canada

OTTAWA AND PRESCOTT

RAILWAY.

JOSEPH MOONEY, *Secretary & Treasurer.*

ROBERT BELL, *President.* B. FRENCH, *Superintendent.*

TWO PASSENGER TRAINS DAILY EACH WAY,

Leaving Ottawa at 7 A.M. and 1.30 P.M., connecting at JUNCTION with the GRAND TRUNK RAILWAY Trains going East and West, and at PRESCOTT with the

Royal Mail and American Line of Steamers,

FOR ALL PORTS EAST AND WEST;

Also, with the N. O. R. R. and R. W. & O. R. Trains leaving Ogdensburgh

FOR

NEW YORK AND BOSTON.

RETURNING:

Will leave PRESCOTT at 6.45 A.M. and 1.30 P.M., on arrival of all connecting Lines, and arrive in OTTAWA at 10.15 A.M. and 4 P.M., connecting with Steamers for Ports on the Upper and Lower Ottawa River.

Not many changes had occurred, either in the Bytown economy nor in the modes of transportation, from the time the canal was finished and 1842, when this scene was drawn by W.H. Bartlett. Soldiers still lived on Barracks Hill, and the square-timber business was booming. Perhaps the only new sight was the active steamer business at the Fitzgibbon Wharf. Courtesy, Public Archives of Canada

had returned to England earlier and gave the press a report that By had misused funds for the canal, resulting in the extra expenses.

In time By was exonerated, but he never recovered from the humiliation and insult to his honour; he died in his home village in England in 1836.

Although originally built by the military, the Rideau Canal was never used extensively by it. Nevertheless, the existence of the canal proved to be an important factor in the development of many communities in Eastern Ontario. The canal had commercial importance as well, serving as a route for ships travelling inland which could not navigate the rapids between Montreal and Kingston; instead they went to Bytown, then south on the Rideau Canal to Kingston.

THE ENTREPRENEURS

When the Rideau Canal was completed, the population of Bytown was nearly halved when the labourers, contractors, and engineers left, but within a few years many other people were attracted to the town. Bytown had begun to survive on its own as a centre for trade; indeed, the lumber industry and all the businesses it

Men with broad-axes square a white pine in the forest near Aylen Lake, Ontario. This log and the one to be cut behind it would have to be hauled by horses to Aylen Lake and, in the spring, floated south to the Madawaska River, and from there to the Ottawa River. Courtesy, Public Archives of Canada

drew had helped to transform the settlement into a busy frontier town with employment for hundreds of people.

There was one reason for this: British shipyards were desperately short of lumber and were anxious for supplies, particularly of the quality of the Ottawa Valley lumber. Squared timber was the principal export product; the squared timber industry peaked during the 1830s, and in 1836 the Ottawa Valley Lumber Association was formed to foster cooperation among the various lumber companies.

The hopes for lasting prosperity were dashed when the British Government imposed a tariff on colonial lumber in 1842. Furthermore, much of the prime lumber in the area had been used up—reforestation was not practiced then—and the Bytown lumber industry seemed to be in serious trouble. Times were uncertain until the end of the decade when markets for Canadian timber in the U.S. began to grow. In 1854 the Reciprocity Treaty was signed, allowing for the duty-free export of lumber from British North America to the United States, heralding a new age for Bytown.

The Bytown lumbermen's timing was perfect: the power of the Chaudière Falls was first harnessed by sawmill owners Philip Thompson and Daniel McLachlin, and soon the sawmills in the area were busy spinning out the spruce and pine planks so much in demand south of the border. On the first of January 1855, Bytown officially became known as Ottawa, a name that came from the Outaouais Indians who had lived in the area. By 1860 the city was among the most important sawmilling centres in British North America.

The lumber industry made millionaires of the men and women who took up its challenge. Ironically, Philemon Wright died without making a profit from his lumber company, but other Americans made a fortune. Ezra Butler Eddy arrived from

Balancing skillfully, lumberjacks with long peavies guide logs into the swift waters. During the winter, the freshly cut logs were piled on the river ice to await the spring thaw. *The Drive* is from *Picturesque Canada,* published in Toronto in 1882. Courtesy, Public Archives of Canada

RIGHT: In this 1862 photograph, lumber is piled near the canal to be used in the construction of the Parliament Buildings. Major's Hill Park had yet to be landscaped, and horses still pulled carts and carriages along dusty roads. The area of Sandy Hill, south of Rideau street, was soon to become a fashionable residential area for members of Parliament and government officials. Courtesy, Public Archives of Canada

Vermont in 1854, the year the lumber tariffs were dropped, and located his mill on the Quebec side of the river, providing employment for many citizens of Bytown. Eddy had very little money when he first arrived on the Ottawa River; he began by making matches, then clothespins and wooden bowls, and by 1863 Eddy was a millionaire. Today, of course, the Eddy name is synonymous with matches and forest products throughout the world.

Other lumbermen such as John Gilmour, John Rochester, John Martin, and Daniel Fisher did well too, but one man, John R. Booth, became Canada's lumber king. It is said that he arrived in Ottawa with just nine dollars in his pocket, but he had initiative. Teaming up with an American to make shingles during that important decade of 1850 to 1860, he established an empire that made him a multimillionaire within a very few years. Booth was also instrumental in developing railroads in Eastern Canada; in the 1880s he built the Canada Atlantic Railroad (along with partner William Perley), which stretched from Ottawa to Coteau, Quebec, near the

LEFT: Ottawa's most brilliant capitalist, John Rudolphus Booth (centre) and his son C. Jackson Booth (left) inspect the last load of white pine to come off their Madawaska limits. Booth came to Ottawa in 1852 with only nine dollars, but left $47 million in cash assets and millions more in investments and property when he died in 1925. Public Archives of Canada/Booth Family Collection

FACING PAGE BOTTOM: From the 1880s until the 1970s, the groundwood process had been used to mechanically produce pulpwood. Steam rises inside the Upper Mill of E.B. Eddy's as men place pulpwood, cut into 18-inch lengths, called blocks, into the pocket grinders on either side of their aisle. Courtesy, of E.B. Eddy Forest Products Ltd.

St. Lawrence.

It was not only the lumbermen who found success. Contractor Thomas MacKay, who had come from Scotland to build the canal, had moved quickly after his construction work was finished to establish his own empire on the eastern side of the Rideau Falls. Believing in diversification, MacKay built what was virtually an industrial complex, including two sawmills, a grist mill, a cloth factory, and facilities for the manufacture of shingles, doors, and window sashes. By 1837, much in advance of the lumber barons' success, MacKay was a wealthy and influential man. He decided to build a house suitable to his position and wealth, a limestone mansion with 11 rooms. After his death the house, which his family called Rideau Hall, was leased by the government for the Governor General. The house, though much added to, and surrounding property are today the home of Canada's vice-regal representative.

As the city's population increased, other entrepreneurs took advantage of the need for building materials, and several brickyards were established, such as that

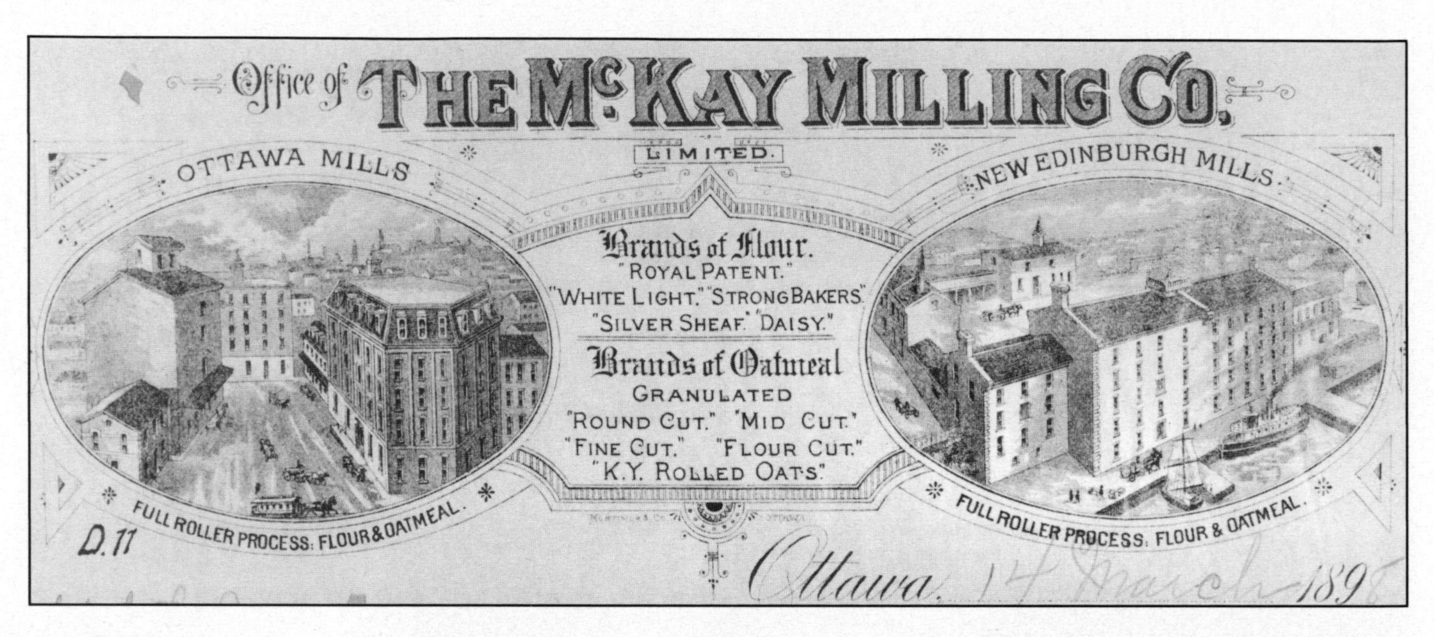

ABOVE: William Cameron Edwards, later Senator Edwards, bought the New Edinburgh and Ottawa grist mills in 1894 from the family of the original owner, Thomas MacKay. The New Edinburgh mills, located on Green Island, and the Ottawa Mills, located to the west of the Rideau Falls, existed until the early twentieth century. The other MacKay Mills on Chaudière Island were destroyed in the Great Fire of 1900. Courtesy, Historical Society of Ottawa

of Enoch Walkley, after the first brick house was built in Bytown in 1833.

What remains notable about the city's entrepreneurs is that although some of them came to Canada with money and a plan to start a business, many others built their fortunes literally from the ground up. Even the lumber men, whose wealth must have been fantastic for their times, began by working for monthly wages in the lumber camps.

By 1871, Ottawa was a bustling commercial centre; the seven lumber mills employed 1,200 men, and that year produced lumber worth more than $1.5 million.

THE QUEEN'S CHOICE

In the middle of the eighteenth century, discussions about the location of a capital city for Canada began. At this point there were five cities under consideration as the site for the government: Quebec City, Montreal, Kingston, Toronto, and Ottawa, which was known as Bytown until it became the City of Ottawa in 1855.

The controversy fairly raged for more than 10 years and almost everyone had an opinion about which city was best suited to be the capital; Toronto was thought to be too far west of the centre of what was then the Province of Canada, while Quebec City was too far in the opposite direction. Montreal was a very unsettled city then, and Kingston was on the St. Lawrence, too close to the border with the United States. Ironically, the only consensus among all the disparate groups arguing their choice for the location of the capital was that Ottawa was everyone's second choice!

It was, after all, an industrial town, with little of the accoutrements of culture that

LEFT: Families stroll and relax on the grounds of the rustic Victorian summer house at the Lookout on Parliament Hill. This print entitled ***Looking Up the Ottawa, from the Parliament Grounds,*** is from ***Picturesque Canada,*** published in Toronto in 1882. Courtesy, Public Archives of Canada

BELOW: Large rafts were a typical and attractive sight below Parliament Hill in the nineteenth century. In this 1882 photograph, cribs are being reassembled into rafts in Rafting Bay beyond the Hill. The small boat with pointed ends, appropriately called a pointer, aided in the manouvering of the sections. Courtesy, Public Archives of Canada

were present in Quebec or Toronto. Goldwin Smith wrote from England that Ottawa was little more than a "subarctic lumber village"—despite the fact that the city was closer to the tropics than he was in Oxford, and that the "village" was in the middle of an industrial boom—and this view of Ottawa as a primitive small town was echoed by many, including elected representatives and newspaper editors.

Finally, Ottawa won out. Queen Victoria's decision was officially announced in 1858. A story appeared in the *Ottawa Tribune* on January 30, 1858, proclaiming that "Ottawa is now destined to advance with rapid strides on the road to prosperity. Her natural advantages will be brought prominently before the country."

True enough, the coming of government brought rapid change to Ottawa, not the least of which was an incredible

This rattan-brush snow sweeper of the Electric Street Railway Company proved to be an excellent invention considering the conditions around the turn of the century. Courtesy, Public Archives of Canada

LEFT: By 1893, the Ottawa Electric Railway had established the Ottawa Electric Parks at either end of the line—at Britannia Bay and Rockcliffe—to encourage weekend use of their service. Here, members of the Anglican Church, Christ Church, fill the cars to brimming as they set off on their sunday school picnic in 1893. Courtesy, Public Archives of Canada

building boom as government buildings were constructed. The city became home to people of varied backgrounds. To the established social order of wealthy families who had made their fortunes in the lumber trade, the successful merchants, retired military officers, and professional people, the presence of the vice-regal court made for very exciting times.

The years after 1859 saw a flurry of construction as government buildings rose in the centre of the city, not the least of which were the Parliament Buildings themselves. Other important structures included the beautiful and intricate Library of Parliament with its 16 sides, built between the years 1859 and 1877, and the Central Chambers, finished in 1890. The latter building was the first commercial structure in North America to use bay windows to enhance illumination of the interior space.

The last decades of the nineteenth century also represented the great age of railways in Canada. The first passenger train arrived in Ottawa in 1854. However, the terminus was in New Edinburgh, and passengers had to be ferried across the Rideau River to Ottawa. Eventually, each of the rail lines—and there were many, crisscrossing the city to the east, south, and west—built its own station in the city. J.R. Booth, whose Canadian Atlantic Railroad extended from Lake Champlain in the United States across Ontario to Georgian Bay, had promised the government to build a central station, but he never did. The grand Union Station was finally finished in 1912 on the site of Booth's old station, built by the Grand Trunk Railway. Another vestige of the great age of railways is the Chateau Laurier, a magnificent structure built in the chateau style, also built by the Grand Trunk Railway, which maintains to this day its status as a luxury hotel.

The railways brought Ottawa—and Canada—into the twentieth century, connecting people and cities, buyers and markets, across the land. By the year 1900, Ottawa was a very different place from the little settlements once known as Richmond's Landing and Bytown; the streets lit by lamplight and travelled by electric tramways were a far cry from the brush-covered wilderness of just a century before.

The nineteenth century had been one of dramatic change for Ottawa. Once an insignificant community, known only to voyageurs and then to enterprising lumbermen and courageous settlers, the city was now the capital city of a vast and promising country.

It has been said that the twentieth century would belong to Canada. Of all the cities in Canada, none has a better chance of proving this prophecy than Ottawa, for no other city is as representative of the country as a whole—still close to the savage beauty of Nature, while enhanced by the civility and refinement of culture, but most important, a place of endless opportunity.

FACING PAGE BOTTOM: This Royal Mail car, photographed in 1894, was specially designed by the Ottawa Car Manufacturing Company, and travelled the tracks of the Sappers Bridge away from the Old Post Office. Courtesy, Public Archives of Canada

LOVE PRINTING

Love Printing's new plant and offices at 5977 Hazeldean Road in Stittsville.

"Quality and service is our business" is the adage painted in huge letters on a Wall of Love Printing's new headquarters and plant. This is more than a slogan; it's a promise and the cornerstone on which Love Printing has established its position as the largest printer in the National Capital region. The expansion of Love Printing's business is reflected in its new, modern, climate-controlled 85,000-square-foot building in Stittsville that is far removed from its former downtown location in both distance and space.

All of this is no small achievement for what was a comparatively small printing operation with 35 employees until taken over by Ian and Karen McJannet in 1980. Today there are more than 200 people employed by Love Printing.

The McJannets are perpetuating the line of local ownership that started when Love's predecessor, Miller Printing, began serving the community in the 1930s. The change to the current name occurred in 1962, when Gordon Love purchased the company.

Continuing that same local entrepreneurial spirit, Ian and Karen McJannet "put everything on the line" in 1980 when they purchased the operation from Gordon Love, the former president to whom Ian McJannet had been assistant. The takeover was part of the firm's natural evolution. McJannet's interest, dedication, and untiring efforts toward the success of Love Printing have not dimmed since they purchased the business.

Considerable effort is placed on team effort and co-operation among all those who work for the company. "When people say this is a family operation because a husband and wife run it, I like to point out that we consider all of our staff part of a family," Karen McJannet says, "These people all played an important role in making Love Printing the success it is today."

Roles in the family-owned operation are clearly defined. Ian McJannet has a keen understanding of the preparation, production, and printing operations. He oversees the technical side of the plant.

Karen McJannet runs the business side, including pre-production, accounting, sales, public relations, marketing, personnel, and Love Printing's involvement in many community projects.

The family attitude is evident throughout Love Printing's operations. Ian McJannet is on a first name basis with everyone on staff. "Nobody works for us," says McJannet, "but everyone works with us. Business is a people thing. It's the people that matter, and we're one big family at Love Printing."

This attitude is reiterated by Karen McJannet. "After acquiring the company, Ian and I knew we had to establish a reputation," she says. "The way to do that was through the people we employed and the work they did." "The rest followed," Karen McJannet emphasizes.

What followed was the growth of the firm's reputation and a rapid ex-

prominently in the front reception lobby, attesting to the quality of work produced by Love Printing.

The firm's success also has provided flexibility to respond to perceived needs of clients in the area. A new multi-unit, roll-feed Web press has been installed. This new press will help cope with the rising demand for service from clients from across Eastern Canada and the United States. Some work has come in from such far-off spots as

"Quality and service is our motto" is in huge letters on the wall at Love Printing and is reflected in the team effort and cooperation evident throughout the company.

pansion in business. Love Printing's offices and plant on Gladstone Avenue in downtown Ottawa that had housed the company soon became too crowded. Lack of space and year-over-year growth of more than 30 percent led to construction of the new plant and offices at 5977 Hazeldean Road in Stittsville, Ontario, west of Ottawa.

Love Printing's operation is an impressive array of computerized accounting, estimating, costing, and delivery tracking systems in the front office operations through to the latest in high-tech typesetting, design, and layout equipment in the preparatory stages and the best of printing and bindery machinery.

The company has an expert design team that is complemented by state-of-the-art computerized typesetting. Experienced operators can either key text into the system, accept material on small or large computer floppy disks, or receive it on line by telecommunication modem. Accurate work, quick turnaround time, and lower costs all lead to satisfied customers.

The spaciousness of the plant adds to the sense of care for work and individuals. Apart from the quality Heidelberg presses that turn out high calibre multi-color work, the bindery is the largest in the region.

Adjacent are two auto stitchers capable of collating, stitching, trimming, and cover inserting at a rate of 10,000 magazines per hour. The company also has two binders capable of running 5,000 and 8,000 books per hour, either slot bound or perfect bound, up to three inches thick.

Several first-place awards and letters from satisfied clients hang

Australia and Ireland.

But the secret of the McJannets' success is more than a simple extended family operation that places a strong emphasis on quality printing and good customer service. It lies in their ability to achieve and exceed detailed plans. This has been done with hard work and commitment by all who work for Love Printing.

BA BANKNOTE

BA Banknote, Ottawa.

British American Bank Note has a long history of providing currency and security printing services—a history older than Canada itself.

Founded in 1866, a year before Confederation, the company was formed through the merging of two competing operations, which brought together the skills of Ottawa's master engraver, William Smillie, and Montreal lithographer George Burland.

From that start—and with a nominal $100,0000 in capital—British American Bank Note was ready to print currency for an emerging nation. In May 1867 the firm was selected to engrave its first currency issue—one-, two-, four-, five-, and 10-dollar notes for the Canadian Imperial Bank of Commerce. The Government of Canada soon became a customer, a relationship that has weathered more than a century of technological change.

Upon his retirement from British American Bank Note in 1881, William Smillie sold his company shares to George Burland and immediately formed the Canada Bank Note Company. Government orders remained with British American Bank Note, however, and Smillie's enterprise was absorbed into the older concern after 10 years. In the interim another rival, the Dominion Bank Note Company, had also been acquired.

Business slowed for British American Bank Note at the turn of the century, when 25 Canadian banks either went out of business or were absorbed by other financial institutions. The slump was followed by a boom during World War I, though, when the firm received orders for war and victory bonds.

The upturn continued through the 1920s, when huge quantities of bonds, municipal debentures, and stock certificates were needed. While these orders slowed to a near halt during the Great Depression of the 1930s, the company was able to offset the setback through increased demand for the stamps it supplied to the Canadian post office. In fact, British American Bank Note's Cartier Quadricentenary stamp, issued in 1934, was selected by the prestigious *Gibbons Stamp Monthly* as the best philatelic design of the year.

World War II brought another financial boost to the company, which became responsible for the engraving and printing of currency for a number of Allied nations. The additional volume increase in Government of Canada bonds, bank notes, and revenue stamps pushed the firm to the limit and necessitated a move to larger facilities.

British American Bank Note relocated to its present site at 975 Gladstone in 1948 and incorporated a number of new features, including wire mesh partitions between departments, improved operating efficiency, temperature and humidity controls, and tighter security.

The high steel fences, electronic surveillance equipment, and posted guard at the Ottawa plant all demonstrate that the corporate tradition in security printing has not only been maintained, but improved. Security is equally as tight at the several other plants located nationwide.

That security is important because inside those walls, half of Canada's currency is printed, along with those of Portugal, Oman, Bangladesh, Cyprus, and other countries. But British American Bank Note prints more than just bank notes and currency; the company is involved in virtually every aspect of printing where security is necessary.

Its engravers and production staff produce government and corporate bonds, share certificates, postage stamps, travellers' cheques, drivers' licences, passports, identity documents, lottery tickets, prospectuses, corporate annual reports, and financial documents—in each case incorporating techniques that make successful forgery extremely difficult.

The company recognizes that such documents demand the same type of security control as its currency operations. At the same time, British Bank Note meets its customers' deadlines and continues to improve on its high standards of quality.

That type of dedication to detail has served the firm well. In 1986 revenues were $79.1 million, an 18-percent increase over the previous year. Plans for further growth and an expanded role in the European market are now in progress.

Now a member of the Quebecor inc., BA Banknote's role in the world of security printing continues to grow. The affiliation with the country's largest printer ensures that its success will continue.

Much may have changed since Smillie and Burland started out with $100,000 more than a century ago, but the success of British American Bank Note should be no surprise in a world where security is more important today than ever.

Trusted leaders in security.

DOLLCO PRINTING

After a recent move into a spacious new 86,000-square-foot plant, Dollco Printing is ready to build on its reputation as one of Eastern Canada's finest printers.

Originally known as Dominion Loose Leaf Company, the firm was purchased by G.H. "Gerry" Nicholds in 1956. The name Dollco, an acronym of the original, was coined six years later.

Today the growing operation is owned and managed by Gerry's sons "Hap" and Barry, who purchased the business in the late 1970s. Dollco now has its head office and plant in Ottawa, and sales offices in Toronto and Kingston.

Most of the firm's business is in commercial printing and specialty carton manufacturing. According to company president Hap Nicholds, the company has succeeded by pinpointing its target market and providing it with impeccable service. The strategy has attracted local, national, and international publications.

"The work our people do is what makes us stand apart," says Nicholds, and Dollco's growing reputation bears out the words of its president. Publications demanding high resolution and superb four-color printing—*Canadian Geographic* is just one example—are finding that Dollco's printed product meets or surpasses their expectations.

The same is true for the folding cartons, annual reports, and promotional materials that are also part of Dollco's business. Many nationally recognized consumer products, including national brand lingerie and cosmetics, rely on Dollco to produce eye-catching packaging that will stock retail shelves across the country.

"We're client-driven," Nicholds explains. "We're successful because we try to be flexible and because each department has confidence in the others."

Fortifying that confidence is a modern plant with equipment that has the company ready and eager for the 1990s. Dollco has recently installed a computer-controlled, full-size Harris heat-set web press. Coated stock speeds through its rollers at almost a quarter-mile per minute. The plant also operates a half-size web press, various sheet-fed presses printing in one to five colors, a UV high-gloss coater, as well

Above: Dollco's move to a new 86,000-square-foot plant firmly establishes the company as one of the pre-eminent printers in Eastern Canada. With sales offices in Kingston and Toronto, the firm is ready for continued growth.

Left: A five-color Komori Lithrone-40, sheet-fed press is one of four new Komori presses in Dollco's plant.

as die-cutting and foil stamping equipment. The plant floor is immaculate, and all customers are invited to tour the facilities.

"When we print a booklet or magazine for a customer, we realize that people have spent a lot of time doing the writing, research, and photography that have gone into it," Nicholds says. "We're the end of the line for that product, so it's up to us to make sure it reflects the effort the client has put into it."

Dollco's operation also includes a fully equipped bindery and finishing department. There the cutters, folders, perfect-binding machines, and saddle stitchers (with inserting and blow-in capabilities) ensure that quality printing becomes quality finished publications. Gladstone Press, a division of Dollco, works out of separate facilities, specializing in smaller jobs such as stationery, business cards, and forms. Gladstone also has complete typesetting services.

The move to a new plant has given Dollco the opportunity to expand its business to meet new customer requirements. The firm has added a mailing and polybagging operation to better serve the publications industry and direct-marketing clients.

Although it's part of an industry that relies heavily on sophisticated technology and equipment, Dollco hasn't lost sight of the human side of the business. "We don't use the word 'quality' to describe our printing because our work has always spoken for itself," Nicholds states. "We use the word 'quality' to describe the people who work here. What's good for them is good for Dollco and our customers."

According to Dollco controller Reid Hodgins, "In the printing industry today it's very hard to get experienced help, especially in the prepress area. So we hire young people and train them. They have a good future with a growing, adaptable, and modern company."

This dedication to people, including 130 employees and a diverse group of customers, has been a key ingredient in Dollco Printing's winning formula. "Our motto is 'We make good impressions on paper,'" Nicholds adds. "But we've succeeded because we also make a good impression on people. That has been the key to our success."

Above: Dollco operates two heat-set web presses to meet the needs of its client publications. Here the signatures are checked in detail against proofs, ensuring that they meet Dollco's philosophy of "good impressions."

Right: Skilled craftsmen and the latest equipment combine to create a superior product. Here two crew members ink up a four-color press.

OTTAWA-CARLETON BOARD OF TRADE

One of the oldest non-governmental business organizations in Canada, the Ottawa-Carleton Board of Trade has made a lasting contribution to Ottawa and environs over more than 132 years. The summer-long Changing of the Guard ceremony on Parliament Hill is but one initiative of the Board of Trade that has become symbolic of the nation's capital.

Other Ottawa attractions, such as the Festival of Spring, are manifestations of the visible, public efforts of the organization. While these successes are a considerable achievement, perhaps they deflect attention from the less visible—but equally successful—activities the board carries out on an ongoing basis in the vibrant business community in the region.

The Ottawa-Carleton Board of Trade is the unified voice for the business sector in the Greater Ottawa area. Activities undertaken by the board to ensure that business in Ottawa-Carleton is able to operate in a viable environment include: speaking on behalf of business so that there will be an uninhibited voice in matters affecting its well being—this includes lobbying for small and medium-size businesses to federal, provincial, regional, and municipal governments; participating in the process of legislative, administrative, and bureaucratic decision-making by governments so that such decisions are promulgated in a way that enhances the local entrepreneurial climate; promoting public recognition of the principle that business creates the wealth of employment and social benefits necessary to the Canadian way of life.

With Ottawa-Carleton one of Canada's major high-technology centres, the Board of Trade fulfills a vital role on behalf of the region's business community. The organization represents more than 1,000 member firms and has more than 2,000 individual representatives participating in its activities. The considerable expertise that exists in the business community is harnessed in a comprehensive committee structure to address many issues of mutual concern. Besides the many projects directed toward the improvement of the business environment, there are six policy committees and three service committees that help formulate well-researched, succinct policy positions and lobby strategies.

Noteworthy among the Board's many activities is the Student Venture Capital program. As the local operator of this joint effort between the Ontario government and the Royal Bank of Canada, the board studies proposals, makes recommendations, and provides advice from members who volunteer to help students developing summer businesses.

By providing an information service to its members and the public, the Ottawa-Carleton Board of Trade communicates business views while creating a forum for the business community to develop opinions and programs that contribute to the social, economic, and physical betterment of the region. To that end the special services provided by the board, such as a group insurance benefit plan, long-term disability insurance, and a retirement plan, are all attractive additional features of membership.

The Board's facilities are also well suited for periodic private business seminars and meetings. The dining room is a popular meeting place for members over the lunch hour and is sometimes used for special breakfast meetings. The Board offers catering and banquet facilities for special occasions, too.

The Ottawa-Carleton Board of Trade's facilities are available for private business seminars and meetings (below), and the dining room (left) is a popular meeting place for members over the lunch hour and is sometimes used for special breakfast meetings.

CENTRAL PRECAST PRODUCTS (1979) LIMITED

Bongard Avenue—the administration offices and main manufacturing plant of the company in the foreground with the concrete pole plant in the background.

In April 1954 young Luigi Mion stepped off the boat from Italy and onto the soil of Canada, where he would make his fortune.

Arriving in Halifax, he immediately boarded a train for British Columbia with a group of 500 other Italians who had been hired to work on the CN Railroad nationwide.

"Italy at the time was a bit short of work," explains Mion, who will never forget the seemingly endless eight-day train ride from Nova Scotia to New Westminster, British Columbia.

"When we got off the train," he continues, "we were walking like ducks." Mion had originally planned to work on the railway for a year, but after two months he headed for Ottawa, where a distant cousin of his was working for a tile and marble contractor. There, Mion landed in the nation's capital exhausted and broke, but the next day he began toiling as a laborer for his cousin's employer—at one dollar per hour.

"I worked 100-hour weeks to make $100," says Mion, who asked his boss for a raise after a year of backbreaking work and was turned down. That was it for Mion; he decided to start his own business.

He considered opening an Italian restaurant, but the estimated cost of such a venture proved prohibitive. Instead, for the price of a bag of cement, a load of stone, a pile of sand, a wheelbarrow, some shovels, and a telephone, Mion and a partner formed Central Precast and began making patio blocks and steps in a two-car garage on Booth Street in June 1956.

Since then Mion has spread his business wings in a number of different directions to the point where his company now is a virtual shopping mart for concrete produced of every description. It manufactures and supplies such items as underground structures for storm and sanitary sewers, architectural panels (which comprise the outer shell of such developments as the new Minto Place in downtown Ottawa), light standards and transmission poles (used throughout the region and across Canada), interlocking pavers and patio slabs, and highway barriers.

Although Central Precast has grown to 150 employees (a spectrum of 12 nationalities working in harmony), it remains privately owned. Mion, who bought out his partner in 1976, runs the booming enterprise from a gleaming, 100,000-square-foot facility on Bongard Avenue in Nepean. Central Precast is presently expanding its underground structures and manufacturing operations by constructing a 40,000-square-foot plant, on Carp Road in the township of West Carleton, to house state-of-the-art equipment.

The company is a family operation. Mion is president; John Mion, the oldest of Luigi and Ada Mion's four children, manages the firm's pole plant, while son Rodolfo and daughters Marcella and Anna work in administration. Mion's brother, Gustavo, serves as general manager/production, while Frank Berardini, Mion's brother-in-law, supervises the company's architectural production department. To complete the Mion clan, Luigi and Ada are the proud grandparents of Vanessa, John, and Marco.

Mion is a former director of the Ottawa Construction Association and is active in the city's Italian community. He explains that the key to success in his business—in any business—is good money management, "growth through diversification, quality products, and superior service."

CENTRAL PRECAST
PRODUCTS (1979) LIMITED

Downtown Ottawa with the impressive Minto Place complex in the foreground and the Carlyle Building in the background.

OTTAWA HYDRO

Ottawa Hydro has been meeting the electrical power needs of customers in the capital region since 1915, when a rivalry among several local power companies and Ontario Hydro led to the creation of the Hydro-Electric Power Commission of the City of Ottawa.

Originally established to guarantee a supply of energy to the growing city, the company today provides 4 billion kilowatt hours of energy annually to more than 125,000 commercial and residential customers.

Operating under the authority of the Power Corporation Act and the Public Utilities Act, Ottawa Hydro is the sole retailer of electricity within Ottawa, Vanier, and Rockcliffe Park. Customers in those communities pay among the lowest power rates in the province—and the nation.

Under contract the company purchases wholesale power from Ontario Hydro at 12 transformer stations located in the city. At these sites power is transformed from 115 and 230 kilovolts to 13.2 kilovolts, and then transformed to 4.16 kilovolts, the distribution voltage, at 44 substations. A 10-year plan is currently under way to upgrade the system's distribution voltage to 13.2 kilovolts.

As well as the energy purchased through this wholesale network, the firm supplements its power supply with the power generated at two commission-owned hydroelectric stations at Chaudiere Falls within the city. A computerized control system monitors voltage, indicates service failures, switches circuits, and warns of system abnormalities throughout the service area.

The commission structure, established in 1915, remains the governing body of Ottawa Hydro. Consisting of the sitting mayor of the City of Ottawa, a provincial appointee, and an appointee of the city, this board is responsible for carrying out the corporation's three objectives: to supply power at the lowest-feasible cost, to provide a secure supply of electricity within a safe working environment for its employees, and to promote the wise and efficient use of electricity throughout the service area. The commission is owned by its customers, is self-sustaining, and derives no revenue from taxes.

Ottawa Hydro's customers include 110,000 residences, ranging in size from single-family houses to large apartment complexes. Twenty thousand of these customers use electricity for general heating and 66,000 use it for water heating.

Average annual household power consumption through Ottawa Hydro is nearly 10,000 kilowatt

Above left: Since 1915 Ottawa Hydro has been serving the city's electrical power needs.

Above: The waters of the Ottawa River provide a continuous and reliable energy source for Ottawa Hydro.

hours per year, in keeping with Canada's status as one of the world's largest per-capita users of electrical energy. While this residential energy is conveyed largely through an overhead distribution system, the standard delivery route for new residential construction is underground.

The firm's 15,000 business customers make special demands on Ottawa Hydro's services and account for 62 percent of all kilowatt hours sold. The requirement for power in the city centre alone exceeds 100,000 kilowatts, and the underground distribution system used is a complex one by any city's standards. The maximum individual commercial load available from the secondary distribution system is 50 kilowatts, although higher loads are supplied through transformer vaults located within buildings.

Along with keeping the homes and businesses of the city both warm and bright, Ottawa Hydro is also responsible for maintaining the City of Ottawa's more than 22,000 streetlights. As in the company's other areas of operation, changing technology has meant ongoing improvements, and the city's existing mercury vapor lights are gradually being replaced with energy-efficient high-pressure sodium units. The reduced operating costs afforded by these units have allowed the city to expand its street lighting program, keeping Ottawa one of the best lit—and safest—cities in Canada.

Maintaining low costs has meant more for the firm than just satisfied customers. It has also helped growth in the Ottawa business community, as companies are attracted to the city because a major operating cost—energy—is kept lower than in almost any other metropolitan centre in the country.

Ottawa Hydro is instrumental in the city's economy in other ways as well. With more than 400 employees, the firm pumps more than $180 million into the capital city each year.

In its ongoing effort to provide power for a growing city economy, Ottawa Hydro is actively involved in a number of co-operative efforts with other utilities to promote load management and the efficient use of electrical power.

Right: Twenty thousand streetlights brighten the streets of Ottawa each night, thanks to Ottawa Hydro's power and maintenance.

Below: Plant conditions are monitored and managed at Ottawa Hydro's computer centre.

RICOH CORPORATION (CANADA) LTD.

Ricoh Corporation is looking forward to the 1990s. Already a leader in automated office products, the company is well positioned for the office "facsimile boom" that is under way. In fact, Ricoh Canada is convinced that the facsimile—or fax machine—will even become commonplace in Canadian homes in the coming years.

Ricoh is already the leading vendor of facsimile products in Canada, the United States, and Japan, but that success is likely just the beginning. Industry projections show fax use growing right through the next decade.

"The fax market has doubled and tripled over the past few years," explains Taiji Saito, Ricoh Canada's energetic president. "We expect continued growth of 150 percent per year through to 1990 as well."

Ricoh Canada was established in 1975 and is the only Japanese company to locate its Canadian head office in Ottawa. A major factor in that choice was the proximity of the federal government, a natural customer for facsimile products.

The firm has since grown to include a network of sales and service centres in every major Canadian city. It employs more than 200 people in its national operations, 100 at the Ottawa head office. The parent company was founded in 1936 as an offshoot of the renowned Institute of Physical and Chemical Research of Japan. Today it is a $7-billion corporation employing more than 25,000 people.

Ricoh's leadership in the area of office technology is not new. The company invented the first high-speed digital facsimile machine in 1973 and had made the technology applicable to plain paper by 1983. Ricoh facsimile products are supplied to more than 130 countries and are used by more than one-half of the *Fortune* 1,000 companies.

Among its largest Canadian customers are Bell Canada, with a 2,000-machine system, and four major chartered banks. The company has set a world standard for facsimile equipment. In the 1980s alone Ricoh was the exclusive fax supplier to the Japanese delegation to the World Economic Summit in Toronto, the Canadian Papal Tour, and the Commonwealth Conference in Vancouver.

Among the products that have made the Ricoh name synonymous with quality facsimile is the Ricoh Fax 1000L, a plain paper digital facsimile transceiver using laser technology. Through this revolutionary development, a permanent copy is provided that can be handled continuously without the possibility of degradation due to heat or light, unlike thermal-sensitive paper.

This high-speed unit, weighing only 62 pounds, can transmit an 8.5- by 10-inch sheet in 15 seconds. Capable of polling, the Fax 1000L can "pick up" documents from up to 80 different remote units, and, in turn, transmit to more than 120 stations either immediately or at a later time, using its "send later"

Taiji Saito, president of Ricoh Corporation (Canada) Ltd.

Ricoh offers a full line of award-winning photocopiers.

At Ricoh's Canadian Communications Centre, service calls are received and, in turn, dispatched using state-of-the-art communications equipment.

feature. Its large, 60-page memory can store confidential documents, allowing retrieval only through the use of a programmed password. Like most Ricoh machines, it can also conveniently be used as both a fax and a telephone concurrently, thereby eliminating duplicate calls and saving not only time but money.

Beyond striving for quality, though, Ricoh is determined to make the fax machine more accessible to all users. "We think our products can contribute a great deal to the efficiency and productivity of Canadian business," Saito says. "We want to make sure that businesses at all levels can afford the technology."

To that end, Ricoh has developed a complete line of full-featured facsimile machines. Starting with its RF800, which, at less than 10 pounds, combines the most popular fax and telephone features, Ricoh offers an additional five portable business fax: the Fax 15, Fax 25, Fax 35, Fax 65, and the Fax 75. Weighing less than 18 pounds, each of these units is fully featured and can poll other machines and even send documents later, allowing users to take advantage of lower evening or night telephone rates by transmitting documents after hours. In addition, the Fax 75 allows users to broadcast to numerous units at once. Rounding out the line are Ricoh 510, 610, 830, and 2100 fax machines specially designed with high-end commercial users in mind. The company believes that the many features and high usability of its product line will increase facsimile use by both businesses and individuals alike.

The firm's expertise in producing images is also being applied to other areas. In October 1987 Ricoh Canada introduced a line of photocopiers. Once again, diversity was the key, what with 12 models from which to choose. From basic units to models that reduce or enlarge, adjust margins automatically, copy on both sides of a sheet of paper, to a unit that "memorizes" frequently used copy jobs, Ricoh has exactly what small businesses as well as large corporations are looking for.

Ricoh Canada does more than $50 million of business in the country each year. Its sophisticated computer systems are linked to Ricoh USA's New Jersey head office by a series of dedicated lines.

"We are quite excited by the opportunities and challenges in both Ottawa and Canada," Saito says. "By continuing our pursuit of excellence, Ricoh can be a major contributor to the success and growth of Canadian enterprise."

Ricoh offers the widest range of facsimile products in Canada.

BRISTOL-MYERS PHARMACEUTICAL GROUP

The head office building at 2625 Queensview Drive, Ottawa, Ontario.

Bristol-Myers Pharmaceutical Group is one of the Canadian divisions of Bristol-Myers Company, New York, a worldwide organization engaged in the manufacturing and marketing of pharmaceuticals, nutritional products, medical implants, medical instruments, diagnostic tests, household products, toiletries, nonprescription health products, and beauty aids.

The Canadian Pharmaceutical Group, headquartered in Ottawa, manufactures and markets pharmaceutical and nutritional products through three operating units: Bristol Laboratories, Mead Johnson Canada, and Bristol Oncology. The group has manufacturing facilities in both Belleville, Ontario, and Candiac, Quebec.

Bristol Laboratories markets drug therapies for diseases related to the cardiovascular system, central nervous system, and antibiotic use. The major products in the cardiovascular field are Questran, a cholesterol reducer, and Sotacor, a beta blocker. Bristol's antidepressant drug Desyrel, a new chemical entity, was the number-one prescribed drug in its class in North America. The anti-infective products are Duricef, an oral cephalosporin, and Amikin, an aminoglycoside used in hospitals for serious infections.

Mead Johnson is the market leader in the field of pediatric nutrition, vitamins, and analgesics, as well as having a wide range of specialty adult nutritional products. These specialty nutritional products address the specific needs of the postoperative and cancer patient, and the special nutritional requirements of the geriatric.

Mead Johnson is known to Canadian parents with its market-leading infant formula, Enfalac, as well as for its leading pediatric analgesic and vitamin products, Tempra and Tri-Vi-Sol. Products supporting the special needs of infants, adult patients, and geriatrics are ProSobee, Isocal, Flexical, Sustacal, and Sustain.

Bristol Oncology is the leading Canadian company in the field of chemotherapeutic agents for the treatment of cancer. Major products

Below: Bristol oncology anti-cancer products.

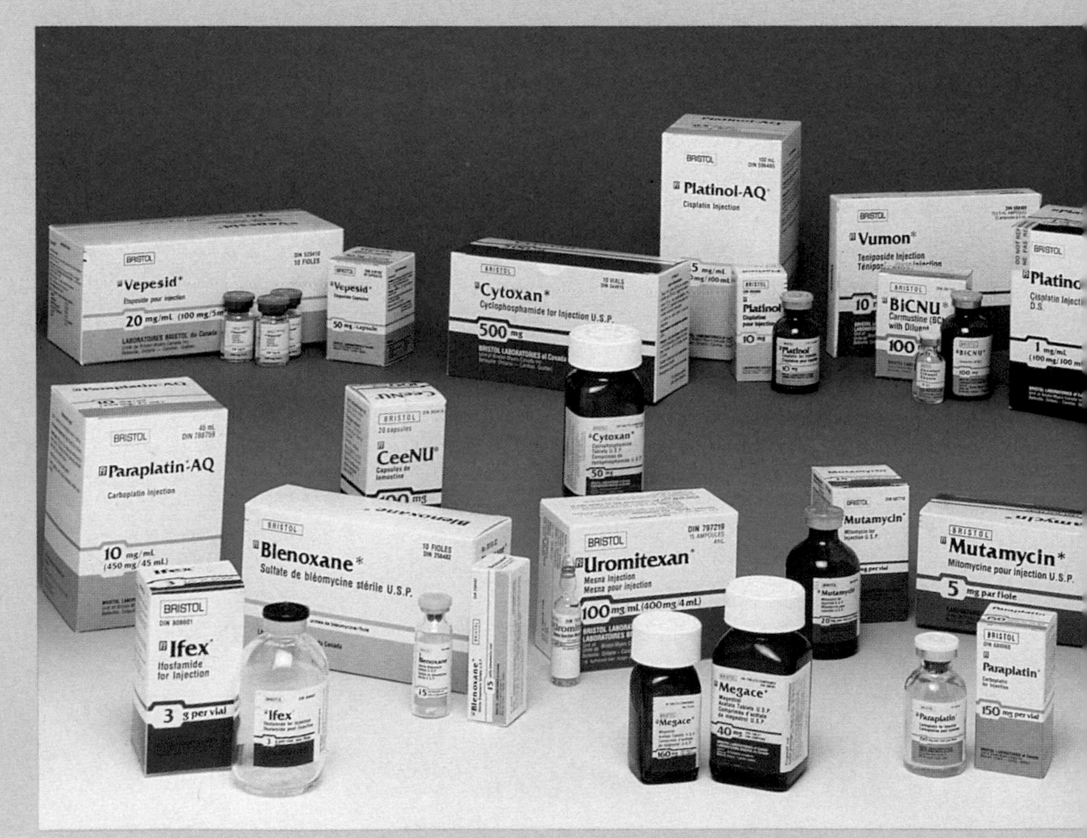

are Megace for the treatment of breast cancer, Vepesid for lung and testicular cancer, and Paraplatin, Platinol, Blenoxane, Mutamycin, Ifex, and Uromitexan, among the many products for use in the treatment of various types of cancer.

The Bristol-Myers Company celebrated its 100th anniversary in 1987, having grown out of a small failed drug company in Clinton, New York, to a *Fortune* 500 corporation with worldwide sales approaching $6 billion. Beyond its contributions to medicine and its research and development programs to improve the health and quality of life, Bristol-Myers is satisfying consumers' needs with such well-known products as Keri Lotion, Presun, and Alpha Keri for the skin; Windex, Javex, Fleecy, Scrub 'n Shine, Drano, Vanish, Behold, and Mr. Muscle for the home; Excedrin and Bufferin for nonprescription health care; toiletries such as Ban, Vitalis, and Clairol's Nice 'N Easy, Loving Care, and Miss Clairol; and beauty aid appliances.

The Bristol-Myers Company is committed to research and development with annual expenditures exceeding $394 million in 1988.

In 1989 Bristol-Myers has committed to spend in Canada approximately $7 million in research and development, with a further commitment through the Patent Legislation Act Bill C-22 to spend $42 million over the next four years. Pharmaceutical research will concentrate on the development of new therapeutic agents in five major areas: anti-cancer, central nervous system, anti-infective, cardiovascular, and dermatology. Basic research will be conducted in molecular biology, immunology, and the development of novel drug delivery systems. The Canadian research facility is an active member of these research efforts, along with the other Bristol-Myers facilities in the United States, Belgium, France, and Japan. The company is also involved, through acquisition, in the development of monoclonal antibodies and diagnostic tests using advances in biotechnology and genetic engineering.

Bristol-Myers Pharmaceutical Group, employing more than 500 Canadians, believes in supporting the communities of its employees. Examples of this are the contributions to such programs as Ronald MacDonald House, with facilities in cities across Canada, and in the fight against drug abuse by being one of the founding board members of the Alliance for a Drug Free Canada activated by Carleton University.

Mead Johnson's infant formulas.

Bristol Laboratories' Questran.

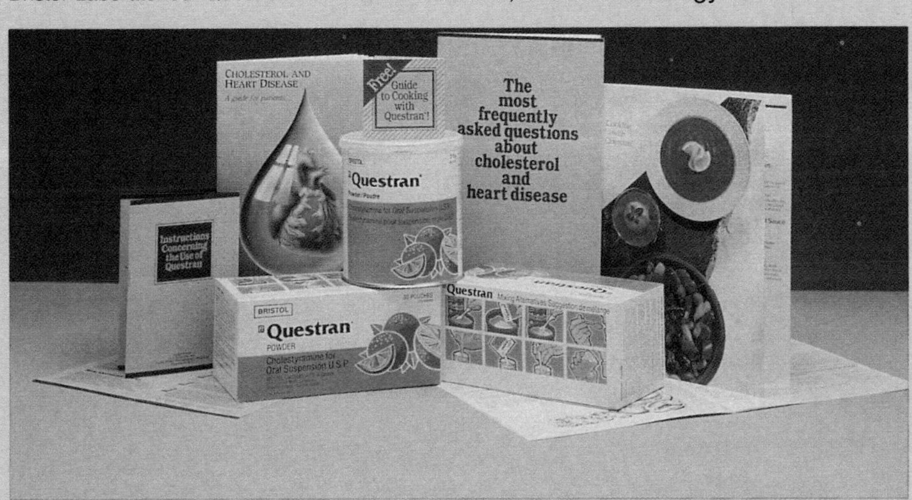

ALPHATEXT

Alphatext, a member of the Quebecor family of companies, was the first high-technology company to make Ottawa its home, launching its operation—and Silicon Valley North—in 1969.

Marrying the art of the type compositor and graphic designer with modern data-processing technology, Alphatext's electronic typesetting and page make-up facilities offer reduced costs, improved production time, and excellent quality.

The company's specially engineered vibration-proof building, adjacent to Ottawa's Queensway, is a downtown landmark—the unique lettering up the side of the building reflecting the firm's graphic arts capabilities.

There is an Alphatext product in virtually every home. Used extensively in the production of telephone directories—the company sets and designs phone books for clients as far away as Trinidad and Tobago—Alphatext is also a problem solver for magazines such as *Time, Saturday Night, Reader's Digest,* and others. Clients also include large industrial companies with complex product catalogues.

Alphatext was initially established by Glen McInnes to provide text-processing and typesetting services to the federal government. A Windsor office, which later moved into Detroit, was also established to offer catalogue production services to the automotive industry.

In 1983 it was purchased by Bell Canada and took over preparation of all Yellow Page and white page directories. In the process it became necessary to expand operations into Toronto.

In a business that relies on marrying technologies, Alphatext has continuously searched for innovative new ways to serve the business community. It is presently offering 200,000 pages of Yellow Page information to on-line customers and has announced its intention to become the leading direct marketing bureau in Canada.

Its leadership in its field was recognized by the Canadian government when it was called upon to assist the Free Trade negotiations by providing statistical information that was couriered overnight to Washington. In addition, Alphatext prepared the largest single federal government publication, the *Access to Information* and *Privacy* publications.

In 1988 Alphatext was part of a major acquisition by Quebecor Inc., a large printing, publishing, and forest products company in which BCE took an equity position.

Having grown from a text and typesetting shop, Alphatext now offers a wide range of services, including information capture and diskette conversion, editorial and graphic services, composition, electronic output options, and printing and distribution.

Alphatext's vibration-proof building—an Ottawa landmark.

Above: Alphatext's high-speed typesetter composes 18,000 characters per minute of camera-ready pages.

Below: Alphatext's technologists on-line to the integrated data-processing/typesetting system.

THE JWI GROUP

The requirements of the papermaking industry are constantly evolving through both technology and the changing demands of consumers. For Canada's JWI Ltd., this evolution has meant 200 years of challenge.

JWI Ltd. is one of the largest companies in the world devoted exclusively to the manufacture of paper machine forming fabrics, press felts, dryer fabrics, filtration media, and drainage equipment. It is a leader in developing and patenting innovative products that have become industry standards and state of the art worldwide.

Among those innovations is the removable T-bar-mounted foil blade that enables papermakers to change drainage blades without costly machine shutdowns. During the past two decades the company has been prominent in developing woven single- and multi-layer synthetic forming fabrics, which have replaced traditional metal wires in papermaking worldwide.

Each of JWI's innovations has led to improvements in the papermaking industry's ability to produce high-quality paper at a lower cost. The firm's reputation comes not only from its tradition of development but also from the high standard of quality and service it sets in the industry.

JWI's facilities in Kanata house administrative and executive offices, a well-equipped research and development laboratory and pilot plant, and central engineering. The firm also operates 12 manufacturing plants in Canada, the United States, and England, and has sales agents worldwide. Company products are at work in more than 30 papermaking countries.

JWI Ltd.'s roots go back to Manchester, England, during the industrial revolution. The company's forerunner became associated with the paper industry by providing woven metal screens for the newly invented Fourdrinier paper machine. In 1901 a wire-weaving plant was established in Montreal to serve the fledgling Canadian paper industry.

The rapid growth of the Canadian industry led to the steady expansion of the Montreal plant. Since 1957 JWI has built new plants in Vancouver; Atlanta, Georgia (three); Kanata, Ontario; Burlington, Vermont; and Pittsburgh, Pennsylvania, to meet the increasing needs of the industry. Equipment plants were also established in Montreal and in Springfield, Massachusetts.

Today The JWI Group of companies is constantly improving product quality and performance to meet the challenges of the papermaking industry. A privately owned Canadian company, JWI and its more than 1,400 employees are looking ahead to new growth opportunities and the future development of innovative products that will keep the Canadian paper industry healthy and competitive and assist papermakers worldwide.

From its head office in Kanata, JWI Ltd. operates 12 manufacturing plants in Canada, the United States, and England and has sales agents worldwide.

This experimental loom is used by JWI R&D to develop new, innovative weave designs (inset) for paper machine fabrics.

EASTCAN BEVERAGES LIMITED

Eastcan Beverages Limited employs more than 300 people in its 158,000-square-foot Belfast Road plant. Another 62,000-square-foot expansion is anticipated to meet the demand for EBL products.

Since its purchase by a management group of four people in June 1988, Eastcan Beverages Limited (EBL) has become the fastest-growing soft drink bottler in Canada. This marks the company's evolution from a small, family-owned bottler through to ownership by one of the giants of the industry, Pepsi International, and its final entrepreneurial evolution to the operation purchased in 1988.

Today's impressive operation got its start with the seed of an idea sown in the fertile mind of a young serviceman, Mervin Mirsky, as he boarded his ship for the return to Canada at the end of World War II. Mirsky watched dozens of cases of Schweppes Ginger Ale being loaded for export to Canada. He thought there was no reason for ginger ale to be imported by Canada. At that moment the young serviceman became an entrepreneur.

After his return to Ottawa, Mervin convinced his father that they should get into the bottling business. Pure Spring thus was born, the name originating with another flash of flair from the pure spring running behind the Mirsky home on Wellington and Preston streets.

Today the operation is a 158,000-square-foot plant on Belfast Road that employs more than 300 people. What is more, the plant is about to undergo a 62,000-square-foot expansion to meet the demand for EBL products.

The new management quartet of Bruce Quincey, president and chief executive officer; Dave Reid, vice-president/sales and marketing; Mario Galang, vice-president/operations; and Jeff Fleming, vice-president/finance, brought extensive experience in the industry when they purchased the operation after Pepsi Cola, New York, divested itself.

Since June 1988 EBL has expanded rapidly beyond its immediate Ottawa market. Plants were purchased in Renfrew, Belleville, and Oshawa in October 1988. Those

This fleet of trucks delivered the company's first product, Pure Spring Ginger Ale.

were followed by acquisitions in Smiths Falls and Kingston in March 1989. Nor does it end there: EBL is looking at future regional acquisitions as the opportunity arises.

With the addition of 62,000 square feet of space, EBL is taking the opportunity to replace two existing bottling lines with new ones while also adding a new canning line. The more than $15 million investment will be completed by August 1989.

Expansion of the Ottawa operation has had several impacts. Soft drink product growth from 30 to 100 percent of needs is a major development. That total self-sufficiency in bottling and packaging eliminates reliance on imports to the region from Montreal and Toronto.

Since June 1988, under the new ownership of Pepsi International, EBL has expanded rapidly beyond the Ottawa market, and the new fleet of trucks is a familiar sight throughout the area.

EBL's employee roster has grown from 225 in the Ottawa area to more than 350 in its operating region. The Ottawa production plant operates with two shifts a day, five days a week. That level of production is needed to meet the needs of the 2.2 million people serviced in EBL's sales territory.

The Ottawa plant will service the entire region without causing layoffs and disruptions in the markets where existing operations have been taken over. EBL's purchases have been timely from the perspective of the Ottawa plant expansion and the need for either significant outlays for new equipment or closure of plants in those communities. EBL has retained sales depots in each area superior service to the local communities.

"We have been lucky in the acquisition we've made," says Dave Reid, vice-president/sales and marketing. "There has been an exceptional personnel base in each of the communities—really dedicated soft drink people."

From its Ottawa plant the company's production and distribution has grown from more than 180 million individual soft drink servings annually in the Ottawa area to in excess of 410 million servings in its sales territory.

EBL products include the leading brands in the industry today—Pepsi, Seven-Up, Pure Spring, Hires, and Crush, along with their corresponding diet versions. It is also a local distributor for Perrier and other waters and a number of fruit juices. EBL's association with Pepsi, as well as the area licences for Hires, Crush, and the original Pure Spring, have given it the complete line and marketing capabilities needed to compete for prime positions in retail stores.

With a market population in excess of 2.2 million in a region larger than some nations, the company's sales staff is always eyeing new promotion methods and new markets.

One of the fastest-growing markets to emerge during the past eight years is diet soft drinks. Instead of just drawing consumers solely from other flavors, the diet soft drink is actually drawing a new group of people into the soft drink market. Market surveys show these consumers to be health conscious, upscale, and demanding of quality—something not lost on the Ottawa bottler.

This direction has meant keeping an eye on trends and on developing flavors and sweeteners. It also calls for the aggressive marketing of its diet products. The diet drink share of the total soft drink market is currently 30 percent, but industry analysis sees that number rising to 50 percent in the near future.

EBL is also active in marketing its non-diet drinks, becoming involved in tours and promotions for David Bowie, Tina Turner, and Michael Jackson, and regularly sponsoring sports events. A strong advertising presence supports this activity.

Restaurant sales are also important to success in the soft drink industry. EBL is a leader in the area market, serving countless restaurants, including the Fat Albert's and Burger King chains exclusively. Restaurant sales at present account for 20 percent of the Ottawa operation's annual business.

The management quartet brings a strong entrepreneurial spirit to EBL. Through employment, purchase of supplies, and other elements of business, EBL puts back more than $15 million into the communities where there are operations. The 350 employees, a fleet of more than 80 delivery vehicles, and soft drink promotion campaigns create a ready EBL presence in the region.

The commitment to community and people is another mark of EBL. The company is an active participant in the Pepsi "Stars" program, with its strong anti-substance-abuse message, that targets schoolchildren. EBL is targeting the program into more than 300 schools in the region.

As with any successful company, close attention is paid to technical advances in the industrial sector while also being attentive to other necessary attributes such as packaging and the firm's fleet of vehicles.

Growth of the soft drink industry has meant concurrent growth for the bottler, from its fateful observation and inception by Mervin Mirsky in the 1940s through to today's quartet of owners. EBL is continuing the tradition of innovation and community involvement. It is active in the National Capital Commission, the Exhibition Association, and the Ottawa Rough Riders. It is also a major sponsor of the Ottawa Symphony Orchestra.

Because Canadians drink 460 servings of soft drink per capita per year, there are constant challenges for the bottler—riding new trends and providing the product the market desires. At Eastcan Beverages Limited, meeting that challenge is part of a tradition—one that keeps it at the head of its industry.

EBL products include the leading brands on the market today.

Photo by Wayne Eardley/
Burke Communications
Photography

Although major changes have occurred in most Canadian cities following World War II, this area of Ottawa around the Parliament Buildings and Confederation Square has remained much the same. Courtesy, Public Archives of Canada

THE INTIMATE CITY

At the turn of the century, Canada, which was then a relatively new country, and its capital city offered great promise for prosperity. The new federal government had begun to grow, and the population of the City of Ottawa grew with it as people came to take positions with the civil service.

Growth, of course, meant construction, and Ottawa saw plenty of that after Confederation. Eleven major government buildings were constructed in the years between 1896 and 1913 as well as landmarks such as the Chateau Laurier and the Union Station. As the nineteenth century became a memory, Ottawa was an energetic little metropolis, with the new Parliament Buildings at its heart.

Significantly, however, the first year of the twentieth century in Ottawa was also the year of a great fire. Early one April morning sparks from the chimney on a house in Hull flew to a pile of pulpwood nearby;

Confederation Square was photographed just as World War I was beginning in Europe in August 1914. From the left are the Chateau Laurier, the Rhea Building, and the Grand Trunk Railway Station. Courtesy, National Archives of Canada

LEFT: This was the rear of the match factory in Hull after the fire of 1900. The destruction of the city was unequalled, even when compared to the earlier and more notorious Chicago fire. Courtesy, National Archives of Canada

FAR LEFT: The region from the Chaudière south to Carling Avenue resembled a bombed-out area after the Great Fire which destroyed 1,900 buildings in a 440-acre area. Fearing more fires in the area, many residents moved to Sandy Hill or Centretown, and the razed area never regained its former fashionable status. Courtesy, City of Ottawa Archives

The Great Fire reached the corner of Wellington Street and Pooley's Bridge turn-off in this photo taken on April 25. Seven people died in the disaster, and more than 8,000 Ottawans were left homeless. Courtesy, Public Archives of Canada/ Booth Family Collection

Seven lives were lost when fire destroyed the Centre Block of the Parliamentary Buildings the night of February 3, 1916. The structure was entirely gutted and arson was suspected, but never proven. Courtesy, Public Archives of Canada

in no time at all most of the City of Hull had burned. The Chaudière Bridge caught fire too, spinning the flames across the Ottawa River to the J.R. Booth sawmill, just west of Ottawa. Historical accounts describe the sawmill as a blazing inferno from which fire spread to the wooden houses in LeBreton Flats. The glow from the spreading flames was seen as far away as Brockville, 100 miles to the south.

Although the City of Ottawa proper was saved from destruction because the wind propelling the fire finally changed direction, some 15,000 people on both sides of the river were left homeless, and the settled area known as LeBreton Flats was completely devastated.

It was a fact of life in which one could find some irony that wood, which had figured so strongly in Ottawa's beginnings, was the fuel for many of the city's early disasters. People then were dependent on wood for fuel and as a building material. Fire usually spread from wood stoves and caused the destruction of many buildings in Ottawa, such as the Russell House hotel, the original Ottawa City Hall, and the Parliament Buildings, which burned in one terrible night in 1916.

THE NEED FOR CHANGE

Fire was one force in the eventual rejuvenation of the city; the other was the growing realization among residents and government officials alike that the city's appearance in its early years did not become that of a capital city. Ottawa, picturesque as it is today, was not a pretty sight over 80 years ago. Dirt from the streets swirled up in clouds of dust, irritating the eyes of pedestrians, blowing in through shop doors, and covering everything in grit. The cityscape was marred by numerous telegraph wires hanging from unsightly poles; the Rideau Canal was little more than a water-filled ditch, a railroad on its eastern bank. And everywhere piles of lumber littered the ground and grimy smoke polluted the air.

The city had developed almost haphaz-

In the early 1900s, a number of large federal buildings were constructed to house a growing civil service. Chief Federal Architect David Ewart designed this structure, the Connaught Building, in 1913 on Mackenzie Avenue. It houses the Department of Revenue's Customs and Excise Branch. Courtesy, Public Archives of Canada

ardly on the basic grid first laid out for Bytown, but the fact that there was just one bridge across the Rideau Canal meant that new development had taken a sort of hourglass shape, with the bottleneck at Sapper's Bridge.

Prime Minister Mackenzie King is reported by his biographers to have remarked that the City of Ottawa was "not a pretty place, save for the Parliament Buildings." Actually, the need for a plan for the city had been recognized much earlier as the city changed gradually from a trade centre founded on the lumber business to the seat of the national government. The Ottawa Improvement Commission, forerunner of the present National Capital Commission, was founded in 1899 with the goal of maintaining the city's best attributes. Citizens were concerned too that the rapid proliferation of government buildings would adversely affect the business environment of the city.

PLANS FOR THE FUTURE

The first real plan for the city's future growth was developed by Nowlan Cauchon who noted the difficulties the presence of numerous railways in the city presented; he outlined a plan for encouraging the growth of industry in the eastern portion of Ottawa. It was clear, even at the time of Cauchon's report in 1912, that something needed to be done, but it was not clear who would pay for the necessary modifications; consequently, nothing was done.

Nothing, that is, until Prime Minister Mackenzie King decided Ottawa deserved

ABOVE: Sir Wilfrid Laurier, Prime Minister of Canada, stands in the front row beside Governor-General Lord Grey during a 1910 ceremony on Parliament Hill marking the death of His Majesty King Edward VII. Courtesy, Public Archives of Canada

better treatment. In 1928 the Russell House, a hotel serving members of Parliament and a meeting place for society people, burned to the ground. The federal government expropriated the land because the Prime Minister wanted the northernmost end of Elgin Street to be redeveloped as a stately approach to Parliament Hill. In a speech to the House of Commons that year, King explained that Ottawa may not be "the largest, the wealthiest or the most cosmopolitan Capital in the world, but I believe that with Ottawa's natural and picturesque setting . . . and a little careful planning, we can have the most beautiful Capital in the world."

For the "careful planning" King had requested Jacques Gréber, a world-

Despite the prosperity of Ottawa in the 1920s, an alternative lifestyle existed on the banks of the Rideau River, where today stand vacation homes and hotels. Courtesy, National Archives of Canada

FACING PAGE BELOW: William Lyon MacKenzie King is among the many Ottawa citizens who had bought recreational land in the Gatineau around the turn of the century. In this 1901 photograph taken at Kingsmere, King (in rear, with girl on shoulder) is pictured with family and friends. Courtesy, Public Archives of Canada

renowned urban planner and architect to visit Ottawa, which he did a year after the two men met in Paris in 1936. The war years intervened but the Prime Minister repeated his invitation to Gréber to act as a consultant with a group of Canadian planners. Work began on the assessment of the capital in 1946, Gréber being assisted by Edouard Fiset and John Kitchen. Kitchen had worked with Nowlan Cauchon decades before on the first plan.

The Gréber Report, presented in 1949 and regarded even today as an international benchmark in urban analysis and design, stemmed in some ways from Cauchon's work decades before. The report crystallized in prose both the beauty and the problems of Ottawa as both a capital city and a centre of trade and industry. The city, Gréber wrote then, had a "strongly conjuring character which has not yet been divested of the charm of its large wooded vistas, its picturesque canals and falls, the grandeur of its monuments and parks. A bird's eye view of the city leaves the impression that it is wrapped in green."

The problems, Gréber and his associates noted, were many: stately government buildings were situated across the river from grimy factories; 11 railroads dissected the city into utterly unrelatable parts; there was no architectural control as to development on city streets; and pressure from development in the core was affecting the residential areas of the city.

Gréber and his colleagues drafted an elaborate plan for the 900-square-mile capital region. In specific, it called for many improvements, including the relocation of the rail lines and the freight yard downtown, the construction of new bridges and parkways as well as a new boulevard in Hull to enhance the riverside setting of that city. Also suggested were industrial zones in Hull, the reservation of land in both Ottawa and Hull for government buildings, and the construction of a parkway through the Gatineau Hills, north of Hull.

Interestingly, Gréber remained entranced by the fact that even in fully developed sections of Ottawa, there were many

A Jockey Club member purchases war stamps from a "Miss Canada" at Connaught Park Race Track in August of 1942. Photo by A.E. Armstrong. Courtesy, Public Archives of Canada/National Film Board Collection

By the time of this 1926 photograph, the Chateau Laurier had become part of the chain of Canadian National Railway Hotels. The Union Station, also built by the Grand Trunk Railway, had likewise been nationalized. Courtesy, Public Archives of Canada

species of trees. In a visionary passage of the report, Gréber and his associates wrote about the importance of trees in contemporary cities; they "should not be the privilege solely of residential areas, parks and parkways. They should be integrated in the design of industrial centres as well as commercial areas. The mania for the 'megalopolis,' the super-densely built self-contained block, is disappearing gradually, and the aspirations of the people are tending toward a more natural way of living."

The timing of the Gréber Report was excellent, for in 1950, Canada was embarking on a decade of prosperity and the federal government could well afford to enact the proposals made by the urban planners. It helped too, of course, that Gréber, Fiset, and Kitchen's work was supported by three prime ministers, all of whom saw the great need for a reorganization of the capital city.

Within 16 years, all five of the planners' chief proposals—the establishment of green space throughout the city, the planning of government buildings away from the heart of the capital, the relocation of rail lines and the establishment of a "green belt" around the region, and the acquisition of a park in the Gatineaus—were realized. A few years more brought additional changes: the view from Parliament Hill across the river to Hull was no longer a glimpse of piles of pulpwood through factory smoke, but a clear vista of a glittering complex of government buildings. To the west of the city, yet another government complex was built on a site that was once a farm and is still known as Tunney's Pasture; to the east of the Rideau Canal, a grand rail station is now seen to sit not at the end of a rail line but at the waterside and plays host to visitors from across the country. And readily in view is the pleasant green of mature trees and the calming proximity of the rivers and canal.

THE FACE OF DOWNTOWN

Because of the presence of the federal government and the many businesses that have located in the city both to serve and to deal with government, Ottawa's economy is very obviously centered in offices, much more so than other cities of its size; in fact, about two-thirds of all the jobs in the City of Ottawa are office-based. Within six blocks south of Parliament Hill and from the Rideau Canal in the east to Bay Street on the west is a conglomeration of commercial and retail buildings, including office towers and hotels with shopping concourses, government buildings and complexes, and street level stores and businesses.

Far from being a jungle of high-rise towers looking down on darkened, windy streets, however, Ottawa's downtown is characterized by a juxtaposition of architectural styles and economic purpose and by a sense that the streets invite one to walk along them, to explore new sights and

A blissful curtain of falls forms sculptured patterns at the mouth of the Rideau River. Photo by Wayne Eardley/ Burke Communications Photography

Farms dot the Ottawa River valley near Gatineau, in the shadow of the Gatineau Hills. Photo by Wayne Eardley/ Burke Communications Photography

A variety of pastimes are available at Lac des Fees in Gatineau Park. Photo by Justine Hill

Above: The water is cool and fresh at the Prince of Wales Falls, at Hog's Back. Photo by Justine Hill

An audience listens with unbroken attention to a noon-hour concert on the Sparks Street Mall. Photo by Justine Hill

activities. There are modern, shining, steel and glass buildings, of course, such as Place Export Canada, the Journal Towers, Place de Ville, and L'Esplanade Laurier which are government-occupied, along with private sector developments such as Place Bell Canada, the Metropolitan Life complex, Constitution Square, and 99 Metcalfe, all sleek and attractive structures.

But what makes the core of Ottawa so vital are the open spaces, such as the newly renovated Sparks Street pedestrian mall, where hundreds of office workers take their lunches on summer days, enjoying the sunshine and the splashing of nearby fountains. Confederation Square is the focal point of what Prime Minister Mackenzie King hoped would be a dramatic approach to Parliament Hill and a public square not unlike London's Piccadilly Circus. (That effect has been heightened by the use of distinctive red double-decker buses during the summer months by a local tour bus operator.)

And of course there are the many buildings downtown that are part of Canada's history: the huge, imposing structures that were built in the first decades after Ottawa was designated the capital city, such as the stately Langevin Block, now the home of the Prime Minister's Office, the Central Chambers, and the Central Post Office. The Post Office Building that now stands opposite the Confederation Square was built in 1937, replacing the original which was demolished to make way for the Square and its monument to the many Canadians who died in the two World Wars.

In truth, there isn't just one "downtown" in Ottawa, there are two: longtime denizens

Mail collection by pickup truck was a common sight in Ottawa in 1938. Courtesy, National Archives of Canada

LEFT: The Central Post Office has been a splendid landmark for decades, with its copper roof and elegant, strong, vertical lines. Photo by Jessie Parker/ First Light

BELOW: This photo of the Old Post Office, between the Sappers' and Dufferin Bridges, was taken shortly before the turn of the century. Courtesy, National Archives of Canada

ABOVE: Under colourful awnings, local farmers offer fruit and vegetables, flowers and plants to shoppers in the Byward Market. Photo by Cosmo Condina/ The StockMarket

ABOVE RIGHT: Dewy local Lobo apples await Market shoppers who have visions of pies or applesauce in mind. Photo by Devries Mikkelsen/ First Light

RIGHT: Fresh fruit and vegetables tempt Saturday shoppers in the Byward Market. Photo by Mihok/ The StockMarket

FACING PAGE BOTTOM: The Old Fish Market is one of many Byward Market area restaurants, offering the best of the world's cuisines. Photo by Jessie Parker/ First Light

of the city refer to the two parts of the inner city where they love to socialize and do their shopping as Uptown and Downtown. Uptown is Bank Street and Sparks Street, south of Parliament Hill. Although it would be difficult to say whether Ottawa in fact has a single "main street," Bank Street is one of several principal thoroughfares that see plenty of activity, day and night. Bank Street became a centre for commerce when the tram lines were first laid out in the city before the turn of the century, and shopkeepers opened their businesses progressively southward along the street; today there are high fashion furriers, bookshops, restaurants, and clothing stores side by side to attract shoppers and pedestrians.

Downtown, on the other hand, is centred on the Byward Market, the farmer's market that has been at the heart of Ottawa since it was Bytown in the mid-nineteenth century. In the age-old tradition of urban development around a market square, the Byward Market sits with its brick Market Building, ringed by farmers' stalls of fresh produce and flowers, in the part of Ottawa that began as Lower Town.

Once the home of the French-speaking labourers who came to work on the Rideau Canal, Lower Town remains home to many of their descendants, as well as a popular destination for Ottawans looking to spend a dewy Saturday morning shopping for just-picked vegetables or an evening out in a café or supper club.

Many of the city's best restaurants are located in the Market area, offering cuisine from Japan, Holland, France, Italy, India—even Afghanistan—as well as classic Continental and traditional North American food. Often, cooking staff can be seen traipsing across Clarence or York Street to pick up another carton of fresh lettuce from a local farmer or a basket of steaming rolls from one of the several bakeries.

The Market area is more than a farmer's market, however; it has also become a haven for those who appreciate the unique in life, whether it be a designer dress, an antique book, or hand-made jewelry.

The centre of Ottawa is distinctive from many other North American cities in that people both live and work in it; there have been a number of luxury condominium developments built recently, and there is rental housing available as well, appealing to the many Ottawans who love to walk, jog, or cycle to work.

BILINGUALISM IN THE CAPITAL

One of the reasons Ottawa was considered a prime candidate to become the

TOP: Byward Market was the commercial centre of Ottawa in the 1920s. Today, it is a lively night-spot with restaurants and clubs, and is known as the most "old world" section of Ottawa. Courtesy, National Archives of Canada

ABOVE: A noon-hour concert on the Sparks Street mall delights the crowd. Photo by Wayne Eardley/Burke Communications Photography

The City of Nepean is a fast-growing network of neighbourhoods. Photo by Wayne Eardley/ Burke Communications Photography

capital of Canada was its location. Situated on the border between Ontario and Quebec, it straddles the meeting place of Canada's two predominant cultures with their two languages: French and English. Although bilingualism is a fact in many European cities, North American cities in which people work in two languages, and in which two cultures interact to their mutual benefit, are not common. Thus Ottawa is uniquely fortunate, thanks to the cultural richness and versatility its bilingualism provides, in North America.

Outsiders may assume that the Ottawa River forms a tangible boundary between the English and French cities of Ottawa and Hull; however, this is not in fact the case. There are settlements on the Quebec side that historically were settled by English-speaking people, and similarly, villages and towns on the Ontario side that were populated originally by French-speaking settlers. The City of Aylmer in Quebec is a case in point; originally "an English town" Aylmer is today a community in which both French-speaking and English-speaking Canadians live side-by-side.

Typically, telephone calls to businesses in the capital are answered thus: "Dicom, *bonjour,* "a greeting that signifies a willingness to speak either language. Many people who are in regular contact with the public are bilingual. (Or trilingual, in the case of the many businesspeople who have emigrated to Canada from Lebanon, Italy, or the Far East.)

Much of the drive toward complete bilingualism has been evidenced in the Ottawa school system. Until the late 1960s, education in French at the secondary school level was provided only by private schools run by religious orders; at the same time, publicly funded elementary level education was available in French and in English. The net result of this situation was that the French Catholics experienced an obstacle to higher education; in 1984, of course, the Ontario government extended funding to Catholic separate schools right through to the Grade XIII level.

When the federal civil service began to institute its policy of bilingualism, the effect on Ottawa was dramatic. Suddenly, French-speaking citizens (who were frequently bilingual out of necessity) were in a favoured position to compete for government jobs.

With the extensive language training programs and the French immersion programs in the schools, many citizens of Ottawa are now at ease in either official language, and business is conducted in both French and English from one part of the region to another, according to preference. It is possible, for instance, to telephone the City of Hull and ask for information on a cultural event and to receive a reply in English; meanwhile, public employees in the City of Ottawa can offer assistance in either French or in English.

THE NEIGHBOURHOODS

It's a saying among the people who live in Ottawa that you can't go anywhere in the region without seeing someone you know; whether you're at the theatre, finishing Sunday brunch at a café in the market, browsing through the antiques at the Stittsville flea market, or just doing the grocery shopping, Canada's fourth largest metropolitan area is in many ways just another small town.

In large part it's Ottawa's many neighbourhoods that give people this feeling, as each neighbourhood has its own distinctive character. Historians have noted that the neighbourhoods in Ottawa tended to develop according to the characteristics of the civil servants who would buy homes in them; some of the houses in Rideau Gardens, for example, a quiet part of the city nestled between Rideau River and the Rideau Canal, were originally bought in the 1920s by senior staff from Agriculture Canada, who then planted perennial gardens and trees not usually seen in city landscaping.

Until the 1960s the term 'neighbourhood' just meant where a person lived in Ottawa, but in the wake of the tremendous redevelopment of the National Capital Region due to the Gréber Plan strategies, city planning in the sixties was oriented more toward expansion than preservation. This trend was not accepted wholeheartedly, and various citizen groups began to band together to oppose certain forms of development that would, in their opinion, destroy the very nature of the neighbourhoods these developments were intended to exploit. To this day redevelopment in Ottawa has to be sensitive to community concerns, particularly where heritage properties are concerned. For the most part, however, developers have responded by offering designs for new projects that integrate well with neighbourhood context.

Of all the neighbourhoods in the City of Ottawa, the best known are Centretown, the Glebe, Sandy Hill, New Edinburgh, and Island Park.

Centretown, which lies immediately to the west of the Rideau Canal, south of the city's commercial centre, is living proof of the vitality of downtown Ottawa. This neighbourhood is where many of Ottawa's young urban professionals have chosen to live. Centretown is Sunday brunch in a sidewalk café on Elgin Street with a copy of the *New York Times,* or an ice cream cone and a stroll past designer clothing shops, century-old brick Victorian houses and tree-shaded streets, and bunches of laughing children in the parks.

Elgin Street has become much livelier in recent years and now boasts theatres, a supper club that often features Ottawa's famed Skit Row comedy troupe, restaurants, and cafés, as well as bookstores, art galleries, and gourmet food shops. A

Hot air balloons are a common sight over the city on a summer day; in the centre is the YM-YWCA. Photo by Paul von Baich/ First Light

relatively recent phenomenon in tourist accommodation in Ottawa can be found in Centretown, namely Bed and Breakfast establishments, which are usually turn-of-the-century mansions that have been renovated and function now as guest homes. Here tourists can enjoy the flavour of the city as the residents do, by staying in a real home.

The Glebe is the neighbourhood for the young affluent Ottawa family; it has been said that the people who choose to live here tend to be nostalgic about the past and want good, solid, old-fashioned houses as well as that feeling of belonging to a small community. In the Glebe you'll see small food shops where "natural" food and organically grown produce is sold. You'll also find busy newsstands where magazines from all over the world are available, antique stores, and designer dress shops, and one of the city's busiest toy stores.

Community activities centre on the many interesting programs for people of all ages offered by the city at the Glebe Community Centre and on the two neighbourhood public schools, Mutchmor School and the classically renovated First Avenue School. Also in the Glebe is a senior citizens development called the Glebe Centre; residents live in a high-rise apartment building which is attached to a splendid

ABOVE: First Avenue School is one of the oldest in Ottawa, and today offers a program of early French Immersion. Photo by Jessie Parker/ First Light

LEFT: Mutchmor Public School bears the name of a prominent Ottawa family, once headed by pioneer James Mutchmor. Photo by Jessie Parker/ First Light

ABOVE LEFT: A Victorian house on McLeod Street serves as a cosy Bed and Breakfast house, where guests can enjoy an Ottawa family's hospitality. Photo by Devries Mikkelsen/ First Light

FACING PAGE TOP RIGHT: The Bank Street Promenade is a walkway past some of the city's most interesting shops and services, past old-fashioned street lamps, and flower-filled planters. Photo by Justine Hill

stone house called Abbotsford, built in 1872 by Alexander Mutchmor. The Glebe Centre is the focal point for many community activities, and residents benefit from being able to remain in their old neighbourhood, close to familiar places and people.

People in the Glebe know their auto mechanic or the man behind the newsstand by his first name; many of the shops and services on Bank Street in the neighbourhood have been there for decades, while others are enthusiastic newcomers. Names such as Herb & Spice, Loretta's Bakery (rumoured to have the best Gâteau St. Honoré this side of France), and the Glebe Meat Market readily evoke the image of a tightly knit community within a busy city.

There is an interesting little community of English nannies in the Glebe too, many of whom congregate with their tiny charges around the fountain at Fifth Avenue Court, a small but cheery grouping of neighbourhood shops with an enclosed brick courtyard.

Sandy Hill is another well-known neighbourhood, east of the Rideau Canal. It was originally the estate of Louis Besserer, who was a veteran of the War of 1812 and a member of the House of Assembly. Lots were sold and development initiated in the 1860s, when housing was much needed by the many families who came to Ottawa after the city's designation as capital.

Although Sandy Hill was originally where high level civil servants and members of government lived, today its residents come from all levels of society, attracted by the University of Ottawa, the focal point of the neighbourhood. Senior citizens, civil servants, families, and univer-

A peaceful summer afternoon is spent under the willows in a New Edinburgh park. Photo by Wayne Eardley/Burke Communications Photography

sity students and professors all live in Sandy Hill, appreciative of its rolling topography—unique in Ottawa—and the stimulating variety in housing styles.

Sandy Hill is one of the oldest neighbourhoods in the city, and many houses were built before 1900; because the houses are architecturally significant, they have been preserved and updated. Some, as in the case of the award-winning Portals development, have been used as the cornerstone for new development that effects a seamless imitation of the old housing styles.

One of the most interesting houses, and a "must-see" for residents and visitors alike, is Laurier House, the only private residence in Canada which has the distinction of having been home to two prime ministers. Originally the home of Sir Wilfrid Laurier, the house was also occupied by Mackenzie King from 1923 until his death in 1950. Aside from being a charming home, in which many beautiful furnishings and works of art are displayed, Laurier House offers a fascinating view of the private life of a head of state.

Although Sandy Hill doesn't have retail shopping strips to the extent that other neighbourhoods in Ottawa do (and being perhaps five minutes from downtown, doesn't need to) there are interesting shops and restaurants on Rideau Street, as well as the famed Rideau Bakery, where one can get a cup of superb coffee and a croissant or muffin just out of the oven.

Not far from Sandy Hill is New Edinburgh, once known as the Village of New Edinburgh. This area of the city started life as the lands owned by Thomas MacKay, the stonemason who worked with Colonel By on the Rideau Canal. MacKay Street is named after him, and four of the streets in New Edinburgh—Charles, John, Victoria, and Alexander—are named after his children. New Edinburgh, of course, was also home to the MacKay mill and industrial complex, as well as to the labourers who worked for MacKay.

FACING PAGE: Verdant Brantwood Park is located next to the Rideau River, with its wading pool and tennis courts. City-owned swans often stop at the shore to receive bits of bread from children. Photo by Paul von Baich/ First Light

All that has now disappeared; what remains is a very attractive neighbourhood so quaint one might think the clock has been turned back a hundred years. This effect is seen in the beautiful Minto Bridges, the lovingly renovated frame and brick homes, and the intricate network of lanes throughout the community. As well, many descendants of the families who first came to Canada from Scotland to work for MacKay still live in New Edinburgh, giving the village within a capital a strong sense of Scottish heritage.

Residents of New Edinburgh today are both francophone and anglophone, and many of them are young professional couples who have children. Residents are very keen on preserving the unique character of the village and so ensure through community activity the appropriateness of new developments.

Although not at New Edinburgh's geographic centre, certainly the centre of life in the community is Rideau Hall, MacKay's original stone house and now the home of the Governor-General of Canada. Government House, as it's also known, sits in the middle of an 80-acre estate, surrounded by an enormous iron fence; tours of the house and grounds are offered daily for those who are interested.

One cannot describe New Edinburgh adequately without mention of McCreery's Grocery and Butcher Shop on Crichton Street. With its pressed tin ceiling, creaky wooden floor, and old-time serving

A cyclist crosses the Minto Bridges, which were the site of the first rail line into the City of Ottawa. Photo by Wayne Eardley/ Burke Communications Photography

counter, this shop has catered to the needs of local residents, including members of Parliament and diplomatic officials, since it first opened in 1890.

The Village of Rockcliffe Park isn't really a neighbourhood in Ottawa but a municipality in its own right, with its own mayor and town officials. It has no police force of its own, however; instead the Ontario Provincial Police provide police service.

To the casual observer Rockcliffe is a dignified, perhaps even "snooty" area of town, its huge baronial and Tudor mansions inhabited by wealthy old Ottawa families, as well as by diplomats from countries such as Finland, Cuba, and Bulgaria. The winding streets are shaded by trees; there are no sidewalks in Rockcliffe, and

ABOVE: This spectacular view of the Ottawa River and the Gatineau Hills is from the pagoda-like Rockcliffe Lookout. Photo by Wayne Eardley/ Burke Comunications Photography

RIGHT: Alta Vista is one of Ottawa's most attractive neighbourhoods, and was established in the 1950s. Photo by Paul von Baich/ First Light

the atmosphere is really that of a country hideaway, as opposed to an enclave for the elite. Yet although there is no commercial development of any sort in the Village, Rockcliffe is minutes from downtown Ottawa or McCreery's.

Virtually every architectural style in the world is represented in the houses in Rockcliffe, from the imposing stone mansions, such as the Rockcliffe Manor House and Waterstone, to Hart Massey's elegant and intriguing house that seems to float out over MacKay Lake on steel supports. Stornoway, since 1950 the home of the Leader of the Opposition, was one of the first houses in Rockcliffe. In 1942, when it was owned by the Perley-Robertson family, Stornoway was offered to Princess Juliana of the Netherlands as a temporary home where she and her family took refuge in Canada during World War II.

Not all the houses are impressive stone or brick and stucco structures, however; in recent years new luxury condominiums have appeared among the trees around MacKay Lake. Also of note is the O.J. Firestone House, in which a stunning private collection of Canadian art is displayed; Dr. Firestone donated the house to the public, and visitors may arrange tours through the Ontario Heritage Foundation.

With all the trees and the quiet, country ambiance, visitors to Rockcliffe may miss the fact that the village is close to the Ottawa River. That can be corrected with a visit to the Rockcliffe Lookout, which offers a marvellous view of both the river and the Gatineau Hills beyond.

For years, Rockcliffe's reputation for being an enclave for the very rich was heightened by its proximity to Vanier, another municipality next to the City of Ottawa, but which was known for its predominantly French-speaking, working class population. Once known as Eastview, the City of Vanier today continues to resist annexation to Ottawa, and proudly boasts signs on its main thoroughfares that read, "You are now entering the City of Vanier. Bienvenue. Welcome." The recent addition of charming, brightly colored wood benches bearing the city's name also serves to set Vanier apart from its municipal neighbours.

As is the way of such areas, and as housing stock close to the core of Ottawa rises in value, Vanier is gradually becoming a "hot" place to live, while still very much the home of young, mostly French-speaking families.

Luxury condominium developments have appeared in the northern portion of the city, but Vanier maintains an appealingly intimate character, and a good deal of charm. On Beechwood Avenue, for example, new shops have appeared in renovated older buildings, and old favourites, such as restaurant and florist shops, continue to serve people as graciously as they have always done.

Ottawa East is another important Ottawa neighbourhood, one in which lovely farmhouses built in the nineteenth century can be found amid newer homes, and where huge, venerable trees bend over wide streets that slope gently down to the Rideau River.

Ottawa East was settled originally by farmers and owners of small plots of land, as well as by certain religious orders. It was previously known as the Village of Archville, which was annexed to the City of Ottawa early in the 1900s. The Slattery farmhouse, one of the principal homes in the early days, is today still visible on its hilltop setting between Riverdale Avenue and Mount Pleasant. Slattery's Field, just north of the house, was the site from which the first airplane took off from Ottawa, as a highlight of the program offered by the Central Canada Exhibition in 1911.

Ottawa East today, though very different in many ways from that original country setting, in other ways remains the same; Main Street still offers services, with a health food store serving almost as a kind of general store, and Art's Market, a local greengrocer's, still exists as the meeting place for many in Ottawa East. The community is threatened somewhat by its closeness to downtown, however, in that proposed collector lanes for The Queensway may be run through the heart of Ottawa East. Nevertheless, citizens groups endeavour to find the best solution to everyone's needs.

Alta Vista, which lies across the Rideau River and southeast of Ottawa East, is a beautiful neighbourhood of sprawing bungalows and modern two-storey homes. In fact, Alta Vista was where two of Canada's most renowned homebuilders, Minto and Campeau, faced off during the 1950s, and as a result of the competition, produced some of the best housing in the nation. Just minutes from downtown and less time still from Ottawa's hospitals on Smyth Road, Alta Vista is home to a varied mix of residents, from physicians and nurses to the proprietors of many of Ottawa's small businesses.

West of downtown Ottawa are several very interesting neighbourhoods, such as Island Park, another collection of imposing homes set on and near scenic Island Park Drive, and Westboro, a thriving family community that has developed around

The Kanata Square development is an example of the high quality office space in the suburban office market. Photo by Wayne Eardley/Burke Communications Photography

historic Richmond Road.

Westboro was once a village but was annexed to the City of Ottawa, as were other villages such as Hintonburgh, Mechanicsville, and Bayswater, in 1950. Nevertheless, the neighbourhood still retains that village atmosphere, aided in no small part by the focus on Richmond Road, which passes through the heart of the settlement. The area's centre, states renowned architectural historian Harold Kalman, is in fact the former Nepean Town Hall on Richmond Road. The old hall briefly hosted activities for Westboro's senior citizens.

In the late 1970s the area's businesspeople developed a plan for aesthetic improvements, including new sidewalks, streetlamps, and planters, which have done much to enhance the village character of Westboro.

SISTER COMMUNITIES

Around the City of Ottawa are several other municipalities, which are as much a

An incredible view of the Ottawa River Valley can be seen from the Champlain Lookout in the Gatineau Park. Three centuries ago, only the Indians knew it existed. Photo by Wayne Eardley/ Burke Communications Photography

part of life in the National Capital Region as a visit to Parliament Hill. Many people who work in Ottawa live in Hull, Aylmer, or Gatineau, or in a neighbourhood in the growing municipalities of Nepean, Gloucester, or Kanata. Similarly, people who live in Ottawa may travel to their place of work outside the city proper, in a new office park in Nepean, for example, or in the complex of government buildings in Hull.

Aylmer is just one of the towns that lie outside the boundaries of Hull, in Quebec, such as Gatineau and Cantley. Aylmer was once regarded as an English enclave in Quebec West, but today is a community in which both cultures live happily. The *Rue Principale,* or Main Street, has recently been restored and beautified at the urging of the local historical society, and many marvellous stone buildings, such as the Hotel Symmes, have been renovated for present-day use. The Aylmer marina is the site of many activities year round, including the annual festival of the Ottawa River, Festivoile, which features sailing races and other marine-centred events.

The City of Kanata, just 24 kilometres west of the centre of the City of Ottawa, is a new addition to the region, having been formed officially in 1978. Kanata developed as a result of the dreams of several real estate developers in Ottawa, William Teron among them, and was spurred on by the fact that several advanced technology firms chose to locate to the west of the region.

The name *Kanata* is an Iroquois word that means "meeting place"; today Kanata is home to several dozen high-tech companies, including Canadian Marconi, Digital, and Mitel; it is also home to more than 30,000 people.

Nepean is another fast-growing community, which in 1988 opened a splendid civic complex at Centrepointe, including municipal offices, a theatre, and an artspace. Residential construction boomed in

The wide Ottawa River is swathed in red and yellow autumn foliage. Photo by Bill Marsh/ The StockMarket

Nepean in the latter part of the 1980s, but this is no mere bedroom community for Ottawa, not any more; record numbers of building permits were issued in the late 1980s for commercial and industrial construction as well. The Centrepointe Community serves as a shining example of mixed use development, with varied density residential development strategically, and thoughtfully, placed close to office and commercial developments.

But these are just a few of the interesting neighbourhoods and areas in Ottawa; others, like Crystal Bay, have a long history as a summer retreat for the city's families. Britannia, for instance, was once the end of the line for the western tram line from the city; today it boasts a yacht club on sparkling Britannia Bay and houses that vary from quaint cottages to modern, West Coast style homes.

Within a half-hour drive of Ottawa, north of Hull, are certain old villages—Chelsea, Old Chelsea, and Wakefield—where people live close to the Gatineau River in the valley between the river and the beautiful Gatineau Hills.

Beyond the greenbelt that surrounds the region, like the "necklace" Jacques Gréber intended it to be, there are rural communities that still view Ottawa in its traditional role as the central trading place for produce and farm goods. Each year in autumn Ottawans head out for a Saturday or Sunday visit to a fall fair in Richmond, Almonte, or Murphy's Corners.

The people of Ottawa-Hull enjoy the best of all worlds: pleasant neighbourhoods with a strong sense of identity and community spirit as well as a deep-seated respect for history; a busy city that is an international centre for business and the arts; and last, a proximity to the countryside, which is never far from any Canadian's heart.

This view of Parliament Hill reveals this region's timeless beauty. Photo by Derek Trask/The StockMarket

Photo by Wayne Eardley/
Burke Communications
Photography

Photo by Wayne Eardley/
Burke Communications
Photography

Photo by Wayne Eardley/Burke Communications Photography

Photo by Wayne Eardley/
Burke Communications
Photography

Courtesy, Public
Archives of Canada

Courtesy, National Archives of Canada

IBER DEVELOPMENTS INC.

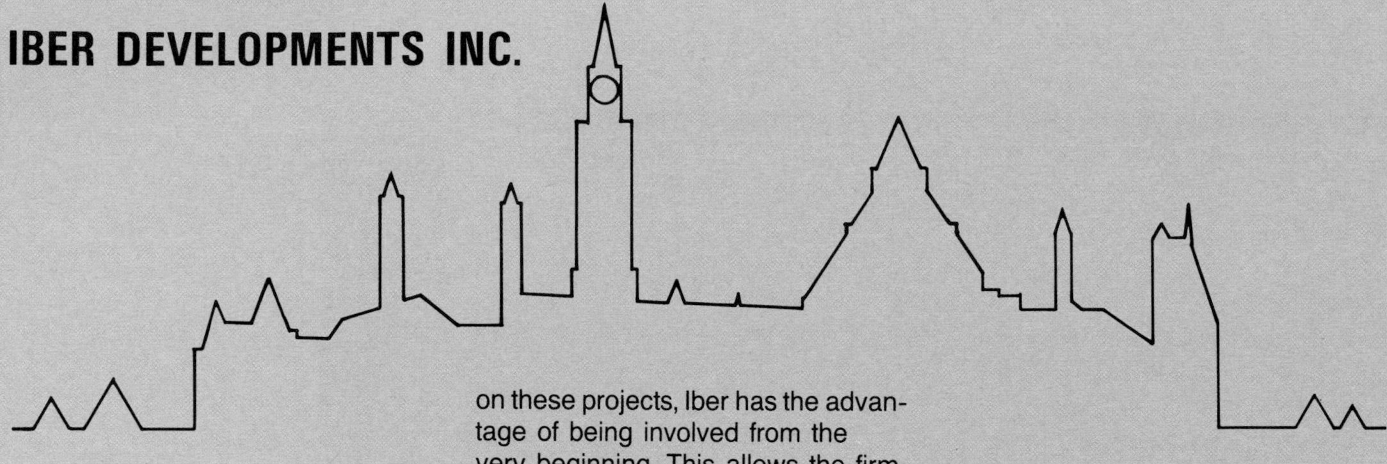

Iber Developments Inc. is a young and dynamic company in the Ottawa-area real estate and land development field. At the top is 39-year-old controlling shareholder Jack Steenbakkers, who assumed the presidency of the firm in 1984.

Behind the youth of the company, however, is a quarter-century of experience as a homebuilder and developer through Iber and associated companies. Success has come as a result of a unique determination to "build communities, not just houses."

"We always try to imagine what a community will look like in five and 10 years and beyond before we undertake any development," Iber marketing manager Teresa Steenbakkers explains. "That way we can build for the right mix, design the streetscape accordingly, and end up with a community package that's desirable to the home buyer."

Iber has developed and successfully marketed a number of communities in the Ottawa area, including the ongoing community of Huntersfield which includes homes ranging in size from executive singles to the unique townhomes in Town Walk III. Other community-style projects completed and sold out by Iber include Rosevale Gardens; Rosevale Park; Fox Hollow, in the city of Kanata; and the 46-lot Beechwood Estates, centrally located near Rockcliffe Park. Iber's Brentwood Park, a condominium community in the city of Ottawa comprising 79 units, was sold out in an amazing 13 weeks.

As both developer and builder on these projects, Iber has the advantage of being involved from the very beginning. This allows the firm to be both flexible and patient.

"As a company, we're not in a hurry to develop projects just for the sake of it. We'd rather build 200 good homes in a year than rush and sell 1,000," Teresa Steenbakkers says. "We plan on being around for quite some time, so patience will pay off for us."

As well as having an excellent image in the marketplace as a homebuilder, Iber is also involved in other aspects of real estate. The firm's commercial projects include development of an industrial park in Ottawa and a number of commercial buildings.

Iber Developments pumps about $30 million into the Ottawa economy each year through salaries and capital expenditures. It employs 35 people year round with as many as 75 on staff during the active season.

After building more than 1,500 homes in the Ottawa region Iber Developments is confident about what lies ahead. "There's no book in the library that can teach what we've learned," Steenbakkers says. "This has been a hands-on education—one that has prepared us very well for the 1990s."

The Chesapeake—Iber's most popular model.

BAYSHORE SHOPPING CENTRE

The recently renovated Bayshore Shopping Centre conjures up an image of upscale fashion. The three-storey centre houses 165 businesses, including four major department stores and more than 160 quality shops and services. The many local and national stores offer a wide range of merchandise, and the new third level features a variety of high-grade fashion boutiques.

A classic when it was built in 1973 housing 100 stores and services, the centre was totally renovated in September 1987. A third floor was added to the two-storey structure, and the centre was brought into the 1990s with skylights, soft colors, and modern lines. The skylight, running the entire length of the centre, creates a bright environment. The exterior retained "a touch of Ottawa," with dormer windows reflecting the architecture of Ottawa's Parliament buildings. The design is simple, but effective, eye catching but not distracting.

Located just west of Ottawa in the city of Nepean, the centre is directly accessible from the Queensway. Bayshore's success is attributed to its location in a rapid-growth area and the convenience of free parking in its multilevel, 4,000-car-capacity lot. Away from the bustle of downtown, customers can shop every weeknight until 10 p.m. in "the best selection of stores in Ottawa."

Above: Bayshore's modern architecture is pleasing to the eye but not distracting. The patron's attention is drawn to the centre's myriad of fine stores. Photo by Philippe Landreville

Left: Bayshore Shopping Centre is prepared for the 1990s with its new third floor, which features skylights and dormer windows.

Despite the fact that Bayshore is a large regional centre, it is very community minded. Many of the centre's promotional events include fund raisers for local service clubs, the Kidney Foundation, and the Children's Hospital of Eastern Ontario, to name just a few. One of its major events is devoted to senior citizens. Each November Bayshore hosts a Seniors' Day, treating thousands of its elderly shoppers to discounts, lunch, entertainment, and a day filled with memories.

Most shopping centres serve customers within a five-mile radius; Bayshore attracts clients from as far away as Perth, Pembroke, Smith Falls, Carleton Place, and its neighbors across the river in Quebec. Bayshore Shopping Centre is truly a shopping experience as well as an exciting attraction to Ottawa residents and its tourists.

THOMAS C. ASSALY CORPORATION LTD.

Albion Place, a $105-million multiuse development completed in 1988, is the largest single project the company has ever undertaken.

Thomas C. Assaly, president and chairman of the board.

Thomas C. Assaly makes his own breaks.

From the time he first broke ground in real estate in 1953, Assaly and his family have believed that hard work, determination, and ingenuity are the benchmarks of a successful company.

Their drive for success has reshaped the role of developers in the national capital region. With one eye on the future, they have refocussed attention on multiuse developments in the mold of Albion Place, the firm's flagship. The 300-room hotel, condominium apartment tower, apartment-hotel, recreational centre, office tower, and expansive commercial parking garage—a $105-million project—is the largest single endeavor the company has ever undertaken. Albion Place was completed in October 1988.

Mega-projects, which have generated more than $300 million for the corporation in syndicated real estate sales, are the offspring of humble beginnings. Assaly's first large-scale housing venture came in 1960, when the company was contracted to build 550 multi-homes at CFB Uplands. Today Thomas C. Assaly Corporation Ltd. is among the largest and most respected real estate companies in the national capital region.

Since its inception Assaly has acted as a mirror and voice of the community. As a gesture of good will, the company has donated one million dollars to the building of an institute for neuromuscular research. The complex will be built at the Ottawa General Hospital.

Organizing and promoting events such as the Festival of Spring and Winterlude are other examples of how Thomas C. Assaly Corporation Ltd. returns to the community the good fortune it has received.

With high-volume construction a modern-day reality for developers, Assaly has not compromised quality. A quality-control department was set up to ensure the strict standards set by the company are followed by all contractors.

With Thomas C. Assaly Corporation Ltd. projects as far west as Alberta and as far south as Florida, the company is clearly willing to expand. "Wherever there is a profit to be made or income to be earned, that is where we are going," says Assaly, age 65, who, to this day, remains president of the company and chairman of its board.

With projects ranging as far west as Alberta and as far south as Florida in the United States, Thomas C. Assaly Corporation Ltd.'s headquarters is still in Ottawa where it began in 1953.

Phase I and II of Viewmount Woods offer 280 apartment units in a mid-rise setting.

CAMPEAU CORPORATION

Les Terrases de la Chaudiers in Hull is one among many of Campeau's prestigious developments.

The story of the Campeau Corporation is one of the outstanding Ottawa business success stories of this generation. Now a leader in retail real estate and commercial development in North America, the company traces its beginnings to 1949, when founder Robert Campeau turned a profit on the first home he built in the capital region.

Still guided by Campeau's firm hand and vision, Campeau Corporation has long since grown away from residential development, while at the same time maintaining a strong Ottawa presence. The list of projects the firm has developed in the capital region includes some of the most prestigious office and retail complexes: Place de Ville, Journal Towers, Centennial Towers, Pinecrest Office Park, Les Terrases de la Chaudiers in Hull, and the Cognos Building, to name a few.

Place de Ville, to which a 600,000-square-foot third phase is currently being planned, is particularly outstanding. Proposed and promoted by Campeau himself in the mid-1960s, this development was genuinely ahead of its time and changed the face of the city centre when it was completed in 1972. It is still the largest development of its kind in Ottawa.

That type of forward thinking has allowed Campeau's Ottawa operations to thrive years after the chairman of the board moved on to other projects. Commercial and residential land purchased 25 years ago by Campeau in Kanata and the south and east ends is only now coming on stream and turning a healthy profit.

The Campeau Corporation is currently responsible for more than 6 million square feet of office and retail space in 50 buildings in the capital region. Area assets total well in excess of one billion dollars, a figure that is expected to grow as the company looks at new ways to enhance its portfolio.

One of the areas of particular interest to the firm is the development of a third major shopping centre in the city, on the south end. With the parent corporation now owning some of the largest department store chains in the United States, Campeau Corporation is well positioned to develop a unique and profitable retail complex, again using land acquired by the company founder years ago.

Planning for the future has been the Campeau Corporation's central philosophy from the very beginning, and as this future has unfolded, it has brought with it more success. That is why the company is eagerly looking forward to the 1990s.

The glamorous Place de Ville changed the face of downtown Ottawa when it opened its doors in 1972.

ANNIS, O'SULLIVAN, VOLLEBEKK LTD. ONTARIO LAND SURVEYORS

Annis, O'Sullivan, Vollebekk Ltd. is the Ottawa region's largest private land surveying firm with 85 full-time employees, including seven Ontario land surveyors. The company has expanded steadily since its founding in 1964 by George Annis and Michael O'Sullivan. Today it provides, along with its partner company, Photomap Air Surveys Limited of Toronto, a full range of services, including cadastral, geodetic, topographic, and photogrammetric surveys.

Within the corporation, all the technicians and surveyors are responsible to one of three departments: Legal and Condominium Surveys, Construction and Urban Development Surveys, and Mapping and Major Utility Surveys.

In order to provide the best service to its clients, the firm has remained abreast of the latest computer technology and survey instrumentation. State-of-the-art, onsite instruments record data electronically and link directly to the office computers and automatic plotters. Because of this commitment to new technology, the firm is now involved in the data gathering for Ontario's futuristic Land Related Information System, a comprehensive, automated database of all property-related records.

Clients include municipalities, federal and provincial government agencies, large utility companies, as well as land developers, lawyers, architects, and the general public. Within the Ottawa region, the firm has offices in Nepean, Embrun-Russell, and Orleans. Its work, however, is not limited to Ontario, as several of the company's surveyors are commissioned as Canada Land Surveyors. Projects can be undertaken within federally administered lands throughout the country.

In addition to the firm's sense of professionalism, there is also a sense of responsibility toward the communities in which it works. The company actively supports local events, charities, and amateur athletics, as well as service organizations and hospitals.

This sense of community, along with its dedication to quality and service, assures Annis, O'Sullivan, Vollebekk Ltd. continued success.

Left: Field survey crews electronically measure and store data using an advanced electronic surveying system. Three-dimensional co-ordinates and point attributes are identified by an onboard microprocessor.

Below: The office staff of Annis, O'Sullivan, Vollebekk Ltd. uses fully automated computer drafting systems to produce plans.

ASELFORD-MARTIN LTD.

Since 1966 Aselford-Martin Ltd. has been building on its reputation for delivering buildings and building services of an exceptional quality.

Founded by Garth Aselford and John Martin, the company started out in the residential construction market. While it continues to excel in that area, Aselford-Martin has since become known for its work in developing office towers, retail and commercial plazas, shopping centres, and public buildings.

Aselford-Martin has also expanded into fields closely related to the development industry. Centurion Property Management Corporation was founded in 1974 to provide management services for a number of residential and commercial properties. Two years later the Enviroplan Ltd. division was created to provide project planning services to the business of community development. In 1987 the corporate family was rounded out with the formation of Aselford-Martin Shopping Centres Ltd., created to consolidate and build upon a decade of experience in shopping centre development.

The Aselford-Martin residential experience includes the conceptual development, individual building, design, and construction of more than 2,000 apartment units, 1,000 townhouses, and hundreds of custom- and semi-custom-built homes in the capital region.

The company's first residential housing development, the 200-acre Westwood, was completed in its first year. Its first institutional building, Norwood High School, was completed in 1972.

According to company president Aselford, the growth and success of the firm is based on one word—quality. "The prudent and selective purchaser looks for value, asking: 'Will the product stand the test of time? Will it increase in value?' We have always built for that discriminating buyer," he says. "We believe that our work should have inherent value."

Both Aselford and Martin, who serves as corporate secretary/treasurer, have maintained a direct and continual involvement in the company, lending their expertise to its expansion. "The personal, hands-on style of management we've adopted is based on the conviction that details really matter," Martin explains. "Well-chosen sites, excellent design, sound construction techniques, and painstaking finishes are crucial to lasting customer satisfaction. The product is only as good as the sum of its parts, so we make a point of seeing that each part is exactly right." This approach has meant success not only for the development arm of the firm, but for the newer Enviroplan and Centurion as well.

Enviroplan specializes in the assembly, planning, and development of land throughout the capital region for use in Aselford-Martin construction and for sale to other leading developers. The division has a record of developing communities designed to meet residents' needs and goals.

In addition, Enviroplan provides planning consulting services to a number of the region's more discriminating land development companies. A team of skilled professionals have earned a reputation for transforming vacant land into prime building lots. Enviroplan's excellence was recognized in an official commendation for a unique single-family subdivision encompassing

the most exclusive lots in the Ottawa area.

The Centurion Corporation division of Aselford-Martin manages many thousands of rental townhouse, apartment, and condominium units throughout the capital region. Services offered by this division include rental and financial management, supervision of physical properties by a skilled team and grounds and maintenance people, and the provision of all support services.

The Aselford-Martin corporate family's most recent addition, Aselford-Martin Shopping Centres, is expected to be an area of growth for the firm over the coming years. Aselford-Martin's first shopping centre development, Greenbank Square, was accomplished in 1978, and its success led the parent company to explore retail development further.

This division is currently developing the Meadowbrook Mews Shopping Centre at Cyrville and Meadowbrook roads on the city's east side. The division has also identified several market areas across North America as promising targets for future expansion.

"As building owners as well as developers, we know the importance of building for the long term," Martin says. "This approach is characteristic of every member of our staff. That personal touch, we are proud to say, has become our trademark—in every division."

ASELFORD MARTIN

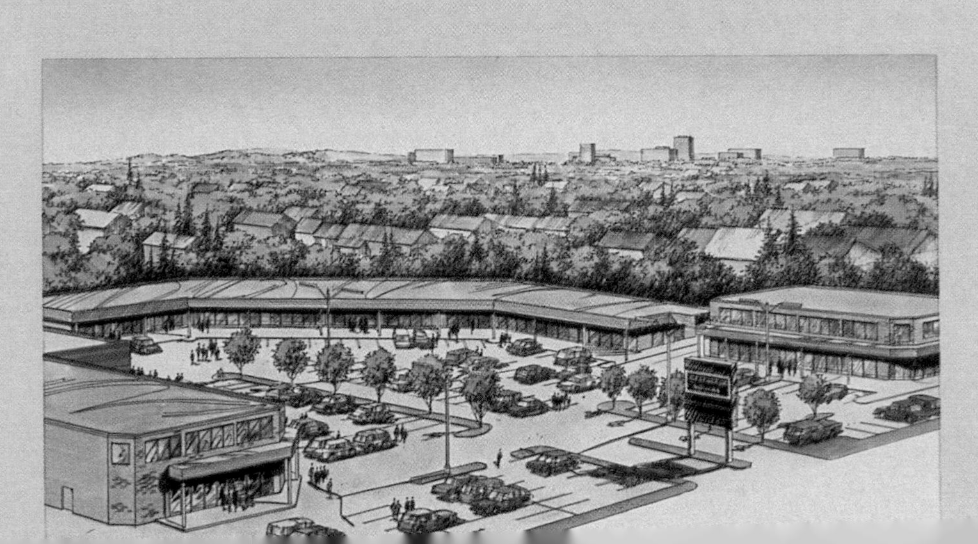

M. HOLITZNER LIMITED

Manfred and Cecilia Holitzner arrived in Canada from Germany in 1957 and founded their company the following year at 338 Somerset Street East, Ottawa. Manfred Holitzner bought his first truck and became a subcontractor in the housing business, undertaking framing and exterior and interior finished carpentry for other home builders. As a subcontractor he started with only one helper and eventually employed up to 40 carpenters. As M. Holitzner Limited grew, Manfred and Cecilia Holitzner invested in land to build their own houses.

Their first house was built for their own growing family in 1959. Holitzner custom-built homes soon followed. The first of the firm's big residential developments started in 1967—mainly in the west end of Ottawa and also south of the city. The Holitzner name soon became synonymous with quality. Manfred Holitzner's reputation as a quality builder grew from his quality homes in Stittsville, Munster Hamlet, Nepean, Kanata, Manotick, and Gloucester. His objective was always to ensure that he uses only the best materials and craftsmanship, and that Holitzner homes are designed with the most up-to-date features.

The company statement—"There is nothing like a masterpiece by Holitzner,"—is not a mere slogan but a statement frequently expressed by Holitzner home owners, by people whose goal is to own a Holitzner home, and also by many other home builders.

Manfred Holitzner was invited to become president of the Ottawa Home Builders' Association in 1979, in recognition of the position he had established both as a widely respected member of the community and as a leading quality home builder in the national capital region.

A second generation of Holitzners is already established in the company. Manfred and Cecilia Holitzner direct a management team that includes their daughters Carmen, who is the chartered accountant; Heidi, who controls the ordering of building materials and estimating of building costs; and their son-in-law, Barry Flegel, who is the construction manager.

In 1986 M. Holitzner Limited diversified from building single-family homes to apartment buildings and commercial construction. Poole Creek Manor was the second low-rise rental building to be constructed on Main Street in Stittsville. A 50,000-square-foot shopping centre is planned for Stittsville's Main Street. Continued growth obliged the company to build new and bigger office facilities in the Rideau Business Park, where it moved in April 1988, to 10,000 square feet of space, from its old 2,000-square-foot office in Nepean.

M. Holitzner Limited has won numerous awards for building tract housing in a variety of sizes from approximately 1,300 square feet to more than 3,500 square feet. It has also won specific awards for the designs of its kitchens and bathrooms.

In 1989 M. Holitzner Limited was actively building residential developments in Kanata, Barrhaven, and Stittsville. It builds approximately 150 single-family homes annually. In 1987 it was the second-largest builder of single-family homes in the west end of Ottawa, as well as being engaged in the construction of multiple residential units and commercial developments.

Poole Creek Manor on Main Street in Stittsville, built in 1986, was among M. Holitzner Limited's first commercial projects.

The Ravenscroft was awarded first place by the Ottawa-Carleton Home Builders' Association in 1986.

RICHCRAFT HOMES

Kanata Mayor Des Adam assisted with the ribbon cutting at the official grand opening of the Richcraft model homes in Kanata Lakes on Sunday, October 16, 1988.

Kris Singhal is proud of the accomplishments of Richcraft Homes. On the reception desk at the company's Nepean offices sit some of the trophies the firm has won in the Ottawa-Carleton Home Builders' Association's annual awards competition. Newspaper clippings about Richcraft's people or projects hang on the waiting room wall.

Singhal thinks Richcraft has a lot to be proud of—growing from a small one-person operation in the mid-1980s to a major developing force, with more than 40 full-time employees. Sales in 1988 exceeded $40 million, and the company has become the region's second-largest developable landholder, with more than 1,000 acres under its umbrella.

The road to the top has been based primarily on the hard work and determination of its founder. Singhal arrived in Canada in 1974 with a dream of success as a new Canadian. After earning accreditation in accounting, he took a position with Northern Telecom and reached the position of assistant comptroller. After working for Northern Telecom for four years, Singhal joined the federal government's supply and services department and worked there for another four years.

But a sense of adventure and of wanting to be his own boss soon returned to Singhal, and, following an unsuccessful foray into the import-export business, he purchased two run-down properties, improved them, and re-sold them for a profit.

It was then that the real estate bug bit Singhal, and he proceeded to buy small one- and two-lot packages, develop them, and build custom homes. A major turning point came in 1984, when the company acquired a large property in Orleans and successfully built and sold 92 homes.

The size of Richcraft's projects is larger now. The company built more than 300 units in 1988, including single-family homes and freehold town homes. Plans are also under way for the development of a highrise, and the firm has established a busy commercial and industrial developments division.

Richcraft's biggest current project is in Hunt Club Park where it plans to build more than 2,000 units over the coming years. The company is also excited by its Kanata Lakes developments, which will feature 185 luxury single-family homes of up to 4,300 square feet, located along the driveways and waterways of a Kanata golf course. Richcraft is also building 270 single-family and town-house units in the Spruce Grove development, also in Kanata.

Richcraft's commercial division is presently developing three properties for commercial and office purposes in the Ottawa Business Park on the city's east side.

Singhal takes the success of his business in stride and points out that it has been a shared honor. "If one makes it, there are so many people behind him to support his efforts. It is never one man's story," he says. "Hard work, good wishes, the luck factor—all play an important role."

Singhal and Richcraft Home make many large donations to charities and community services each year, but usually on the condition that they are anonymous. "What you take in makes a living," the successful developer explains. "With what you give out you make life."

Kris Singhal, president of Richcraft Homes, addresses the guests who attended the grand opening.

Visitors are entranced by the perpetual flame on Parliament Hill. Photo by Wayne Eardley/ Burke Communications Photography

3

THE CENTRE OF GOVERNMENT

Every year, hundreds of thousands of people flock to Parliament Hill on Canada Day to celebrate in grand style. Photo by Paul von Baich/ First Light

It's not uncommon for cities in which there is one industry that seems to overshadow all the others in terms of visibility, employment, and general importance to the citizenry, to be called a "one-horse town." Ottawa—Canada's capital city and home to the federal government—has been called that too. Is it a one-horse town? Well, maybe . . . but what a horse!

Since Confederation in 1867 and throughout the twentieth century, the federal government grew from a few buildings on the Ottawa River where several hundred people worked to become the major landowner and employer in the National Capital Region and to have enormous influence on the day-to-day activities of every Ottawan.

Today, although dependence on the government has diminished somewhat and the city's economy shows new signs of diversification each year, the Government of Canada remains an integral part of the city's character, and its activities frequently exert a strong pull on the direction of development in the capital region.

The most obvious and perhaps the most positive effect of the presence of government has been its stabilizing influence on the economy in Ottawa. First, the presence of a large and stable population has meant generally prosperous times for retailers and service industries alike. Despite the government's commitment to stemming the growth of the bureaucracy and controlling government spending, the annual growth of employment opportunities within the civil service continues to grow at a rate of between one and two percent each year. At present, the federal government employs more than 30 percent of the total regional work force.

What this slow but constant growth has meant in turn is that the city seems almost protected from the dramatic swings that sometimes occur in economic conditions elsewhere in the country or, indeed, in North America and the world. The price

ABOVE: A Mountie bows his head in a moment of silence at the War Memorial at Confederation Square. Photo by Devries Mikkelsen/ First Light

of real estate, for example, usually remains stable, increasing incrementally year after year in a calm, almost orderly fashion.

The most visible way in which the government exhibits its presence in the capital is through its role as the principal landowner. About half the vacant land in Ottawa is owned by the federal government, and government agencies—most notably the National Capital Commission—own perhaps a tenth of the land in the greater National Capital Region. Much of that, of course, is the scenic Gatineau Park north of the Ottawa River and the Greenbelt area that circles the city.

Besides being the major landowner in the area, the federal government is also the tenant most often listed on rent rolls in Ottawa. Of the city's more than 25 million square feet of office space, the federal government either leases or owns about two-thirds.

Beyond the federal government's physical presence in the city and the region, its influence is felt in many other ways. Because Ottawa is the city where the most significant of decisions and policies are made—those that affect the rest of the country—many business enterprises and professional associations or lobby groups that have frequent contact with the government have chosen to locate in Ottawa.

There are more than 20 government departments that are considered major employers in the capital, and at least six Crown corporations or federal agencies.

The Department of Communications is

FACING PAGE RIGHT: The most imposing sight in the capital is the Parliament Building. Photo by Wayne Eardley/ Burke Communications Photography

From the west side of the Parliament buildings, one can survey the Parliamentary precinct; the Westin Hotel is in the distance. Photo by Wayne Eardley/ Burke Communications Photography

ABOVE: Once known as Barrack Hill, the promontory of land just west of the entrance to the Rideau Canal is now Parliament Hill. The House of Commons is in the Centre Block, and the splendid Library of Parliament is behind. Photo by Paul von Baich/ First Light

easily identified by most people passing through Ottawa as the department responsible for the huge research centre just west of the city at Shirley Bay, where satellite dishes tilt toward the sky and the landscape is dotted with communications towers.

In fact, much of this department's work—like the radio waves it monitors—goes by unseen by most Canadians. Basically, there are several categories of responsibility in the department's activities in Ottawa; one is spectrum management of the airwaves, a field in which Canada is an acknowledged world leader. Anything that uses radio waves—whether automatic garage door openers, mobile telephones, police radios, or radio-operated industrial machinery—comes under the jurisdiction of the Communications department, which

ensures that all such uses conform to federal regulations.

The federal government, not surprisingly, is the largest single user of telecommunications in Canada, and the department provides such services through the Government Telecommunications Agency. Helping others use telecommunications is yet another goal; the department has been behind many Canadian firms involved in "high technology," by supporting their initiatives or by developing new technology in government facilities and then transferring this knowledge to private industry.

A prime example is the Department of Communications' role in Canada's space industry. Not many people in the world are aware that Canada was the third nation, after the United States and the Soviet Union, to operate a domestic satellite. Can-

ABOVE AND LEFT: The ceremony of the Changing of the Guard attracts huge crowds seven days a week. Photos by William P. McElligott

FACING PAGE: The monument to Samuel de Champlain catches the explorer holding his astrolabe to the heavens. Photo by Cosmo Condina/ The Stock-Market

ada was third then, but has since been first in many other initiatives in space; Canada was the first country in the world to establish a commercial satellite communications system, first to experiment with direct broadcast satellite systems, and first to implement a mobile communications system using satellite technology. The goal of the Department of Communications is to use space technology to serve national needs via systems under Canadian control and to support Canadian research and development in order to create a viable space manufacturing industry in Canada.

So far, so good: today Canada excels in the development and manufacture of space communications satellites and earth stations. The industry is growing at an incredible rate, with sales increasing at a rate of 50 percent a year.

Canada's first satellite was the Alouette I. Designed and built in the government laboratories at Shirley Bay, just west of Ottawa, the Alouette was launched by the U.S. National Aeronautics and Space Administration (NASA) in 1962. Three other satellites have been launched for scientific use, as well as the commercial Telesat satellites. Communications had another world first in 1975 when the Hermes demonstration satellite was launched, which pioneered new frequency bands and exemplified the feasibility of direct broadcast television satellites.

Satellites are "road-tested" in the world-famous David Florida Laboratory at the Communications Research Centre at Shirley Bay. The laboratory has extensive facilities used for the assembly, integration, and environmental testing of spacecraft and spacecraft components. Built in the early 1970s specifically for the program that produced the Hermes satellite, the laboratory was expanded in 1980 to incorporate testing facilities for the new generation of satellites.

Freedom of speech and assembly is a right in Canada; here, a demonstration is held protesting the imprisonment of political prisoners in Iraq. Photo by Devries Mikkelsen/ First Light

At the lab are five thermal vacuum chambers which simulate the environment in space; here satellites from Canada, the United States, and Europe are subjected to an ordeal of vigorous vibration and alternate chilling and heating—literally a "shake and bake" test.

The facility is one of the largest in the world and features not only special systems for balancing spacecraft but also two high-bay spacecraft assembly areas with specialized dust and contamination control. In 1984 some 30 companies and agencies used the laboratory for more than 70 projects, including the European Space Agency's Olympus I satellite.

The Department of Communications has influence on Canada in another way, through its support of cultural programs. In the portfolio of the Minister of Communications are Telefilm Canada, which in turn gives grants to Canadian film projects; the Canada Council, which gives grants to drama, art, and literature; the National Arts Centres; and the Canadian Broadcasting Corporation (CBC).

Also reporting to Parliament through the minister are the National Museums of Canada, most of which are located in Ottawa and are an integral part of Ottawa life. Virtually every child in the city (and his or her attendant grown-ups) who has been to the National Museum of Science and Technology on St. Laurent Boulevard clamours to return to the "Crazy Kitchen," a delightfully tilted room that plays with human perceptions and sets children into gales of laughter.

While the Department of Communications in Ottawa develops policy and sponsors space-age research, another government department has its eyes closer to earth. The Department of Agriculture (known in governmentese as "AgCan") is among the larger government departments located in Ottawa. While most Ottawans know the Sir John Carling Building which overlooks the west end of

RIGHT: The Main Barn at the Central Experimental Farm was first built in 1887, and rebuilt in 1914. Today it houses the showcase herd of purebred cattle. Photo by Wayne Eardley/ Burke Communications Photography

the city from a hill on Carling Avenue, many visitors and agricultural scientists know the Central Experimental Farm and Research Centre. This centre, situated on nearly 1,200 acres of prime land within the city, has been the site of many important agricultural discoveries. For example, the technology that led to today's freeze-dried foods was developed at the research station, as were instant potato flakes and an early maturing variety of seed corn and soybean that is gradually replacing oats and barley as a crop on many Canadian farms.

The research that is done at this research centre has served to earn Canada a reputation worldwide as a forerunner in the field of agricultural science. There are more than a hundred buildings on the site, some of which form highly specialized and protected environments for studying plants and animals. One such building houses "swine suites," chemically disinfected environments where the feeding and breeding habits of pigs are studied and the statistical information analyzed with the aid of computers.

BELOW: Every child enjoys an outing to the cattle barn at the farm. Photo by Wayne Eardley/BurkeCommunications Photography

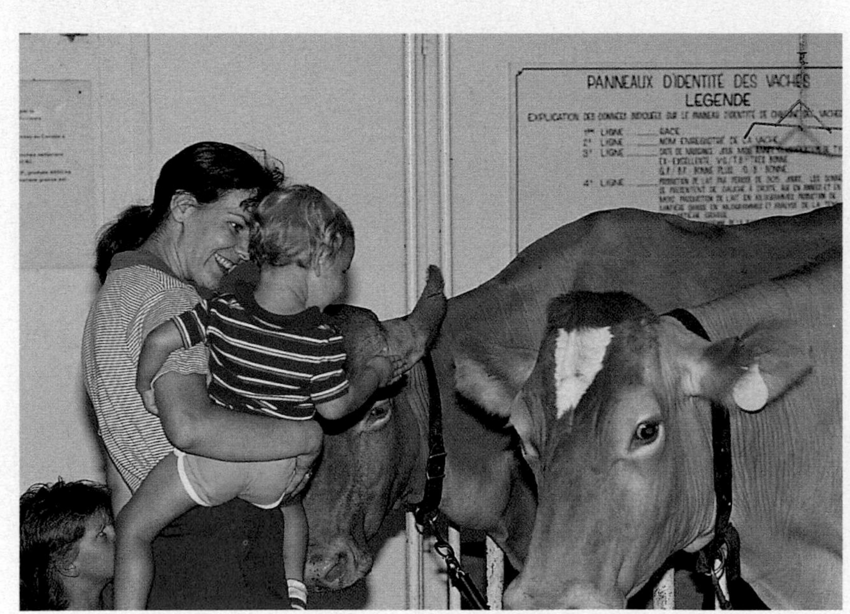

There are stables and a barn for dairy cattle (the Experimental Farm has a herd of more than 50), greenhouses, laboratories, and the Agricultural Museum. Teams of draft horses pulling old-fashioned wagons, usually packed with dozens of laughing children and camera-toting visitors, start on tours of the farm several times a day, except in winter. The wagon rides leave from the Dairy Barn and pass through a portion of the Arboretum.

The Arboretum is a collection of trees and shrubs, some planted decades ago, and species of trees that beautify acres of rolling hills and range from the exotic magnolia to the majestic Norway Spruce.

The mere mention of the word "statistics" in Ottawa immediately conjures thoughts of Statistics Canada which has its headquarters in Ottawa, in the stately R.H. Coats building in the city's west end. To say that the department simply gathers numbers would be an incredible understatement: Statistics Canada today provides statistical information and analysis of both social and economic life in Canada. This

LEFT: A child stops for a moment to watch a frog in the pond at the Ornamental Gardens at the Central Experimental Farm. Photo by Wayne Eardley/ Burke Communications Photography

BELOW: A cyclist uses the bike path through the Arboretum at the Central Experimental Farm, where many different species of trees thrive in an idyllic environment. Photo by Jessie Parker/ First Light

RIGHT: Union Station is now the Government Conference Centre, where federal-provincial meetings are conducted throughout the year. Photo by Devries Mikkelsen/ First Light

information provides the basis for the development, analysis, and evaluation of a broad range of social and economic policies and has many implications for private enterprise. Developers, for example, can get complex demographic data from Statistics Canada together with an analysis of specific geographic areas and can thus plan development projects with a clear idea of market needs.

Included in Statistics Canada's multifaceted mandate is the objective of publishing its information, which it does through printed materials released daily, weekly, monthly, and annually, as well as through its computer information network, CANSIM, a data bank and information retrieval service.

Transport Canada employs nearly 5,000 people in the capital; the department's role, simply stated, is coordination and technical regulation—in matters under federal jurisdiction—to ensure safety and efficiency for transportation in Canada. In a country the size of Canada, that's a tall order: the Airports Authority Group, for example, manages 20 airports across the country, either through direct ownership, as in the case of the Ottawa International

ABOVE AND LEFT: The Ottawa International Airport is among the busiest in the country. Photos by Wayne Eardley/ Burke Communications Photography

RIGHT: An Air Canada jet is serviced before another cross-country flight. Photo by Wayne Eardley/ Burke Communications Photography

Airport, or through financial support. Transport headquarters controls all of Canada's major airport operations, from Vancouver to Halifax.

The Flight Services Directorate owns a fleet of more than 80 aircraft, both fixed wing and rotary; this branch of the department operates from its headquarters at Ottawa International Airport and directs operations at 16 sub-bases across Canada.

The Marine Transport division, also headquartered in Ottawa, develops marine transportation policy and oversees inter-regional and Arctic marine operations. The Canadian Coast Guard has its main offices in Ottawa as well, close to the policy-making functions of the department.

The department of National Health and Welfare has offices throughout the city, including those overlooking the Rideau River from a building on River Road, but most people know the area west of the city centre called Tunney's Pasture as the principal Health and Welfare enclave. Here are located government laboratories in which drugs, cosmetics, and other chemicals and devices related to health are tested and evaluated. Here also technology related to biomedical engineering and diagnostics is developed, and trends in both communicable and non-communicable diseases are monitored. Like the Department of Communications, technology and innovations developed at Health and Welfare are transferred to the private sector, and government enjoys a continuing collaboration with private enterprise and health care institutions.

Drug manufacturers and medical equipment firms regularly meet with officials in the Health Protection Branch to

BELOW: Part of the Minto Place development, the Canada Building houses the headquarters for Transport Canada, which administers Canada's airports and the Coast Guard. Photo by Jessie Parker/ First Light

ensure that pharmaceuticals or items that are considered to be medical devices meet federal government guidelines.

Health promotion activities are also centred in Tunney's Pasture, where health information programs are developed and their implementation evaluated; the branch is also responsible for payments to provincial health care programs for hospital, diagnostic, and extended health care services.

Probably the best-known social welfare programs administered by the Department of Health and Welfare are the Canada Pension plan, Family Allowance, and Old Age Pension.

Less well known by the general and business public is Health and Welfare's Environmental Health directorate; this branch evaluates any possibility of danger to health in a wide variety of products, from pesticides and their residues to water filtration devices to commonly used arts and crafts materials.

ABOVE: The traditions of Scottish heritage are kept alive in colourful fashion today by descendants of immigrants, such as this pipe and drum regiment, who pose on Parliament Hill. Photo by Greg Locke/ First Light

LEFT: The Central Post Office has been a splendid landmark for decades, with its copper roof and elegant, strong, vertical lines. Photo by Jessie Parker/ First Light

ABOVE: Ottawa's City Hall, attractively set on Green Island, is a fine example of the International style of architecture. Inside is a marble lobby, and a dining room with beautiful views of the Ottawa River and Gatineau Hills. Photo by Justine Hill

RIGHT: Statues of Truth and Justice stand before the magnificent Supreme Court of Canada building. Photo by Jessie Parker/ First Light

FACING PAGE: The Canadian War Museum contains valuable military artifacts from the history of Canada, up to the Second World War. Photo by William P. McElligott

Supply and Services Canada is the business arm of government; no matter what the government needs—a new computer terminal, the services of a management consultant, or a $100-million nuclear-powered submarine—Supply and Services is the department that does the purchasing. As well, the department looks after much of the government's publications. A huge undertaking, the production of publications for both the public and private sectors by the Communications Services Branch (formerly called the Queen's Printer) is a profitable enterprise, returning several million dollars to the Canadian government each year.

Of all the government departments, large and small, the largest and most visible department in Ottawa is that of National Defence. Of more than 120,000 employees Canada wide (both military and civilian personnel), more than 14,000 work for National Defence in Ottawa. The department, which occupies some 50 buildings in the National Capital Region, has its headquarters in a striking office tower in downtown Ottawa at 101 Colonel By Drive.

Generally, the objective of National Defence is to meet Canada's military obligations both around the world and within Canada and to provide specialized military assistance to civilian organizations when needed.

Ottawa is headquarters for the Communication Command which operates and maintains strategic communications systems for the Canadian Armed Forces and, during emergencies, for the federal and

ROYAL MINT

provincial governments.

National Defence is in the forefront of mapping and charting technology; at its Mapping and Charting Establishment, staffed by more than 200 military and civilian personnel, is a modern, semi-automated mapping system and digital map production unit, which was implemented in 1986.

Under the direction of National Defence too is the National Defence Medical Centre, which is a 350-bed, fully accredited general hospital, with more than 900 staff members. The hospital provides tertiary care to all military personnel, members of Parliament, and the Royal Canadian Mounted Police. Since the hospital first opened in 1961, it has expanded and is now a teaching hospital affiliated with the University of Ottawa Faculty of Medicine.

Ottawa is the site chosen for headquarters by many federal agencies and Crown corporations such as Canada Post, the Royal Canadian Mounted Police, the Canada Mortgage and Housing Corporation, Atomic Energy of Canada, the Bank of Canada, and the Royal Canadian Mint.

The Canada Mortgage and Housing Corporation (CMHC) is an agency of interest to everyone, regardless of where one lives or in what type of housing. CMHC is best known for insuring high-ratio mortgages, an activity that has been a factor in the success of Canada's many real estate development firms, but the corporation also maintains up-to-date statistics on housing trends in Canada. These include housing starts, vacancy rates, asking rates in rental accommodation, and the type of housing units being built. As well, it develops policy on the housing industry and on related investment, such as mortgage-backed securities.

The Royal Canadian Mint is a popular destination for visitors to Ottawa, primarily, one supposes, because no one can resist the sight of money! The building itself on Sussex Drive is impressive, having many appropriately fortress-like features, includ-

BELOW: Training courses at the Canadian Police College run the gamut from administration, investigation techniques, and explosives. Also on the grounds are the stables for the Royal Canadian Mounted Police's famed musical ride. Photo by Jessie Parker/ First Light

ing a guard house and tall, spiked fence as well as massive stone turrets. Most of the Mint's operations for making Canadian money have moved to a modern facility in Winnipeg, but the Mint in Ottawa manufactures coins for many other countries from around the world.

The red ceremonial uniforms of the Royal Canadian Mounted Police are known over the world as a symbol of Canada; the Mounties' headquarters and training college are located in Ottawa, employing almost 4,000 people in a variety of occupations, from senior police staff to computer systems analysis to clerical positions.

The fact that the federal government has invested many millions of dollars in research and development, whether in the field of communications, agriculture, or health care, has resulted in Ottawa-Carleton's reputation as a world-class centre for research. Of the federal government's own research professionals and scientists, nearly half work in the National Capital Region. As an example of the funding for research in the region, in the 1983-1984 fiscal period, of a total of $1.6 billion spent on research by all federal government departments, $669 million was spent on research activities and for personnel in the National Capital Region.

The face of downtown Ottawa is reflected in the glass of Constitution Square. Photo by Devries Mikkelsen/ First Light

Computerized information, books and documents aid scientific researchers at the Canada Institute for Scientific and Technical Information, at the National Research Council complex. Photo by Wayne Eardley/ Burke Communications Photography

RESEARCH: THE WAY OF THE FUTURE

The National Research Council, or NRC, has buildings in several areas of the city, notably the headquarters on Sussex Drive, and major laboratory facilities in the east end of the City of Ottawa. In the laboratories a wide range of research activities is carried on, including engineering investigations requiring equipment such as wind tunnels and towing tanks. Scientific equipment, such as optical telescopes for astronomy or stereo loudspeakers for private enterprise, is designed and developed. The NRC's goal is to support private industry by developing and transferring scientific knowledge and specific technology.

The Medical Research Council began as a part of the National Research Council when medical research was considered part of the larger field of scientific research, but in 1949, after medical research had become a much more active field, what was an associate committee became a full division of the NRC. Today, the Medical Research Council has a multimillion dollar budget ($185 million in 1985-1986) and is the major source of federal funding for health science research and for the training of biomedical researchers.

The Department of Energy Mines and Resources research facility, the Canada Centre for Remote Sensing, specializes in data collection and in the analysis of images of the earth's surface that come from scanning systems on the Landsat satellites. The centre aids many private firms in such diverse fields as mining, agriculture, shipping, and forestry. In forestry, for example, remote sensing can show which forests have been logged, where reforestation is needed, and whether trees in a particular zone are diseased. It is possible to distinguish between different tree species on the images, and one can even identify salvageable timber in an area destroyed by forest fire.

Recently, Energy Mines and Resources has been working with private industry to develop Radarsat, a satellite which uses radar images and would provide a significant improvement over current technologies by cutting through cloud cover to provide images both day and night. This technology could continuously monitor ice conditions off the east coast of Canada to assist offshore oil and gas operations. With advances such as Radarsat, businesses in the electronics and survey industries have developed a reputation for first-class products and services.

Access to public sector technology and scientific knowledge is available in Ottawa through offices such as the

Known simply as Building M-58, this building contains the administrative offices of the National Research Council. Photo by Wayne Eardley/ Burke Communications Photography

Technology Coordination Centre and the Canada Institute for Scientific and Technical Information, which is one of the largest libraries in the world of scientific, medical, and technical information. Collaboration between the government research centres and private industry is a common occurrence and is of mutual benefit.

Access to government departments, as well as the ease of access to other related associations, has prompted many national associations and interest groups to locate their headquarters in the City of Ottawa. For example, near Ottawa's "hospital row" on Smyth Road in the southeast portion of the city, are situated the headquarters for the Canadian Pharmaceutical Association, the Canadian Dental Association, the Canadian Medical Association, and the Canadian Red Cross. Within a few minutes' drive of these associations can be found the offices of the Canadian Nurses Association and the Canadian Hospital Association.

In fact, there are over a thousand national associations in Ottawa, including the Consumers Association of Canada, the Canadian Automobile Association, the Electrical and Electronic Manufacturers Association of Canada, the Canadian Chamber of Commerce, the Hotel Association of Canada, and the Canadian Trucking Association.

Staff at the Ottawa General Hospital enjoy lunchtime out of doors on the hospital's park-like grounds. Photo by Jessie Parker/ First Light

Many of these associations produce a variety of publications annually, including monthly professional journals from associations like the Canadian Public Health Association or the Canadian Nurses Association, and thus rely heavily on local graphics arts and printing firms.

Because Ottawa is the capital of Canada, many foreign embassies and diplomatic missions are located in the city. Indeed, many of the city's statelier homes, which are too large for the needs of today's families, are now occupied by embassies. The British High Commissioner, for example, lives in an historic Ottawa house called Earnscliffe. Ambassadors live with their families in beautiful homes in Rockcliffe or in the scenic Island Park area, commuting by limousine to their offices in the city centre.

While the ambassadors represent their people in Canada, many Ottawa firms benefit from the proximity to the representatives of foreign countries. In fact, many countries require that contracts for Canadian goods or services must go through the embassies.

As well, such government agencies as the Export Development Corporation, which promotes Canadian exports to foreign nations and businesses, are located in Ottawa.

A PARTNER IN ENTERPRISE

The Government of Canada is more than a scenic grouping of buildings on a hill with red-jacketed Mounties standing on guard—it is an active partner in Canadian business and in research and development and serves as an integral part of the foundation of Ottawa-Carleton.

Photo by Wayne Eardley/Burke Communications Photography

Photo by Wayne Eardley/Burke Communications Photography

NATIONAL CAPITAL COMMISSION

The National Capital Commission (NCC) is a federal crown agency created by the National Capital Act of 1958. Until recently the Commission's mandate focused on the planning, development, conservation, and improvement of the National Capital Region (NCR).

With cabinet's approval in 1986 and the passage of Bill C-153—an act to amend the National Capital Act—in August 1988, the NCC has expanded its mandate to include three key elements: the capital as Canada's meeting place, communicating Canada to Canadians through the capital, and safeguarding and preserving the capital's natural and built environment, including the national treasures therein.

Since 1899 the NCC and its predecessors, the Federal District Commission and the Ottawa Improvement Commission, have focused mainly on the third element. This has resulted in a beautiful, functional, and appealing capital. In the 1950s, 1960s, and 1970s, the NCC implemented a plan prepared by French urbanist Jacques Gréber at the request of then-Prime Minister Mackenzie King.

The NCC has considerable authority over and significant responsibilities in the areas of acquisition and disposal of property; construction and maintenance of parks, parkways, bridges, and other structures; joint projects with local and provincial governments, private-sector firms, and interested parties; administration, preservation, and maintenance of historic places; and planning related to the proper development of federal public lands in the NCR.

The NCC is the caretaker of federal lands throughout the NCR. This includes the home of the prime minister and six other official residences, recreational pathways and parkways, many of the major parks in the urban core and Gatineau Park, and the lands on which federal buildings are located. Of the 4,662 square kilometres of land that make up the national capital region, the NCC owns some 55,000 hectares (or about 10 percent) in both Ontario and Québec.

In light of the expanded mandate, the NCC has become more involved with programming the capital. Recurring celebrations of national themes such as Canada Day, Winterlude, and New Year's Eve on Parliament Hill are part of the programming.

Another important aspect of the programming is working in cooperation with outside groups to coordinate and organize activities of national and international significance.

The National Capital Commission is headed by a 20-member commission made up of individuals, representing all parts of Canada, who are appointed by the governor-in-council for terms not to exceed three years. The Commission meets three times per year to exercise its authority over the corporation's by-laws, financial affairs, appointments, and corporate plan. Members may hold only two consecutive terms.

Ice skating on the Rideau Canal.

Fireworks light up the sky over the Parliament buildings.

SCOTT & AYLEN

Scott & Aylen, a leading bilingual law firm in Ontario, combines traditional standards of excellence with a progressive, modern practice, using the talents of Ottawa's most respected professionals.

Consisting of two divisions—a firm of lawyers and one of patent and trade-mark agents—together under the name Scott & Aylen, the firm provides general counsel, advice, and expertise in general litigation, intellectual property litigation and prosecution, and corporate-commercial matters.

The names Scott and Aylen have represented distinguished service in the practice of law in Canada for five generations. Colleagues Cuthbert Scott and John A. Aylen set about to develop a practice with high standards for personal commitment and individual attention to their clients' concerns. Both lawyers came from a long succession of prominent Ottawa lawyers dating back in Canada to the mid-nineteenth century. With Scott's expertise in intellectual property and Aylen's in litigation, they formed an association in 1952 that later became Scott & Aylen, Barristers and Solicitors.

Today, with headquarters in Ottawa, the firm's dynamic, progressive team of 33 lawyers and patent and trade-mark agents concentrate on civil litigation and administrative law, intellectual property (IP), corporate and commercial law, and real estate.

Unique in its bilingual practice, Scott & Aylen offers services in both of Canada's official languages to its local and international clients. Whether it is a trial or a real estate transaction, the firm's lawyers can act for clients in English or in French.

Corporate/Commercial Law and Real Estate

The firm's corporate and commercial practice encompasses all levels of business, from personal to multinational, providing consultative services in matters of corporate administrative structure, incorporation, dissolution, amalgamation, and reorganization at the federal and provincial levels.

Scott & Aylen provides legal counsel to business and real estate owners on handling the details and procedures of corporate organization, property acquisition, and management.

For the prospective entrepreneur the firm's general commercial service offers practical advice on partnerships, joint ventures, business acquisitions and dispositions, and trust agreements. The firm also provides financial guidance on tax laws and securities legislation, and advice to lenders and borrowers on commercial loan requirements.

Lawyers in this department also offer advice on estate planning and administration and on the preparation of wills and codicils.

Scott & Aylen offers assistance to clients ranging from first-time purchasers of family homes to contractors of major construction projects.

Patent and Trade-mark Agency

The patent and trade-mark agents conduct business before the Canadian Commissioner of Patents, the Registrar of Trade-marks, and the Registrar of Copyrights and Industrial Design. These professionals have academic credentials and qualifications in specialized areas of engineering, science, and the arts. Their familiarity with intellectual property rights in a wide range of subjects is enhanced by frequent liaison with colleagues and international associates.

The patent and trade-mark agency provides assistance in the preparation, filing, and prosecution of applications for patents, trade-marks, copyrights, and industrial designs. It also provides advice to clients on the selection and use of trade-marks, as well as the intellectual property implications associated with the manufacture, importation, and sale of products and processes.

The firm's automated intellectual property data management system ensures accuracy and speed, with on-line access to worldwide patent and trade-mark database for searches.

Patent and Trade-mark Litigation

The liaison between the firm's intellectual property lawyers and patent and trade-mark agents offers an exceptional advantage to clients. While patent and trade-mark agents acquire and manage IP rights, the IP lawyers act as counsel and advise clients on infringement and licensing issues.

The firm's IP litigation and licensing practice also includes appeals to the Federal Court of Canada from decisions of the Commissioner of Patents and the Registrar of Trade-marks. Lawyers working in this field prepare and negotiate agreements involving the transfer of technology, franchising, character merchandising, and computer software.

Harmonization of intellectual property laws worldwide is of concern to everyone, and Scott & Aylen's intellectual property lawyers and agents constantly monitor and keep clients up to date on changes in Canadian laws.

Civil Litigation and Administration Law

Scott & Aylen represents clients before federal and provincial courts, regulatory boards, and administrative tribunals. The majority of its litigation practice, which represents about one-half of the firm's activity, involves commercial disputes, professional negligence, insurance, and personal injury claims. Other areas of practice include labor relations, human rights, wrongful dismissal, family law, environmental protection, and public utilities regulation.

The firm's extensive research facilities and in-house consultation network result in cost-effective, quality representation at every stage of legal proceedings.

A second office in Toronto serves clients seeking advice on all intellectual property matters. The Ottawa and Toronto offices are linked by a state-of-the-art WANG computer system and a telecommunications network for instant interoffice communication. Professionals and staff have immediate, on-line access to IP client files and accounting data.

Both the Ottawa and Toronto offices have computerized access to Canadian jurisprudence, the Canadian Trade-marks Register, and international patent and trade-mark information that complements an extensive library.

Scott & Aylen's new offices in Ottawa occupy four floors at 60 Queen Street.

Scott & Aylen was one of the first law firms in Canada to publish periodicals for established clients to keep them informed and advised in all areas of law. Its two periodicals are *The Intellectual Property Quarterly* and *The Commentary: A Periodic Review of Current Canadian Law.*

Scott & Aylen's lawyers and patent and trade-mark professionals are active members of national and international associations and committees. They lend their professional expertise in education and through community service.

OC TRANSPO

OC Transpo means business. That's a fact that is well understood by Ottawa-area merchants, employers, and businesses as the transit company's economic influence and importance have grown.

With a daily ridership in excess of 335,000 on 127 routes, the firm's impact on the area economy is already considerable. Thirty percent of all travel in the urban part of the region is on OC Transpo buses; almost 25 percent of all retail dollars spent in Ottawa-Carleton are spent by transit riders; and at downtown's showcase Rideau Centre, more than two-thirds of shoppers use the system as their mode of transportation. In fact, people ride the bus more often in Ottawa than in any other similar-size North American municipality.

But OC Transpo is more than a carrier service. In the past decade of accelerated growth in Ottawa-Carleton, the system has become an important tool for regional planners for whom access to the company's developing transitway system has become a key factor in residential and commercial development.

Thirty-one percent of all jobs in the region are located within walking distance of the transitway, and the region's plans call for that number to rise to 40 percent during the next decade. More than one billion dollars worth of economic development has already been generated around current and future transitway stations.

The 31-kilometre transitway is a system of roads and transit stations designed solely for the use of OC

In fast-moving bus-only lanes, OC Transpo buses bring 20,000 passengers to and from Ottawa's bustling downtown core during daily rush hours.

Tunney's Pasture Transitway Station in downtown Ottawa, where the 100-millionth Transitway rider was celebrated in May 1987.

Transpo and its passengers. Eventually this system will be extended as far as Orleans to the east, Kanata to the west, and Barrhaven to the south. New developments and communities are already being planned along its route.

As well as directly influencing the future of residential development, business location, and consumer habits, OC Transpo is, in its own right, a major economic force in the city. With more than 2,000 employees, the company is a $140-million-per-year enterprise.

OC Transpo's operations are overseen by the Ottawa-Carleton Regional Transit Commission, a committee of the Regional Municipality of Ottawa-Carleton that appoints the commission from among its own members.

SOLOWAY WRIGHT

The firm of Soloway Wright dates back to 1939, when Hyman Soloway opened his practice with the late John Mirsky. From that beginning the firm has evolved into a large and modern full-service law practice.

Today 41 lawyers and a support and research staff of more than 100 offer legal services in all aspects of litigation, real estate, corporate and commercial law, municipal law, labor law, wills, and estate and tax planning. The firm numbers among its clients major corporations, real estate developers, insurance companies, labor unions, government and nongovernmental agencies, and many thousands of individuals. In addition, members of the firm are often retained to act for or advise other law firms both in and outside of Ottawa.

Hyman Soloway, Q.C., LLD

Maurice Wright, Q.C.

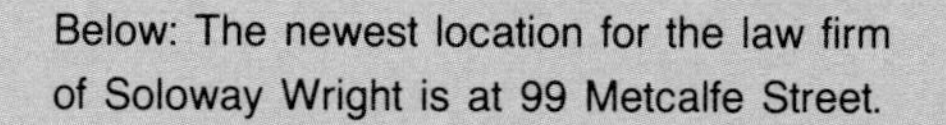

Below: The newest location for the law firm of Soloway Wright is at 99 Metcalfe Street.

Through the years members of the company have been closely involved with many of the important developments affecting the business and legal sectors of Ottawa, eastern Ontario, and the government of Canada and its agencies. Soloway Wright acted as counsel to the National Energy Board, the Tariff Board, the Anti-Dumping Tribunal, the Bank of Canada, and the Canada Council. In addition, its lawyers have always involved themselves in the social and community life of Ottawa. The partners and associates have varied backgrounds and interests and, like their firm itself, have deep roots in the local communities.

Hyman Soloway, who was a leader of the local bar for many years, served with distinction as special counsel to the National Energy Board and as chairman of Carleton University's board of governors. Born in Russia in 1913, he studied law at Osgoode Hall, was admitted to the bar in 1939, appointed Queen's Counsel in 1953, and remains to this day an inspiration and counsel to the firm.

Soloway Wright's litigation department has achieved a reputation for effectively handling court and tribunal cases of all kinds in its role

Articling students hard at work.

as counsel for businesses in Ottawa and across Canada at all judicial levels, including the Supreme Court of Canada.

The firm is involved in every aspect of real property law, from the purchase and sale of residential real estate to the acquisition and financing of major commercial and development properties. The real estate practice is the largest in Ottawa and represents a significant base of new and ongoing clients for the firm.

The corporate and commercial department practises in almost all aspects of business and corporate law, including leasing, franchising, sale and acquisition, business organization, dissolution and insolvency, financing, secured transactions, and contracts.

The municipal law group is one of the largest in Ottawa, with a list of clients that includes individuals, developers, builders, and municipalities.

The firm has a growing and thriving labor law practice that has participated in many leading cases while representing several unions within Ottawa and at the national level.

In addition, Soloway Wright offers complete legal services in the areas of wills, personal and corporate tax advice, and estate planning. These are newly emerging and dynamic parts of the firm that are attracting attention and high regard.

The firm's expertise and reputation gained through experience has meant that its lawyers are in demand as lecturers at the University of Ottawa Law School, Carleton University, the Bar Admission Course, professional development programs, and at various community associations. The firm encourages participation and attendance at the Law Society of Upper Canada and the Canadian Bar Association continuing education programs. "We have a tradition of teaching," says Gerald R. Morin, Q.C., who was for years the director of the civil litigation section of the Bar Admission Course. "The firm is committed to furthering the profession."

Soloway Wright has made significant strides into the age of technology. Computer and word-processing capabilities enable its professionals to practice law in a more efficient and cost-effective manner. The firm has recently enlarged its legal staff and expects to continue the pattern of growth throughout the 1980s and into the 1990s.

Soloway Wright has expanded and succeeded; it recognizes, however, the need for and has retained a strong commitment to its clients.

> "There is no pure law;
> there is only a legal service
> to our clientele to whom we
> owe the highest duty. So
> long as that is fulfilled, our
> community will prosper, and
> we along with it."
>
> —H. Soloway

OSLER, HOSKIN AND HARCOURT

Osler, Hoskin and Harcourt, with nearly 250 lawyers, is one of the largest law firms in Canada. The firm has achieved national and international recognition and has offices in Ottawa, Toronto, and London, England, serving small and large clients worldwide. Osler, Hoskin and Harcourt is a full-service law firm, representing public, private, and Crown corporations; local, national, and multinational enterprises; partnerships; foundations; nonprofit and trade organizations; trusts; investment and mutual funds; municipalities; federal and provincial governments and their agencies; and individuals.

The firm's scope of service and ability to focus extensive and varied resources in almost every area of Canadian and international law are what sets Osler, Hoskin and Harcourt apart.

The Ottawa office, at 50 O'Connor Street, is in the heart of the downtown business community, two short blocks from Parliament Hill. Specializing in matters of law within federal jurisdiction, including federal administrative law and intellectual property law, the office also provides a broad range of legal services in the areas of civil litigation, commercial, corporate, and real estate law.

Osler, Hoskin and Harcourt's history in Toronto dates back to 1855. The Ottawa firm Herridge, Tolmie, which merged with Osler, Hoskin and Harcourt in 1985, was established in 1946. Herridge, Tolmie was widely recognized for its expertise in intellectual property law and federal administrative law, including international trade, trade remedies, customs, and excise; transportation; communications; competition law; agricultural marketing; and energy. Herridge, Tolmie also had an active practice in corporate/commercial law and civil litigation, which has expanded rapidly since the merger. This expertise continued with the merger and has grown substantially in several dimensions.

The Honorable William Herridge, Q.C., now deceased, was Canada's ambassador to the United States during the 1930s. John Ross Tolmie, Q.C., who continues to provide valuable advice to the firm and its clients, was an incorporator and first president of TransCanada Pipelines.

The Toronto office's main area of practice is corporate and commercial law. The other principal areas are litigation, real estate, taxation, research, labor, municipal and administrative law, and personal services.

The Corporate/Commercial Group in both Ottawa and Toronto includes more than half of the firm's partners and associates. The lawyers in this group act as counsel to major Canadian and international corporations, financial institutions, and the investment community. They are equally active on behalf of local corporations, businesses, and entrepreneurs. This group assists in all aspects of business activity. Its members counsel boards of directors and business executives on matters ranging from mergers and acquisitions to executive transfers and personnel problems.

Due to the large number of lawyers in the Corporate/Commercial Group, a series of specialized subgroups, including securities law, bankruptcy and insolvency, banking, financial institutions, competition and trade practices, pensions and employee benefits, and franchising, have arisen.

Clients benefit from both the firm's wide-ranging domestic experience and its business and legal contacts throughout the United States, Europe, and the Pacific Rim.

At Ottawa, the Federal Law Group practises extensively before the boards, tribunals, and courts established by the federal government in areas of federal jurisdiction. Lawyers within the federal law group provide advice on all types of customs and excise matters involving the Canadian International Trade Tribunal. These lawyers represent business and corporations in discrimination complaints under Human Rights legislation and also in access to information legislation. They are involved in oil and gas matters and National Energy Board proceedings and provide a wide range of commercial, administrative, and constitutional law advice to organizations in the agricultural, airline, marine, railway, and trucking industries on matters related to federal transportation, aeronautics, and shipping legislation.

The Intellectual Property Group, active in both Ottawa and Toronto, deals with the entire range of legally protected ideas, inventions, designs, trademarks, and copyrights. The lawyers and agents of the group prepare and prosecute patent, trademark, and design applications; provide infringement opinions; represent clients in infringement, validity, and other legal proceedings; and provide guidance in the licensing and management of intellectual property. Clients include Canadian and international corporations in an array of research and management fields.

The firm has extensive experience in all aspects of trial and appellate litigation in Ottawa and Toronto. The Litigation Group joins the procedural expertise and advocacy skills of trial lawyers with the substantive acumen of lawyers in the partnership, offering clients expert and effective counselling prior to proceedings and ensuring excellent representation before administrative tribunals and courts.

The Research Group acts as the firm's "lawyers' lawyer," finding answers to intricate legal questions in every area of practice and applying those answers to clients' problems. The firm's lawyers are the group's only clients, and the group, consisting of partners and associates dedicated solely to research, serves as an important resource. Established in the 1960s, the group was the first of its kind in the country. Today it has an extensive library and a computer-based information-retrieval system at its disposal.

The firm's Real Estate Group provides services in all areas, including individual home purchases to full-scale development projects. This group deals with condominiums, highrise apartment complexes, hotels, industrial and residential subdivisions, office towers, and shopping malls. The lawyers in the Real Estate Group have broad experience in structuring development agreements involving land acquisition and assembly, zoning matters, joint ventures, ground leases, construction contracts, and property management. This group has been extensively involved in commercial lending arrangements and acts for borrowers and institutional lenders, including banks, trust and insurance companies, and pension funds. The Real Estate Group has extensive experience in all types of leasing transactions on behalf of tenants, landlords, and lending institutions. It advises land owners, developers, and municipalities in such matters as subdivision agreements, expropriation, real property assessment, and environmental protection, and represents clients at tribunals dealing with land-related issues such as the Ontario Municipal Board, Land Division Committees, and Committees of Adjustment.

The Labour Group's lawyers represent clients in hearings and act as negotiators at the bargaining table. They also help clients draft and interpret collective bargaining agreements and keep clients up to date on new legislation and labor relations tribunals' policies. The group is involved in employment law issues, including wrongful dismissal, occupational health and safety, workers' compensation, human rights, job evaluation, and pay equity.

The firm's Taxation Group offers a wide range of services related to Canadian taxation. The lawyers in this group advise corporations and individuals in the areas of tax planning, provide tax opinions, and conduct discussions with various taxation authorities. These lawyers also negotiate tax issues, conduct appeals, and represent clients in tax disputes.

Osler, Hoskin and Harcourt's Community Law Program takes on, at cost or on a pro bono basis, certain clients and/or charitable organizations and certain cases that are of general interest, such as Charter of Rights cases or those that otherwise benefit the community. It also represents certain clients who might otherwise be denied the right to legal advice, such as children in the juvenile and family courts and minority groups. Many of the firm's members are also involved in legal aid and community work.

Osler, Hoskin and Harcourt owns a diverse and extensive Canadian art collection and often contributes works to galleries and public exhibitions.

The firm's Visiting Associates Program provides opportunities for associates to acquire practical experience overseas and develops working relationships between the firm and foreign lawyers. Attorneys from Finland, England, Germany, Holland, and China have worked in the Canadian offices.

Osler, Hoskin and Harcourt is committed to providing quality legal services in all its locations and will continue to expand and diversify its legal practice.

This painting, *Sea, Grass and Sand* by Mulcaster, hangs in the firm's reception area with a plaque inscribed: "To commemorate the merger of Osler, Hoskin and Harcourt (Toronto) and Herridge, Tolmie (Ottawa) November 1, 1985."

The Chateau Laurier stands at the crossroads of Wellington Street and Colonel By Drive. Photo by Cosmo Condina/ The Stock-Market

4

FROM WOODCHIPS TO MICROCHIPS

Hull is well known in the capital for its exciting night life. Photo by Devries Mikkelsen/ First Light

The Ottawa that is the capital of Canada and the centre of the federal government is one city—co-existing in the same space, however, is another Ottawa, with a different reputation and a new image. The other Ottawa is an enterprising city, industrious and innovative, full of promise for new ventures.

Which is only fitting after all, because that's how the city began; from its early history as a trading centre for the Indians and Europeans, and as the heart of the timber industry in Eastern Canada, Ottawa has always been a business centre, long before the bureaucrats arrived and before journalists began using its name as a word synonymous with government.

There are, for those interested in the various categories of commerce, at least four areas of business in which Ottawa actively participates. The City of Ottawa and surrounding municipalities serve as a huge regional market and distribution centre for the Ottawa Valley, from the St. Lawrence River to the city of Pembroke. Ottawa-Hull is also an industrial centre where pulp and paper products are manufactured and where a wide range of service industries flourish, from printing and graphic arts to defence technology and innovations in computer software. Furthermore, Ottawa is the hub of transportation routes for eastern Ontario and the Ottawa Valley, as well as a major centre for research and development in Canada. In fact, so many firms specializing in advanced technology have located in the region that in the 1970s businesspeople dubbed the area "Silicon Valley North."

The dynamics of Ottawa are unmistakeable—this is not a city that has chosen to sit back and admire the indisputable glory of Parliament Hill. This is a city that is open for business.

It would be foolish, naturally, to disavow the effect that the federal government has on the city's business life; although Ottawa's employment base has

tended to diversify and grow in recent years, the government will always be a major force in Ottawa's economy. Nevertheless, no one expects the government to grow significantly (it putters along, at an average growth rate of one percent a year), and as Ottawa develops concurrently, the government's relative share of employment locally will decline.

On the other hand, government has seen fit in recent years to improve its efficiency by contracting out services and by purchasing both goods and services from private enterprise, establishing itself as an ever-increasing market for Ottawa-area companies. Closeness to government counts in other ways too; the fact that Ottawa is important as a centre for national politics fosters complex relationships between government, social organizations, and business. The city, and the region, will continue to be the location of choice for national associations, trade organizations, lobby groups, consulting firms, and specialized business services.

Ottawa is a centre for international relations as well, so that it will long serve as the location for embassies and diplomatic missions, particularly those which require regular contact with major government departments.

Of course, when major Canadian corporations, or the Canadian subsidiaries of foreign-owned companies, have in the past looked for a home for their head offices, relatively few chose Ottawa. Toronto and Montreal have an advantage in that the banking and industrial communities established themselves there in the last century. Nevertheless, more companies are choosing Ottawa today for their corporate head offices, especially those in the field of advanced technology who benefit from the proximity to government and research

FACING PAGE: The copper-roofed towers of the Parliament Buildings are reflected in the glass panels of a nearby office tower, forming an intriguing mosaic. Photo by Didier Dorval/ First Light

A view of the Parliamentary area of downtown, showing the Parliament Buildings (centre), the Langevin Block (left), and the Chateau Laurier and Union Station (right). The photo predates the Rideau Centre and Congress Centre developments. Photo by Bill Marsh/ The StockMarket

The Central Post Office has been a splendid landmark for decades. Photo by Jessie Parker/ First Light

FACING PAGE TOP: Visitors decide where to go next as they pore over a map of the capitol. Photo by Wayne Eardley/ Burke Communications Photography

FACING PAGE BOTTOM: The *Sea Prince II* carries a group of sightseers along the Ottawa River. Photo by Wayne Eardley/ Burke Communications Photography

centres. The fact that Ottawa-Carleton is important as a major market in the Province of Ontario has resulted further in the opening here of a number of regional or district offices for national companies.

These are the major factors that form the foundation of business in the capital, but there is one other important characteristic that distinguishes Ottawa from other Canadian and North American cities—its people. Partly because of the high proportion of civil service jobs, and partly because of the nature of the industries that have chosen to locate in the region, the people who live in Ottawa-Carleton tend to be well educated, earning relatively high incomes. In fact, the average family income for the region has consistently placed in the top five cities in the country.

The benefit of attracting such a population is obvious: while other centres experience highs and lows in, for example, the retail and homebuilding sectors of their economies, Ottawa's stable population base insulates it somewhat from tremendous swings in market activity. The region's growth rate is impressive too: the Regional Municipality of Ottawa-Carleton is the second largest metropolitan area in the Province of Ontario, the fourth largest in Canada, and is among the fastest growing municipalities in the country. Unemployment rates, on the other hand, are well below those of other centres, and housing prices are lower than in other cities, which results in an enviable quality of life.

Although federal, provincial, and municipal government jobs account for about a third of the region's employment, not far behind is the region's service sector, which includes all personal, business, community, and education services. City of Ottawa officials expect that, as the country as a whole, and Ottawa in specific, becomes more dependent on services, this sector will soon equal the public sector in its importance as a local employer.

TOURISM

When you have one of the most beautiful cities in the world, set in one of the most attractive and historic areas of the country, with a pleasant climate and a calendar that boasts virtually nonstop events and entertainment, what can you do but invite people to come and visit?

Tourism is the second largest employer in the region, with more than 25,000 people involved in tourist-related services and activities. More than 3 million people visit Ottawa each year, attracted by festivals such as Winterlude, the Jazz Festival, and the Festival of Spring, and these visitors spend big money in the city—about $400 million a year.

The bulk of tourists here are people who have come to see the capital of Canada and to wander through the spectacular museums, especially the National Gallery, that make Ottawa the "showcase of a nation." Although a good number of visitors arrive in Ottawa to spend time with relatives living in the city (who evidently do a

THE OTTAWA RIVERBOAT CO.
SEA PRINCE II

Tour boats ply the Rideau Canal every hour; here, one is seen passing under the Bank Street bridge, near the New Southminster United Church. Photo by Wayne Eardley/ Burke Communications Photography

wonderful job of extolling Ottawa's many virtues as a safe, clean, exciting place to visit), many others come as part of tour groups—seniors and school groups, particularly. The Canada's Capital Visitors and Convention Bureau says their estimate of 5,000 bus tours in the region a year is a conservative one; they do know, however, that each bus group spends approximately $5,000 a day in the city.

Conventions, particularly, are a big business for Ottawa, a business that's growing each year. The city is seen as a "four seasons" destination for meetings, as there simply isn't any time of the year when there aren't at least a hundred things for visitors to do and see. Visitors from the United States especially seem to appreciate both the safety of walking about in the city's downtown area—something that differentiates it from most other capital cities in the world—and a cultural diversity that compares favourably with many European spots.

In fact, the number of U.S. organizations that choose Ottawa as a meeting destination has jumped from a handful in the early 1980s to more than 50 a year, a change that is due in no small way to the activities of the Canada's Capital Visitor and Convention Bureau (known as the CCVCB for the sake of brevity). The CCVCB acts as a sort of broker for conventions and the local hotels and merchants, helping to match up groups interested in convening in Ottawa with the appropriate facilities in the city. If a group wants to be able to hold a meeting for as many as 3,500 delegates, that can be arranged, and if the delegates or their guests want to take a helicopter tour of the capital region, that can be done too. In turn, the CCVCB advises local businesses on how to use and

Visitors admire a bed of *salvia*, near Dow's Lake. Photo by Wayne Eardley/Burke Communications Photography

More than three million people visit Ottawa each year. Photo by Mihok/The StockMarket

market their facilities for tourism and conventions.

One of the CCVB's goals has been to encourage small groups to meet in the region; the large meetings which bring thousands of people to the city at one time are great, but it's the number of smaller groups that keeps the economy going all year round.

The CCVCB was the first Canadian visitors' bureau to open an office in Washington, D.C., and it has aggressively marketed the city as a place not only where visitors have plenty to see and do, but also where meeting facilities are first-class, and hotel accommodation memorable. A non-profit organization supported by members of the local business community and by the Regional Municipality of Ottawa-Carleton, the CCVCB has succeeded in making Ottawa-Hull one of the top 20 tour destinations in North America.

Hotels, naturally, are an important part of business activities in a city where tourism is significant, and Ottawa has dozens

LEFT: Bank Street, with its office towers and shopping promenade, is one of Ottawa's "main streets." Photo by Wayne Eardley/ Burke Communications Photography

FACING PAGE TOP RIGHT: The Ottawa Westin Hotel is a popular destination not only for visitors to the city, but also for numerous conventions and local social events. Photo by Wayne Eardley/ Burke Communications Photography

The Skyline Hotel is located amid sparkling office towers on Lyon Street, and offers a spectacular view westward. Photo by Wayne Eardley/ Burke Communications Photography

The newly renovated Radisson Hotel serves the heart of the business district in Ottawa. Photo by Wayne Eardley/ Burke Communications Photography

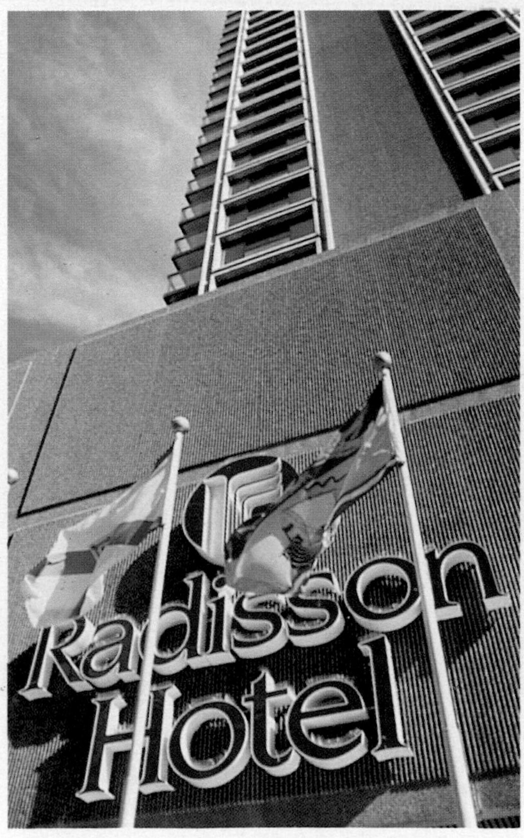

of hotels, from skyscraping chain-operated inns such as The Westin, Radisson, Delta, and Four Seasons, to independents such as the Plaza de la Chaudière in Hull. It's a fact that at any given moment there are about 12,000 business visitors in the city who are here for meetings with business or government, or for seminars and language training; many of these people stay in town for days, even weeks or months, and as a result, Ottawa has a number of all-suite hotels that create a home-away-from-home ambiance for visitors. As well, a number of the city's large, historic homes are now Bed and Breakfast inns, where visitors can enjoy either the quiet seclusion of a private home or the amiability of being welcomed into the innkeeper's family life and getting to know the *real* Ottawa.

In short, there is an almost endless variety in accommodation in Ottawa, and a

full range of rates. In recent years many of the city's older hotels, such as the venerable Chateau Laurier and The Roxborough, have been renovated; still others are brand-new, such as Minto Place, and the Novotel at Albion Place.

Business visitors and tourists alike are further attracted by Ottawa's accessibility: within a day's drive from Toronto, Montreal, and many U.S. cities such as Syracuse, Rochester, and New York City. The city is linked to the rest of Canada by the TransCanada Highway (which passes through its midst), by rail, and by air. Moreover, the design of the newly renovated Ottawa International Airport is quite unlike the rather baffling layouts in other major cities—no lengthy walks to the luggage carousel!

Early efforts at promoting the city to potential visitors and convention groups were hampered by the insistence of some municipal officials in the region that Ottawa be marketed not as the city of Ottawa (which everyone knew really meant the Capital Region as a whole) but as "Ottawa-Carleton," which more often than not had people, particularly in the States, scratching their heads and saying, "Ottawa what?" Thankfully, today everyone recognizes the wisdom of simplicity.

ABOVE: A Bed and Breakfast house in Lower Town catches the interest of two visitors. Photo by Justine Hill

LEFT: The huge pillars that form the *porte-cochere* of the Chateau Laurier make an impressive entranceway. Photo by Devries Mikkelsen/ First Light

The Chateau Laurier—known simply as the "The Chateau"—is more than a hotel; it's a landmark institution in Ottawa, and the site of many gala events. Photo by Wayne Eardley/BurkeCommunications Photography

FACING PAGE BOTTOM: The sun breaks through after a brief shower at a small suburban shopping centre in the city of Kanata. Photo by Wayne Eardley/ Burke Communications Photography

RETAIL

Those who are familiar with the history of Bytown know that when Lieutenant-Colonel John By and his men arrived to build the Rideau Canal, the next event in the area's history was the rapid growth of commercial activity. By 1830 there were stores in both Upper and Lower Town, and Sussex Drive was the city's principal avenue for shops.

Today, Ottawa is still a boomtown of sorts; the stable local economy and a population of well-educated, high-income earners translates into happy, healthy retailers. There are several giant regional shopping centres strategically located throughout the Capital Region—Bayshore, Beacon Hill, and the Rideau Centre to name just a few—as well as smaller shopping centres and a network of retail "strips" in each neighbourhood.

Many of these shopping centres have undergone recent expansion, such as Carlingwood and St. Laurent, as well as Bayshore, which has added a third level of shops and boutiques. Such expansions are just one indication of how much Ottawans love to shop; another is the Statistics Canada estimate that local consumers spend almost $600 million in Ottawa-Hull department stores each year.

That figure is an estimate of only the money spent in department stores; it doesn't include the dollars spent in the

ABOVE: Minto Place opened in the summer of 1988, an all-suite hotel with a difference—every suite is equipped for business travellers who bring along computers. Photo by Devries Mikkelsen/ First Light

"Rendez-vous Rideau!" The award-winning slogan is but one reason for the Rideau Centre's popularity with local shoppers. Photo by Wayne Eardley/ Burke Communications Photography

The freshest of fruit and vegetables are laid out for shoppers in the Byward Market. Photo by Devries Mikkelsen/ First Light

myriad of specialty shops, such as the bookstores devoted to one discipline or another—mystery novels, say, or cookbooks—or the gourmet take-out food shops, or the novelty shops, or the magazine and newspaper stores that carry journals from everywhere in the world except perhaps Tierra del Fuego. Neither does it include what's spent in the clothing stores, in the furniture or decorator accessory shops, or in the outlets for china, porcelain, and crystal shipped to Ottawa from all over the world, or the money that is spent to buy clothes from local designers. One has only to go into the Byward Market or into one of the malls, any day of the week, to see Ottawa shoppers in action; one might wonder if anyone ever stays at home!

Moreover, as housing development stretches across the region from the communities of Orleans in the east, to Barrhaven and Kanata in the west, there has been a concurrent growth in retail facilities, as well as a redevelopment of some areas. For example, to accommodate the commuting homeowners in the east, the area off Innes Road which was once predominately industrial has recently begun to sprout small businesses—many of them aimed at house-proud new homeowners—such as outlets for ceramic tile and wallpaper.

It's obvious, then, that businesspeople in Ottawa are quick to spot an opportunity and to jump on it, usually in a very original way. Ottawa isn't a city where retail strips monotonously offer the same chain stores and restaurants one after another, so that the whole picture looks like a Monopoly gameboard; many small businesses here offer unique products and services, presented in a unique fashion, and each proprietor has a distinctive story to tell.

This market photograph is from May 15, 1954. The two-storey brick market building on the right was built in 1926 after fire destroyed its predecessor. Courtesy, City of Ottawa Archives

ABOVE: This delightful Topley photograph captures the enjoyment of an outing to the Bytown Market. The market has endured and grown since this photo was taken in 1911, despite the threats of removal and the pressures of urban growth. Courtesy, Public Archives of Canada

LEFT: Fresh-picked local corn, heaped in bushel baskets, is ripe for the buying on a late summer day in the Market. Photo by Devries Mikkelsen/ First Light

The architecture of the Constitution Square office development is among the most interesting of the modern buildings in Ottawa. Photo by Devries Mikkelsen/ First Light

CONSTRUCTION

Ottawa's early success as a business centre was based on the region's considerable natural resources, and commerce consisted of supplying other cities and regions with the raw materials to build. The active construction industry in Ottawa today exemplifies how the city has changed from being a producer to a consumer of goods; both residential and commercial development have been strong in recent years, and the expertise of local developers is now known throughout the world.

Ottawa's first association of builders was formed in 1889; however, it wasn't an association in the sense of professional associations today, with meetings between friendly competitors. In those days the construction business was a rough one, and the men in the business were rougher still; relations between the contractors and architects, for instance, were brutal. A story in the June 14, 1892, edition of *The Ottawa Citizen* was just one indication—a contractor and an architect disagreed violently over some matter of construction, and when the architect asked the contractor to "step outside," the contractor replied that he already had one charge of manslaughter against him and he was reluctant to have another. Fortunately the argument was resolved without more drama!

Ottawa experienced a building boom shortly after the city was named the capital, when a series of public buildings was erected. The next significant boom occurred after the Second World War; many more public buildings appeared, as well as large subdivisions of housing. It was during the years from 1960 until 1975 that the Place de Ville complex was built in downtown Ottawa, along with the National Arts Centre, Ottawa City Hall (which remains one of the finer examples of post-modernist architecture in North America), and the Energy Mines and Resources complex, to name a few.

Approval of the Place de Ville project marked an important turning point in Ottawa's development as a city independent of the federal government. For years the National Capital Commission had wielded the deciding vote in the sanctioning of development in the downtown area. The general idea was that no downtown building should detract from the splendour of the Parliament Buildings, which led to the imposition of rather severe height restrictions in what was known as the Parliamentary Precinct. The Ottawa City Council was "pro-development" in the 1960s, however, and it amended these restrictions in 1965; within months the Campeau Corporation proposed its multimillion-dollar Place de Ville office and retail development. Despite the fact that the development's 23-storey towers extended far beyond even the amended height restrictions, the City Council approved the project, which was to

have federal government departments as its principal tenants.

Place de Ville was the city's first highrise office development, to be followed by many more; planners in the 1960s had thought that development in the core would extend southward along Elgin, O'Connor, and Metcalfe streets, but Place de Ville had the effect of directing it westward instead. Within a decade of Campeau's proposal, the City of Hull had its own highrise core, with the construction of the Place du Portage complex and the Terrasses de la Chaudière (the latter having been built by Campeau Corporation, whose relationship with the current authorities was clearly a strong one, perhaps because Campeau's vision of Ottawa-Hull coincided with that of the government).

Since the sixties, commercial properties have developed steadily in the downtown core and, more recently, in Nepean and Gloucester, where large office complexes meet the needs of the suburban market. Although there has yet to be a building boom to rival that of the immediate

A work horse at the National Capital Commission Log Farm greets a tiny visitor. Photo by Jessie Parker/ First Light

postwar period, Ottawa has seen flurries of development, as in 1984-1986, when more than 1.5 million square feet of office space were added to the inventory in Ottawa-Carleton. Several local developers who were perceived by their peers as courageous—an appropriate word for those who speculated on commercial properties when interest rates were over the 20 percent mark—were quickly seen to be astute business practitioners when the vacancy rates for office space began to plummet along with interest rates, sparking a renewed vigour in the economy.

Commercial development continues to flourish in the region, and the coming years will yield tangible evidence of a shift in the pattern of use of office space. While the downtown area of the City of Ottawa will remain as the focus of economic activity in the metropolitan area, the adjacent municipalities are expected to gain their fair share of the economic pie. By 1987, for example, a significant trend had surfaced, in which many local firms were moving to suburban office space, thus leaving the downtown area to the head offices of major companies and key government departments, as well as professional offices and financial institutions. By the mid-1980s, in fact, the City of Nepean's list of the 10 major employers in that city named only one federal government department. Likewise, the City of Gloucester has seen an upswing in development in recent years, including a splendid new office project in its centre.

Meanwhile, many of Ottawa's real estate developers who did so well during the boom years of the fifties and sixties, building homes to meet the pent-up, postwar demand, went on to become highly successful commercial developers of international reputation. Of course, the first name that comes to the tip of anyone's tongue is Robert Campeau, the man who dared to buy out two giant U.S. retail chains, Allied and Federated, in 1986 and 1987.

While it might be unfair to other accomplished developers in Ottawa to single out the story of Robert Campeau (some of which has now ascended to mythological status), it is nonetheless important to chronicle his achievements, if only to demonstrate that rags-to-riches stories do happen off the television screen. Born in Sudbury, Campeau came to Ottawa in 1947 and found work as a machinist; he built and sold one house at a time and became so successful that he soon found himself in the construction business. These were really "boom" times in Ottawa, after the war, when housing was desperately needed, and Campeau met the heavy demand; in 15 years, his firm built 12,000 houses and at the same time gained a reputation for quality that still exists today.

The rest, as they say, is history; the Campeau Corporation went on to build several office complexes in both Ottawa and Hull (its success deriving from the skillful negotiation of long-term leases), and by the 1970s the firm had moved to Toronto. The Campeau name is still a force in Ottawa; the corporation owns a number of office projects and shopping centres and has plans for more, like the South Keys retail development that is expected to have a dramatic effect on development to the south of the city.

Of course, there are other names in Ottawa's construction history: Teron, Minto, Assaly, Tartan, Nicol, and Pérez. Bill Teron, with Sam Shenkman, foresaw the potential of a planned community named Kanata (an Iroquois word for encampment); today, Teron's homes, built in the sixties, form the established "older" neighbourhoods of this pleasant, family-oriented community. Teron's earlier company, Urbanetics, left us with many fine apartment buildings, such as the stately 300 The Queen Elizabeth Driveway. Teron too has assumed international status, and Teron International has been called upon to construct a mega-project in France.

Minto Construction is perhaps Ottawa's best-known homebuilder, though in recent years the firm has gained a reputation not only as a builder of commercial projects—some of which are in the vanguard of contemporary technology, like the "smart" Carlisle building—but also as an international homebuilder with large projects in Florida. Two other Ottawa firms have exported their development expertise south of the border: Tartan and Pérez.

José Pérez's story is not unlike that of Robert Campeau (indeed, the company is now headquartered in Campeau's former head office in Nepean) in that he started out in Ottawa with a small drywall firm and has since escalated his company's activities to large-scale housing developments in Ottawa, Hull, Toronto, and Florida, as well as to several commercial projects. In 1988 Pérez, along with the Toronto-based international Citicom, won the bid to build a spectacular project on the coveted Canlands site, which will overlook Parliament Hill.

Although Ottawa has a reputation as a somewhat conservative—one might venture to say even staid—city, stories such as these create a different picture. In fact, real estate development in Ottawa indicates that the city is quite ready to try new things; for example, Ottawa quickly adopted the concept of condominiums as housing. The first high-rise condominium towers were built in 1967 by Minto; others by R.J. Nicol followed in 1969. Today, residential condominiums are firmly established, and there is a growing tendency toward industrial condominium space, as well as office and retail.

Meanwhile, the growth of industrial development has been much aided by the creation of business parks in various locations in the region, among them the city-owned Ottawa Business Park in the southeast sector of the City of Ottawa.

SERVICES

The second largest industry in the region is the service sector, which includes all business, personal, community, health, and educational services, and which accounts for roughly a third of all the employment in the capital. The national trend is for city economies to become more dependent upon this sector in coming years; this is certainly true for Ottawa, where, within a decade, services are expected to equal the federal government as an employer.

"Services," of course, include a wide range of activities, whether "food" such as catering, or "personal," such as hairdressing, or "business," such as word processing, copying, and printing. One such business service, advertising and graphic arts, offers a good indication as to just how varied the commercial scene is in the region, and how flexible—and accomplished—local businesspeople can be. Ad firms and artists count not only federal government departments and crown corporations among their clients but also numerous real estate developers, retailers, restaurant chains, and shopping malls. Many of Ottawa's advertising agencies are highly regarded in their field, having won local, national, and international competitions. In advertising, however, the bottom line is: What have you done for us lately?—which results in constant competition for innovation.

Another field in which Ottawa firms have made their mark is that of animation and video production. Ottawa is home, for example, to world-famous Crawley Films, whose Atkinson Film-Arts division boasts the largest animation and film studio this side of Los Angeles. The firm has done so well in fact that it was dubbed "Disney on the Rideau" by a local business publication. Indeed, Atkinson has produced animations of some of the best-loved stories in the world—Curious George, The Care Bears, The Raccoons—thus providing cartoon characters that will live in the mem-

A modest building for one of the world's best known film houses is the headquarters of Crawley Films. Photo by Jessie Parker/ First Light

ory of a whole generation of youngsters in the way that Daffy Duck did for children of the fifties and sixties.

And the awards have been plentiful. *The Care Bears in the Land Without Feelings* garnered Atkinson the silver medal in the 1983 International Film and TV Festival in New York. In addition, a Christmas special based on the Canadian "For Better or Worse" comic strip by Lynn Johnston won the company awards at both The Geminis and the Childrens Broadcast Institute, as well as a Blue Ribbon for Best Original Work for Children at the 29th American Film and Video Festival.

Moreover, the National Research Council and the Department of Communications, with help from Crawley Films, is building a multimillion-dollar facility in Hull that will pioneer research and development into the adaptation of computer technology to animation. Canada has long had a reputation for innovation in film, particularly since the debut of the IMAX technology at Expo'67 in Montreal, and now it looks very much as though Ottawa-Hull will be at the centre of breakthroughs in animation in the twenty-first century.

Video technology has also seen advances in Ottawa; local firms have already adapted the use of computers to video production. Thus videos can be produced quickly and inexpensively, but more important, the videos can be updated at minimal cost.

Meanwhile, Ottawa offers a unique opportunity for the makers of feature films in that one has only to travel a matter of minutes to be transported from a busy city street to the tranquil serenity of a wilderness setting. The City of Gloucester in particular has been actively marketing its locale and the sophistication of its local production houses to foreign filmmakers.

Once a sooty lumber town, Hull now boasts several government office complexes and high rise office towers, as well as the new National Museum of Civilization (right). Photo by Devries Mikkelsen/ First Light

ADVANCED TECHNOLOGY

Although Ottawa has been dubbed Canada's "Silicon Valley North," a quick look at the number of advanced technology firms located in the capital region, compared to the number in Toronto and Montreal, reveals that Ottawa is third in the country in terms of a head count of companies. But that's not the whole story.

Although it's true that Toronto and Montreal may have attracted greater numbers of high-tech companies, many of these are in fact sales offices for U.S. or international firms, or they may serve as the location for merely one facet of a company's activities. Many of Ottawa's advanced technology firms, however, are involved in truly innovative work, breaking the ground for revolutionary applications of technology that will affect industry, health care, and communications for decades to come.

Why Ottawa? First, the region has an abundance of resources to offer, not the least of which are the research capabilities of the National Research Council and the city's two universities. As Regional Chairman Andrew Haydon has pointed out, "within a 20-mile drive, it is possible to reach two universities with engineering facilities, a technical college, and some formidable industry and government research and development laboratories. All the companies here are on the leading edge of technology," he adds, "and the amount of technical brainpower is tremendous."

Brainpower—Ottawa's advanced technology firms benefit not only from the quality of the electronics and engineering programs at Ottawa's two universities, as well as the presence of government research facilities and more than 150 research and development technology companies, but also from the expertise and breakthrough-oriented approach of organizations such as the Kanata Enterprise Centre and the University of Ottawa Innovation Centre. Moreover, the competition for all this brainpower is lower than in other world centres for advanced technology, such as California and Massachusetts, because the density of the industry is lower; that means companies can attract the best people, train them, and keep them. Ottawa's singularly attractive quality of life has an impact too; highly trained, virtually irreplaceable staff are content to stay in the city.

And Ottawa has still more in its favour. The price of industrial land, for example, is lower than in other centres and yet, because of the city's size, everything is accessible in minutes, not hours. In addition, most of the advanced technology firms in the Capital Region have had the benefit of constructing their own buildings, using local contractors' abilities to create specialized space, and thus enjoying a unique opportunity for both corporate visibility and identity.

In the 1970s, about 40 advanced technology firms were located in the capital; today, estimates are that there are more than 300 such companies in the region. Although it's difficult to detail these firms' diversity of activities, it is easy to demonstrate the effect their presence has had on the community. For example, several advanced technology firms have grown to become major employers. The three largest

At nursing stations in the University of Ottawa Heart Institute at the Ottawa Civic Hospital, nurses employ sophisticated equipment to monitor their patients' progress. Photo by Wayne Eardley/ Burke Communications Photography

firms, Bell Northern Research, Mitel, and Gandalf, are active in communications; others are involved in the semi-conductor industry, in the aerospace industry, in navigational systems for military applications, and in software development.

The future of advanced technology in Canada is expected to lie in the field of biotechnology, and here again Ottawa has the advantage in that it happens to also be the location for research facilities run by Agriculture Canada, the National Research Council, and the Department of National Health and Welfare. In addition, Ottawa has several major hospitals as well as the internationally known University of Ottawa Heart Institute and the headquarters of the Canadian Red Cross.

The fact that the field of advanced technology is such a strong and significant part of the Ottawa's economy has resulted in a sort of "high tech" community, in which the executives of various local firms can meet and share experiences. As evidence of this, Ottawa-Carleton Research Institute was formed, a non-profit cooperative research facility in which industry, education, and government have pooled resources to develop new technology.

The vision that people in this industry have for the world borders on the miraculous. For example, development of new standards for the integrated system network (ISDN) is an initiative that has involved several local firms. ISDN isn't a *thing* exactly: it's the ability to integrate both voice and electronic data, then to transmit both rapidly over long distances, using telephone lines and a high speed digital format. What this means is that potentially even a large volume of data can be transmitted from one computer terminal to another, thousands of miles away, in a matter of minutes.

COMMUNICATIONS

The history of newspapers in Canada is in many ways the history of Ottawa as the capital of Canada. It was a national obsession with politics that spawned many a newspaper in Canada, and after Confederation many more cropped up to take on position or another in local or national politics.

Ottawa has had one daily newspaper, *The Ottawa Citizen,* which began life in the last century as *The Packet.* Founded in 1843 by a passionate frontier politician, William Harris, the little paper barely subsisted on a very small circulation. It was sold several times and in 1851 was renamed *The Ottawa Citizen.* A new era in Canadian newspaper publishing began when William Southam, who owned a printing business in London, Ontario, bought a share in *The Ottawa Citizen* and sent his oldest son, Wilson Mills Southam, to act as managing editor. At the time, there were two other newspapers in Ottawa, *The Free Press* and *The Journal*, but within months *The Citizen* had garnered a healthy circulation.

The Southam family became a tremendously successful publishing team; Harry Southam, another of William's sons, took over as publisher in 1920, and Wilson Southam assumed leadership of the family company. Southam today, which owns a chain of newspapers across Canada, counts *The Ottawa Citizen* not only as its flagship operation, but its chief profit-making paper as well.

Moreover, *The Citizen* is counted as one of the three best newspapers in Canada, due in no small way to its excellence in political coverage and its enviable collection of columnists, ranging from the sometimes acerbic Don McGillivray to contemporary humorist Charles Gordon. The paper has won numerous awards, for its photography and editorial cartoons as well as for the quality of certain features.

The Journal, meanwhile, persisted as an important Canadian newspaper until its demise in 1979 when, plagued by labour problems and an inability to improve printing processes, it ceased publication. Several groups of investors then tried to publish another weekly paper in the hope of its becoming a daily, to fill the vacuum left by *The Journal.* None succeeded, though, until a group of Ottawa business-people developed *The Sunday Herald,* a weekly tabloid that was born in 1983. Many people predicted the little paper's imminent death, but gave up after its fourth anniversary.

Everyone was surprised, in the summer of 1988, when the Toronto Sun Publishing group purchased the majority of shares in *The Sunday Herald* and promised to turn the paper into a daily, to meet *The Ottawa Citizen* head-on in the local market. Ottawans were treated to a full-scale battle of public relations as each paper jockeyed for position with readers and advertisers.

A number of community newspapers also flourish in the region, including the *Kanata Kourier,* the *Orleans Express,* the *Nepean Chronicle* and *The Leader* in Gloucester. Readers tend to use their community paper as a source of information about personalities and events in their neighbourhood and as a sort of bulletin board for events and programs.

Several business periodicals circulate in the region as well, including the bimonthly tabloid, *Ottawa Business News*; *Ottawa Business Life,* a glossy magazine published eight times a year; and *Business and Leisure,* an annual business publication aimed primarily at the commercial traveller in Ottawa. The Ottawa-Carleton Board of Trade publishes its own business journal, *Byword,* six times a year, featuring news and profiles of local businesses, as well as articles on issues that affect the local business environment. Two other publications, *What's On in Ottawa* and *Ottawa Newcomer,* list events and services for both visitors and newly arrived residents.

Although the City of Ottawa itself has something less than 400,000 residents (perhaps a tenth the size of Toronto's population) it has nevertheless been able to support a high-quality city magazine called, appropriately enough, *Ottawa Magazine.* Actually, the magazine was born out of the ashes, so to speak, of a rather short-lived tabloid called *Ottawa Today*; the fact that advertisers and readers alike have supported a more sophisticated publication, offering features on political issues and life-style, may tell a great deal about Ottawa's citizens.

When it comes to television, Ottawa is ideally suited for channel zappers: situated on the Quebec/Ontario border, within a few hours' drive from New York State, the city offers devotees of the tube an enormous range of viewing choices, particularly if they are subscribers to a cable service. Educational channels are beamed in from Toronto and Watertown, and national networks CTV and CBC maintain stations in Ottawa. Private stations operate here as well, and viewers can choose programs in either French or English.

Several programs seen on national television networks and marketed throughout North America in fact originate in Ottawa TV studios. The award-winning and highly acclaimed program for young children, "Under the Umbrella Tree" is filmed at the CBC-TV studios in Ottawa. At the other end of the spectrum in children's programming is the irreverent but wildly funny program, "You Can't Do That On Television," which is filmed at CJOH studios. The popularity of this program can best be gauged by the reaction of teen girls; one of the young stars took a trip to Colorado with his family and was recognized by avid fans in a shopping centre!

Radio is no different: Ottawa's broadcast market is an active one with a full range of AM and FM stations appealing to every taste in music and serving citizens of both official languages. Carleton University, meanwhile, has its own radio station, which is supported by the community and which features many unique, often experimental, programs as well as offers an opportunity for budding radio stars to develop their skills.

TRANSPORTATION

It's a joke among people who've adopted Ottawa as their home that the region's inhabitants just don't know what a real traffic jam is. And it's true—the relatively uncommon bottlenecks that do occur in Ottawa's traffic rarely cause drivers to measure their progress in hours, rather than minutes, as in other cities.

Part of this happy situation is due to the region's advanced public transportation system, O-C Transpo, and in particular, the Transitway. What began in the last century as a passenger railway is today a $100-million a year operation in which more than 800 buses accommodate more than 90 million passengers a year. The sophistication of O-C Transpo, which was recognized by an international transit award, is evident to passengers in the form of the transit information system. This system generates computerized schedules updated every few minutes and presented on video terminals which are displayed in shopping centres and Transitway stations.

The Transitway is a transportation artery that allows buses to travel at higher speeds than possible on city streets, from Woodroffe Avenue in the west to St. Laurent Shopping Centre in the east. By 1991 it will include a total of 26 stations on 31 kilometres of Transitway. Some stations have as many as four platforms, which are accessible by glass-enclosed walkways and stairs, and elevators for the handicapped. A description of the Transitway appeared in *Bus World,* the North American trade magazine: "a true transit system, at relatively low cost. Undoubtedly other cities will follow, because the Canadians are on to something."

THE OTTAWA-CARLETON BOARD OF TRADE

One of the reasons Ottawa is such a fine place to live, work, and do business is the local chamber of commerce, the Ottawa-Carleton Board of Trade. Many of the board's initiatives have had a dramatic effect on the way the city has developed. Even the Rideau Canal may owe its life to the Board of Trade; in 1910 the Canadian National Railway wanted to close the canal in order to build new rail lines, but the board intervened—wisely—and its campaign to heighten public awareness resulted in CNR dropping the plan.

The Board of Trade was incorporated in 1857, and since then has been instrumental in a number of Ottawa's "firsts." The board organized the first city-wide garbage collection, and put together a group to support public hospitals' care of impoverished patients. The board also instigated the construction of the highway between Ottawa and Prescott, now a major route to the south, and lobbied the provincial government to establish the Eastern Ontario Institute of Technology (now Algonquin College) in Ottawa.

The importance of tourism in the region is indisputable and here, too, the Board of Trade has left its mark; the now fabulously successful Festival of Spring, originally called the Tulip Festival, was created by the board in 1953. The board also developed the ceremony of the Changing of the Guard on Parliament Hill, a colourful military exercise that entrances foreign visitors. The Sparks Street Mall, which was the first pedestrian mall in Canada, was developed by the Board of Trade during the 1960s, and became a huge success within its first few years.

Now one can look down upon the mall from the windows in the luxurious members' dining room at the Board of Trade offices, which are between Sparks and Wellington streets—Parliament Hill faces the board on one side; Ottawa storefronts on the other. The Board of Trade's principal goal is the general improvement of business in Ottawa, which it accomplishes by lobbying various levels of government and by providing local business people a forum in which to discuss new ideas and develop policy.

Networking is an important facet of business today, and the Board of Trade holds various events throughout the year that offer excellent opportunities for both making new contacts and strengthening existing relationships. "Doing" lunch at the Board of Trade ranks high on the business agenda, as do the board's "Business After Hours" gatherings and other receptions. The gala event held annually is the Businessperson of the Year award dinner, when a local business personality is honoured by his or her peers. A recent development has been the annual business story awards presentation, in which the Board of Trade recognizes the quality of writing produced by local journalists, especially the work that puts the spotlight on local business.

A full social calendar does a lot toward furthering business activities, but the day-to-day world of commerce depends primarily upon a healthy economic environment; the Board of Trade offers its members numerous opportunities to make a difference in how business operates in Ottawa-Carleton. The various committees at the board examine issues and develop programs that are as far-reaching as the impact of national issues, such as free trade, upon the local economy, or the effects of tax reform enacted by provincial and federal government; closer to home, the problems that the advanced technology sector faces are discussed, and information on employment assistance programs are distributed to small-business members.

Thus the Ottawa-Carleton Board of Trade has been an important voice for business in the capital from the time Bytown was christened the City of Ottawa.

Of course, most cities can look back to their beginnings and see changes, some more dramatic than others; nevertheless, one has to admit that the transition from the earliest days of Bytown and the grimy, gritty days of the lumber business, to the sparkling office towers and busy shops of Ottawa today, has been a marvel. From sawdust to software, the city has taken its place in Canada not just as a bedroom community for the government, but as a centre of commerce in its own right.

The *Sea Prince II* sails the Ottawa River with a view of downtown and the Confederation building as a backdrop. Photo by Wayne Eardley/ Burke Communications Photography

BNR

BNR engineers have adapted the Northern Telecom DMS-100 telecommunications switch (shown in the background) for fiber-optic technology to the home by developing a special plug-in module. This hand-size circuit pack makes it possible to provide subscribers with value-added features such as digital telephones with 40-character LCD display, videotex services, voice and data interworking features via ISDN, high-quality video pictures, and access to pay-per-view service.

The innovation leader in telecommunications systems and component design, Bell-Northern Research (BNR) is one of the largest privately owned industrial research and development firms in North America.

From the world's first fully digital central office switch to the first telephone calls using the Basic Rate Access (BRA) and Primary Rate Access (PRA) standards of the emerging Integrated Services Digital Network (ISDN), BNR has played a pivotal role in creating the communications networks and services that are dramatically transforming information management capabilities worldwide.

The industry pioneer in fully digital technology, BNR designs products that serve the full spectrum of telecommunications users: public telephone companies, global corporations and small businesses, government and military agencies, and education, health, and financial institutions. The firm also performs systems engineering and long-range network planning for telephone companies, specialized common carriers, and government and military communications organizations.

BNR's more than 6,000 employees are committed to a corporate mission: to use expertise in core technologies to produce the innovative solutions that meet customer needs with quality and speed-to-market unmatched by any competitor. BNR engineers and scientists are constantly extending their track record of world "firsts" and have been granted more than 1,000 patents in the United States and Canada during the past 10 years.

Customer-driven innovation is the vision BNR shares with its corporate parents: Northern Telecom, a global leader in the manufacture of fully digital telecommunications systems, and Bell Canada, one of North America's premier telephone companies. This is the vision of an Intelligent Universe in which people everywhere will be able to exchange, share, process, organize, store, and access information in many forms (voice, data, text, and image) using increasingly intelligent terminals linked by fully digital communications networks.

The key to this Intelligent Universe is networking. BNR engineers excel in the design and development of products and systems that allow customers to configure dynamic communications networks—using any combination of public networks and privately owned equipment.

The organization's roots in telecommunications go back before the turn of the century. It was in 1958, however, that Northern Telecom first established a division specifically dedicated to research and development. In 1971 the research and development operation was formally constituted into a separate subsidiary company, BNR, which is 70 percent owned by Northern Telecom and 30 percent by Bell Canada.

BNR's close relationship with telephone operating companies helped it to anticipate the benefits that digital technology would offer telecommunications. BNR's applied research into the semiconductor and software "enabling" technologies involved in digital communications allowed Northern Telecom in 1976 to announce Digital World—its commitment to become the first manufacturer to offer a complete range of fully digital switching and transmission systems. Through products such as the DMS family of switches, BNR helped secure the parent corporation's position as a world leader in fully digital telecommunications, with systems in use in more than 70 nations.

Today the company operates a computer-linked network of laboratories in seven locations in the United States, Canada, and the United Kingdom. Its annual budget exceeds U.S. $600 million. More than 65 percent of its employees have university degrees, with almost 25 percent holding a master's or Ph.D., including some 140 doctorates in electrical engineering and computer science.

BNR designs account for more than 90 percent of the products and systems manufactured by Northern Telecom, and are in use throughout North America and the Caribbean, and in countries such as Japan, China, Turkey, and West Germany. BNR is also an industry leader in the design of proprietary semiconductors and in the generation of sophisticated software. Through a range of company-evolved techniques and internal disciplines—such as its "gating system" approach to new product development—BNR has been able to continually reduce the design-to-manufacture interval, while simultaneously improving design quality.

A BNR designer works with an advanced CAD system, one of the many in use at BNR to shorten design cycles and improve design quality. BNR uses these systems to design high-quality and complex products and services.

A BNR technologist monitors a computer-controlled voice simulator, shown moving in an arc above Northern Telecom's Meridian Norstar M7310 telephone. This testing verifies that the telephone's built-in microphone, used during hands-free operation, transmits a caller's voice with maximum clarity. Here the telephone is being evaluated in BNR's anechoic chamber, where the sound-absorbent walls eliminate all echoes that may interfere with testing.

As an industrial research and development organization, BNR does not concentrate on theoretical research, but directs its international resources toward high customer-value innovation—applying advances in key scientific areas such as semiconductors into top-quality, cost-effective systems and service features that telecommunications users need. The company's work is focused on three major product streams:

Network products—switching and operations systems for telecommunications carrier markets. BNR system designs have included the DMS (Digital Multiplex System) family of central office switches that control local, long-distance, and international telephone traffic, the Autovon military switch, and DMS SuperNode, an integrated network node; Meridian Digital Centrex, offering an unequalled range of business communications features through the public network; and the DPN family of data packet switches with a capacity surpassing 30,000 standard packets of data per second.

Business communications systems—private switching systems, local area networks (LANs), and terminals that control voice and data communications for businesses and institutions requiring from two to thousands of telephones. BNR-designed systems include the Meridian SL family of private branch exchanges (PBX) that support a full range of enhanced calling features and voice mail capabilities; Meridian Customer Defined Networking, a broad portfolio of products, applications, and customer support tools that establishes for the first time a peer-to-peer level of interworking between private and public networks; the DMS-MTX cellular mobile communications system; the Meridian Norstar digital key telephone system, a feature-rich system that brings all-digital switching technology to small businesses. Norstar allows them to

A BNR technician removes a gallium arsenide wafer from an ultrahigh vacuum plasma deposition unit in BNR's Advanced Technology Laboratory, where the world's most advanced monolithic optoelectronic transmitter was fabricated.

enjoy features that were previously available only on PBXs.

Transmission and fiber products—telecommunications transport and access products ranging from voice frequency equipment through microwave radio systems to optical transmission systems.

BNR's advanced systems and technology group is responsible for the application of microelectronics. The group supplies its partner divisions with leading-edge custom semiconductors, printed circuit boards, computer-aided design (CAD) systems, and hardware prototype and test and verification services. It undertakes advanced technology research and development in such areas as the gallium arsenide (GaAs) family of semiconductor materials and optoelectronics.

Critical to the success of this development activity is the ability of BNR's researchers to contain and manage systems and technology of dramatically increasing complexity. A significant portion of BNR's annual capital expenditures (which exceed $100 million) is dedicated to maintaining a world-class computing capability, including the advanced CAD tools that support error-free designs that can be rapidly transferred to Northern Telecom's manufacturing divisions and on to the customer marketplace. The firm deploys more than 380 MIPS (millions of instructions per second) of mainframe-based computing power, 11,000 terminals, and 800 gigabytes of storage.

Integral to the process of top-quality, rapid-to-market design for both hardware and software products are advanced testing and verification procedures. BNR has developed a range of specialized tools needed for the exacting evaluation of system prototypes in the lab. BNR scientists created the world's first computer-aided design tool that could identify and analyze electromagnetic emissions during the design phase of electronic circuit packs. Used in integrity testing for the DMS family of switching systems, TATS, its test and traffic simulation system, helps software designers conduct load testing by simulating up to 300,000 telephone calls per hour under demanding and diverse real-world conditions.

BNR has established "captive offices" at lab locations in the United States, Canada, and Maidenhead in the United Kingdom. These facilities are fully operational central office nodes, especially constructed as test sites for the evaluation and enhancement of prototype hardware and software products. BNR has also developed a series of interactive computer-aided engineering tools that virtually eliminate the need for traditional hardware prototypes as the primary means of design verification.

Linked together in a network covering 24 BNR and Northern Telecom design and manufacturing centers worldwide, these proprietary tools and their associated design data integrate the capture, simulation, and testing phases of hardware design. This integration, combined with a hierarchical design approach, allows engineers to simulate the behavior of integrated circuits and printed circuit packs at each step in the development process, before the product is frozen in hardware.

BNR focuses on designing and implementing networks that serve not only growing volumes of traffic, but also the demand for a wide array of new services made possible by the convergence of telecommunications and computing. Central to the organization's design philosophy is its commitment to helping customers successfully manage change—both in telecommunications technology and in their ways of doing business. The company incorporates the principles of modularity and design continuity into all its products and systems. Northern Telecom products and systems can be enhanced easily and quickly to take full advantage of technological evolution, protecting customers' investments in their existing systems. BNR's researchers do not design isolated pieces of equipment, but bring to bear an overview of the entire telecommunications network and process.

BNR's success in telecommunications research and development was built directly on its ability to master and apply advances in core information technologies. Chief among these critical building-block technologies and processes are semiconductors, optoelectronics, software development, and test and verification tools.

As microelectronics has merged with telephony, advanced microchips have become key enabling components driving telecommunications systems. BNR has been working on applications of silicon devices for some 20 years.

In 1979 BNR seized world leadership in the telecommunications industry when it developed the E-99 filter codec, the first single-chip coder-decoder capable of converting analog voice signals into digital bits and back again. Now silicon development at BNR focuses on advanced CMOS (complementary metal-oxide semiconductor) technology that can accommodate circuitry spaced 1.2 microns apart, tripling the capacity of a chip. While silicon-based integrated circuits will continue as the workhorse technology for BNR system designs, the company is also developing a variety of other chip compounds. Prime among these materials, GaAs is capable of carrying electrical signals at least 10 times faster than silicon.

BNR has constructed a special laboratory with such specialized research tools as molecular beam epitaxy and metal-organic chemical vapor deposition. In 1988 the firm announced the development of an exploratory GaAs circuit that can handle signals at five gigaHertz—believed to be the fastest chip of its type for potential application in high-speed telecommunications.

The combination of high-speed semiconductors with lasers and optical fibers of ultra-pure glass has emerged as the primary telecommunications transmission technology of the future. The advantages of optoelectronics includes virtually unlimited bandwidth, allowing the transmission of extremely high volumes of information at very low cost and with a high degree of message security.

It is in optoelectronics that GaAs circuits carry special potential, because the circuits emit light in response to electronic signals, and generate electronic signals in response to light. BNR's leadership capabilities in GaAs circuits and optoelectronics were demonstrated in 1988 when its scientists processed the world's most advanced monolithic optoelectronic transmitter, which converts digital signals into light pulses at speeds exceeding two gigabits per second.

A central factor behind the success of Northern Telecom's DMS family of switching and transmission systems is the ability of BNR to design and manage the large, real-time software systems that control telecommunications equipment and provide additional service features. These computer instructions to the switching systems are continually augmented as enhanced network features are introduced; all newly written code is fully compatible with previous software.

ISDN—the Integrated Services Digital Network—is a vision of a universal set of standards and protocols for establishing end-to-end compatibility between telephone networks and the connection of various new data terminals and access devices. BNR has established a leading position in developing, trialing, and delivering ISDN capabilities and applications. BNR is active internationally to secure industry-wide agreement on ISDN standards and protocols, working through bodies such as the CCITT, a Switzerland-based international standards organization.

But even ISDN is only a building block toward the goal of the Intelligent Universe. The constant evolution of technology in microelectronics and computing—including speech and text recognition, new computing architectures such as neural networks, and new programming languages such as Prolog—carries with it the promise of a constantly expanding range of telecommunications-based services providing new dimensions of capability and productivity.

A commitment to innovation and achievement, a total dedication to customer needs, a strategy based on networking, a mastery of core technologies, a team of people who see quality as the only acceptable standard—these are the attributes that propel BNR to its goal of undisputed leadership in the design and manufacture of telecommunications equipment into the next century.

A BNR scientist examines a semiconductor wafer made of gallium arsenide (GaAs), containing thousands of the world's most advanced monolithic optoelectronic transmitters. Each exploratory transmitter merges laser technology with microelectronics, converting digital electronic signals into light pulses at speeds exceeding 2 billion bits per second. Transmitters are a key technology in providing voice, data, and video images to the home and office over a single optical fiber.

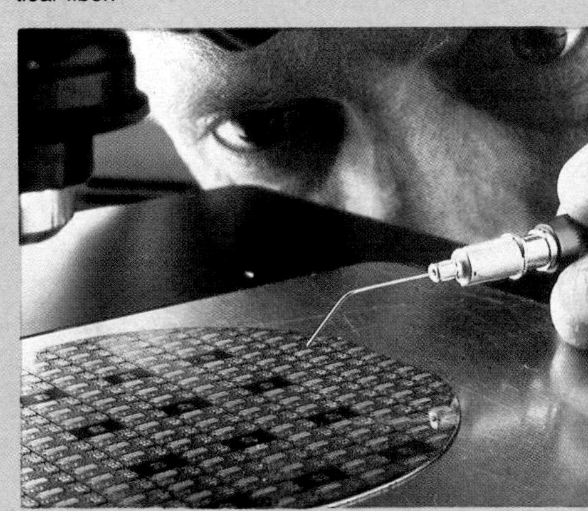

NORTHERN TELECOM ELECTRONICS LIMITED

A technician (foreground) supervises the patterning of images on a silicon wafer.

Thinking small at Northern Telecom Electronics Limited is limited to the size of its product. When it comes to drive, vision, and innovation, NTE, a wholly owned subsidiary of Northern Telecom Limited, thinks big—very big.

The size of its Nepean facilities matches its vision. The state-of-the-art, 500,000-square-foot complex houses 900 employees devoted to producing custom microchips for the exclusive use of Northern Telecom products.

Undoubtedly, NTE's most significant and boldest contribution to this growing and competitive field is the Advanced Semiconductor Technology Centre, which cost $105 million to construct and equip. In addition, millions of dollars are spent every year to help fuel the research and development of advanced processes for producing custom microchips at this complex. The 86,000-square-foot centre—the largest manufacturer of microchips in Canada—features the most dust-free environment in the country.

The centre's 22,000-square-foot clean room, where the microchips are produced, is ventilated by 16 fans that circulate 1.5 million cubic feet of air through the room every minute, making it 10,000 times cleaner than office air. During the fabrication process, the chips are notoriously sensitive and can be easily destroyed by foreign substances otherwise as innocuous as dandruff or microscopic flecks of human skin.

So, just how do NTE's custom chips outclass the competition? In a variety of ways, ways that are constantly being upgraded, challenged, and improved upon. NTE's custom chips, used in a wide variety of products such as telephone sets, switching systems, and voice/data terminals, give Northern Telecom a secure competitive edge by increasing the processing power, intelligence, and functionality of its products. In addition, the product's size and power needs are simultaneously being reduced.

NTE's ability to produce custom microchips has proven beneficial in penetrating the marketplace by filling a crucial demand for the unique combinations of semiconductor technology needed for telecommunication applications.

That in-house capability also results in faster, more economical introduction of new technology to the hungry marketplace and it allows Northern Telecom to retain the proprietary nature of its systems.

NTE's mandate will not allow it to bask in its past glories. Yet they are numerous and frequently have set technical milestones. In the 1970s the development of the filter-codec chip resulted in a world first by allowing analog and digital signals to be mixed on the same chip. As a result, telephone users are now benefitting from higher quality voice channels and from a host of telephone services previously stymied by technical or economic realities.

The march of technology is especially rapid in the semiconductor industry. In 1980 NTE's CMOS1B (Complementary Metal Oxide Silicon) technology enabled the production of circuit lines six microns wide

A technician prepares to transfer a load of wafers into a nitride deposition furnace.

and chips featuring 10,000 transistors.

By 1984 that technology had been fine tuned again, and it, along with the ability to reproduce larger chips, meant 80,000 transistors could be fitted into a chip—eight times the number of the CMOS1B process.

The push is now on to produce chips with circuit lines and elements 1.2 microns in width (one micron is one-sixtieth the thickness of a human hair), which would feature several hundred thousand or more transistors.

The 1990s promise the introduction of chips with circuit lines less than a micron wide. The new and improved advanced chips will allow the parent company to market even more powerful, compact, and intelligent products.

NTE will maintain its leadership role in the semiconductor market for telecommunications by producing mixed analog/digital devices such as the filter/codec chips. Research and development continues on mixed CMOS/Bipolar or BICMOS devices. BICMOS technology marries the lower energy consumption of CMOS with the current drive capability of bipolar structures, and is destined to play an integral role in mainstream technology.

An equipment technologist tests the wheel of a high-current ion implanter. After the wheel is loaded with wafers, it is spun up and scanned across an ion beam. The ions implanted in regions of the silicon wafers will alter their ability to conduct electrical current.

An equipment technologist programs a robot to transfer 150-millimetre silicon wafers into a special furnace, where they will be coated with "dielectric" layers.

Speed and reliability are also key words in the development of on-chip memory, another important focus of NTE's development activities since it eliminates the need for separate memory devices and, therefore, reduces the number of connections between chips.

The meticulous, innovative Advanced Semiconductor Technology Centre and Northern Telecom Electronics Limited's proven track record in its field, and its bold determination and vision, are but stepping-stones to its corporate goal for the year 2000—to achieve world leadership in telecommunications for Northern Telecom.

PRIOR DATA SCIENCES

PRIOR Data Sciences is a software company headquartered in Kanata. In its 13th year of operation, the company specializes in real-time software for military, air traffic control, and imaging applications. PRIOR's business interests centre on air traffic control, system design and development, international military programs, and software product development.

PRIOR offices within Canada are located in Toronto and Halifax, servicing the increasing needs of both these regions. Future plans see PRIOR operating facilities in Montreal, the United States, and Western Canada. The firm is totally employee owned. Some 225 employees work for PRIOR, and most of these are either scientists, engineers, or computer specialists.

In the field of air traffic control PRIOR Data has provided enhancements of the communications link between Prestwick, Scotland, and Gander, Newfoundland, to manage air traffic-control over the North Atlantic Ocean. The firm also provided the Common Controller Workstation and Test Facility, which was developed to identify what information should be displayed to air traffic controllers to meet increased demand.

The firm provisioned all of the software for the Modular Aeronautical Communications Switch. It provides air traffic controllers and flight service specialists with the capability to operate various radio, hotline, interphone, telephone, and intercom systems.

In conjunction with the Canadian Aviation Safety Board, PRIOR designed and developed a system that projects a reconstructed three-dimensional image of an aircraft flight onto a computer video terminal. With this data an aircraft crash investigator can piece together the cause of the catastrophy more accurately and timely.

For the military programs field, PRIOR Data provisioned the display subsystem for the Maritime Command Operational Information System. This system allows Canadian Navy personnel to monitor air, surface, and subsurface traffic of the eastern sea coast of Canada and the United States. The data gathered will be analysed for strategic importance.

The firm also provided the software for the Military Aeronautical Communication Switch. This system is designed to control radio communication between ground sites and military aircraft. PRIOR Data also provisioned the display subsystem for the NATO Saclant project. Supreme Allied Command Atlantic is an establishment responsible for monitoring air, surface, and subsurface traffic for the Atlantic Ocean. Its operation centre collates data and analyses it to glean strategic data that will be forwarded to other NATO agencies for action.

In the software products field, PRIOR Data developed GKS, a programmer's tool. GKS is a subroutine library that contains 220 subroutines. PRIOR's implementation is known for both its conformance and performance to the standard.

InterMAPhics is an interactive mapping and graphics presentation system. It extracts digital maps from a map database and displays graphic symbols of aircraft, ships, and land-based vehicles.

Although a Canadian company, PRIOR conducts 30 percent of its business in the international arena. It has partnered itself with several prestigious "500" club members to provide a solution to complex problems.

PRIOR Data Sciences is recognized as a world-class software supplier. This reputation has evolved from its emphasis on reusable software developed to exacting quality standards.

Canada

BELL CANADA

Bell Canada's operations in the Ottawa area are probably the most advanced for any community of its size anywhere. Satisfying the constant telecommunications demands of the Government of Canada and the specialized needs of the largest high-tech community in Canada are challenges to which Bell Canada's Eastern Ontario regional office has proven equal.

The combination of the latest in telecommunications products, advanced technology, and highly qualified staff supports the evolving needs of Bell Canada's Ottawa area residence and business customers while also emphasizing the highest quality and reliability of service.

Bell Canada offers an extensive portfolio of products and services to subscribers in the Ottawa region. Efficient and reliable voice and data networks, business communications systems, and residential products are now standard services available from the dominant telecommunications carrier. This has meant capital investments of millions of dollars to meet basic and enhanced services and timely planning to step up network modernization in the area.

Ottawa's Television Operating Centre/Programme Operating Centre. Network programming and special video services are switched and controlled through this operation, which has full access to the broadcast grade facilities of both the Canadian and the U.S. networks.

The network status display at Telecom Canada's National Network Operations Centre located in Ottawa. This centre continuously monitors the continuity and operational effectiveness of the nationwide network of the Telecom Canada members.

More than 70 percent of Ottawa's telecommunication network is now serviced by eight local DMS-100 digital switches—a level of service unsurpassed anywhere. In addition to improving network performance and reducing maintenance costs, these digital switches enable Bell Canada to offer a wider range of advanced services to more customers.

Four of these eight DMS-100 switches are dedicated to the government of Canada to operate its Enhanced Exchange Wide Dial (EEWD) service. It is a unique system designed to meet the government's needs, not least of which is the size of the system, which services 100,000 lines and users. The Ottawa area is the hub of the government's telecommunications network and most of the government's traffic flows through this state-of-the-art system. The government of Canada was the first customer to use this Centrex III-based technology, taking advantage of the latest in network features to help manage its network more efficiently and in a cost-effective manner.

Advanced DMS-200 digital switches handle all long-distance calls in Ottawa. It is also the first major centre to have call-management services, an innovative concept that has profound implications for customers' ability to better control their incoming telephone calls and manage their outgoing calls. Among the services included are Calling Line Information Display, which reveals a local-area caller's telephone number; Automatic Call Setup, which rings when a busy line becomes free; Selective Call Rejection, which permits a user to direct calls from up to 12 numbers to a recorder; and Activated Call Identification, which allows Bell Canada's local office to trace annoyance calls.

Ottawa is also the corporate location of Bell Information Systems, a division of Bell Canada. The Eastern Ontario region covers the area from the Quebec/Ontario border to Oshawa and services a population of 2.2 million and provides a wide range of communication services including the Integrated Services Digital Networks (ISDN) and Integrated Office Systems (IOS) portfolio of products. Both of these are excellent examples of leading-edge concepts that will keep Bell Canada in the forefront in providing customer service.

In one trial, three government of Canada departments are testing numerous ISDN applications that will permit the simultaneous transmission of voice, data, image, and text over the same telephone line, using a single integrated access link. For the customer, ISDN will offer more

Bell Canada's District Network Surveillance Centre/Network Operations Centre in Ottawa ensures round-the-clock reliability and quality of the switching and transmission facilities in Eastern Ontario.

cost-effective communication services, greater network control, and increased connectivity with computers.

In late 1986 Bell Canada began positioning itself as a key player in the IOS marketplace by developing portfolios of leading-edge industry standard products selected to provide Connectivity, Office Services, and Telecom Information Management (TIM). Connectivity enhances communication between voice, data, and image products by providing networking capabilities whether they are within a small work group or among multiple customer locations. The Office Services portfolio allows customers to enhance, expand, and efficiently access existing communication and computer equipment and provides a wide range of information services, including word-processing, messaging, spreadsheet, and data base capabilities. And through the evolving Telecom Information Management (TIM) portfolio, Bell Canada is providing business customers with the information and ability to manage and control their on-site telecommunications and office systems. TIM improves the customer's ability to monitor and control communication expenses and the features, usage, and performance of their systems. For example, with Customer Station Administration (CSA), Centrex customers can easily rearrange the numbers and features on their sets and relocate sets without installer assistance and thereby reduce costs.

Bell Canada has already installed products from these IOS portfolios in numerous locations within the Ottawa area—each representing a "custom-designed solution" from Bell Canada.

Highly qualified business and technical development staff concentrated in the Ottawa area are the cornerstone on which Bell's high level of products and services are based. The presence of corporate family members, Bell-Northern Research (BNR), the largest research and development organization in Canada, and Northern Telecom, the largest telecommunications equipment manufacturer in Canada, ensures that Bell Canada not only remains on its toes but also has access to outstanding expertise.

Bell Canada's Eastern Ontario office works closely with BNR and Northern Telecom in using Ottawa as part of a tricorporate proving ground. The customers' needs provide the impetus for technology which, in turn, is translated into service.

This interplay spawns opportunities for continual evolution of sophisticated products and applications. The ready cooperation of Bell Canada and BNR workers means a constant searching for innovative services and solutions.

But it is not merely the technology and products offerings that keeps Bell so well positioned in the Ottawa area. More than 5,000 highly trained and committed employees ensure that there is a continual striving to provide customers with the most efficient and advanced service possible. Bell Canada's presence in the community is further reflected by the more than $150 million that flows into it by means of salaries and benefits paid to its employees.

Those same Bell Canada employees who work so diligently at providing excellent service to customers are also a veritable army of volunteers when it comes to charitable, community, and institutional activities. Bell employees staff the telephone stations during the annual Children's Hospital of Eastern Ontario Telethon. In the past eight years better than 50 percent of the chairs for the local annual Easter Seals campaign have been Bell Canada employees. Similarly, the Junior Achievement program and the United Way Fund have had strong support from the Eastern Ontario regional office, the former through donations and support of personnel and the latter by achievement of the dollar donation figure established for Bell Canada. The Canadian Institute for the Blind also benefits from the activities of many Bell Canada staff who are members of the Telephone Pioneers of America, the world's largest industry-based volunteer service organization.

These are all signs of Bell Canada's strong sense of good corporate citizenship.

A Bell Canada operator, one of 5,000 employees in the Ottawa area, ready to provide friendly and caring service on the company's state-of-the-art network in the National Capital area.

UNISYS CANADA INC.

Unisys Canada's 2200/600 series mainframe computer.

In 1986 two of the world's largest computer companies, Sperry and Burroughs, joined forces and became Unisys Corporation—the power of 2.

Unisys today is a $13-billion information systems company with more than 90,000 employees and 60,000 customers in more than 100 countries. Unisys Canada Inc., with headquarters at 2001 Sheppard Avenue East in North York, Ontario, has offices, service, distribution, and manufacturing facilities throughout Canada. The company is a leading manufacturer of commercial information systems, defence systems, and related services. It employs approximately 3,000 people across Canada and has marketing and service facilities in virtually every major Canadian city from Vancouver to St. John's.

Unisys Canada is divided into a number of business units:

Defence Systems provides specialized military electronics equipment to both the Canadian Armed Forces and military forces of other countries. A sophisticated defence electronics manufacturing facility employing about 500 people is located in Winnipeg.

Paramax Electronics Inc., a Unisys Canada subsidiary, is the prime subcontractor to Saint John Shipbuilding for the electronics and combat systems management required by the Canadian Patrol Frigate Program. Approximately 600 staff, two-thirds of them engineers, work at the advanced Paramax research and development complex in Montreal. A total of 12 frigates will be built as part of the program.

The Peripherals Group and Power Supply Operations both have worldwide manufacturing mandates. The Peripherals Group supplies disk memory units from its plant in Winnipeg and employs more than 450 people. Power Supply Operations is located in Dorval, Quebec, where the staff of 300 is engaged in designing, manufacturing, and exporting power supplies for many different Unisys products.

Information Systems, employing more than 1,000 people, is the business unit of Unisys Canada that is familiar to most customers. The Unisys strategic approach to the information systems marketplace involves concentrating on particular lines of business and serving each of them in depth. In Canada the company concentrates on health care, finance and insurance, industrial/commercial, government and utilities, transportation, airlines, and education. The mandate of Unisys employees is to apply their experience, technology, and understanding to these lines of business to provide appropriate solutions to the information problems and needs of the company's customers.

In broad terms, the Unisys technology strategy for the 1990s includes three major themes: openness, productivity, and enterprise networking.

Unisys is committed to providing open systems solutions to the information needs of its customers. From microcomputers to mainframes, the company offers a fully integrated and connectable line of products and services. Unisys is also a leader in the development of computer systems compatible with the industry-standard UNIX operating system.

In terms of productivity Unisys leads its competition in the development and application of fourth-generation languages and artificial intelligence. Both are key to allowing customers to streamline and expedite the process of creating computer applications software.

Unisys continues to expand and strengthen its enterprise networking capability in one of the fastest-growing areas of telecommunications—the development of open, industry-standard networks to handle the information management needs of a total business.

The Canadian headquarters for Unisys Canada Inc. is at 2001 Sheppard East in North York.

DIGITAL EQUIPMENT OF CANADA LIMITED

The Kanata, Ontario, facility covers a half-million square feet and houses almost 1,000 workers.

On May 1, 1963, Digital Equipment of Canada Limited opened its doors in Ottawa as a two-person sales outlet. Later that year, with a staff of 10, the company began manufacturing logic modules and computer power supplies out of an old woolen mill in the small community of Carleton Place, 30 kilometres west of the nation's capital. Digital Canada's revenues for 1963 totalled $750,000. By 1988 that figure had reached $964 million.

The firm, which manufactures, sells, and services a broad range of computer equipment, is proud of its history as a computing pioneer in Canada. The Canadian subsidiary of Digital Equipment Corporation of Maynard, Massachusetts—the world's leading manufacturer of networked computer systems—Digital Canada employs 3,200 Canadians working out of 45 sales and service centres from coast to coast.

Digital Canada has a special relationship with the City of Kanata, the site of its headquarters, located just west of Ottawa. "We're deeply involved in this community," says Kenneth Copeland, president of Digital Canada. "Our company philosophy reflects our commitment to be a good corporate citizen and neighbor—in Kanata, and in every community in Canada."

It was 1971 when Digital began construction of a 100,000-square-foot building in Kanata, a structure that included a 67,000-square-foot manufacturing facility. As the company prospered its manufacturing facility underwent considerable expansion, tripling in size during 1977 and 1978. In 1982 a headquarters building was added to the operation, and three years later further expansion brought the total space occupied by the organization in Kanata to a half-million square feet.

The gleaming Kanata facility produces large volumes of interconnect modules, as well as Digital's VAX, PDP, and PRO 38 computers for worldwide distribution.

As a result of these manufacturing "missions," Digital Canada's exports increased by 300 percent between 1982 and 1988, significantly benefiting the country's balance of trade. Canadian suppliers have also benefited from the company's success. In 1988 Digital Canada, which has an official "Buy Canadian" policy, purchased almost $100 million worth of goods and services from more than 1,500 Canadian vendors.

Digital Canada's Agenda for Success, its game plan for becoming a billion-dollar company into the 1990s, emphasizes good corporate citizenship. That commitment takes many forms, but manufacturing for export will continue to be one of its most important focal points—within the corporation, and as part of the Canadian technological community.

VAX 8250 and 8350 processors are readied for shipment from Kanata to the United States, South America, and the Far East, including Japan.

MITEL

Mitel is a tough company, a fact that has been proven throughout its young history.

Founded in 1971, Mitel today designs, manufactures, and markets PBX and key systems, public switching systems, and semiconductors. The Semiconductor Division services both internal requirements and external sales.

Today annual revenues exceed $400 million, and there are more than 120,000 Mitel PBX systems in service worldwide. The company's SX-200 PBX product family set the performance standard for small business telephone systems.

In 1987 the Kanata-based firm supplied about 10 percent of the total U.S. demand for PBX lines, ranking it among the top four suppliers in that country, but the road to success has been a bumpy one.

The company was incorporated in 1971 by Dr. Michael C.J. Cowpland and Terence H. Matthews in order to apply the latest microelectronic technologies to the expanding needs of the telecommunications industry. With the introduction in 1973 of its first major product, a tone receiver, the firm quickly established a reputation for superior design at competitive prices. Capitalizing on its advanced semiconductor technology, Mitel developed a unique crosspoint switch in 1978, enabling the design of a remarkably compact, fully featured PBX, the SX-200 system. This was destined to become the largest-selling PBX in the world in its line size.

Mitel doubled its earnings and revenues annually through 1979 to rank as the fastest-growing telecommunications company ever. After only six years it had captured a 33-percent share of the under-100-line PBX market in the world's most competitive marketplace, the United States.

In 1979 the firm began public trading of its common shares on the Toronto Stock Exchange, later adding listings on the Montreal, New York, and London exchanges. But like many a promising, high-tech start-up of the day, Mitel was ultimately unable to keep pace with its own explosive growth. In 1983 the company reported the first in a series of losses.

That was the period during which Mitel earned its reputation for toughness. Rather than pull back, the company continued to innovate and develop. In 1984 the corporation's first fully digital, integrated voice and data system, the SX-2000 PABX, was launched in three countries simultaneously and achieved first-year sales levels unmatched in the history of large system introductions.

But as the decade continued to unfold, pressure on prices and margins mounted in the company's core markets of Canada, the United States, and the United Kingdom. The result was that even all-time record revenues could not erase the balance sheets' tide of red ink.

Left: The SX-2000 SG and the SX-2000 S PABX's are fully digital integrated voice and data systems.

Facing page: The GX-5000 (one-metre cabinet)—a dial office for small urban and rural communities.

Among remedial actions on a number of fronts, the firm sought an equity partner. That search ended successfully when British Telecom plc, one of the world's largest telephone operating companies with annual revenues in the billions of pounds, acquired a 51-percent controlling interest in Mitel for $242 million in 1986. With this injection of new capital, customer and market faith in Mitel was restored.

What remained to be accomplished was the tough work of developing a strategy to return the corporation to sustained, profit-producing growth. This task was complicated by two factors: flat demand and falling prices worldwide for PBX products. At the time such products accounted for a majority of Mitel's revenue. Clearly, new revenue sources were critical to the company's future.

Two areas were targeted for new growth. One was the public switching business where Mitel offers the GX-5000 community dial office for small urban and rural communities. British Telecom's overseas division, already a supplier of telecommunications equipment to some 80 countries, markets the switch through its distribution network in Africa, Asia, the Middle East, and Latin America.

Other sources of new revenue include peripherals and applications where niche areas show excellent growth potential.

On October 19, 1988, the company announced to its 4,000 employees worldwide a new corporate strategy and the following mission statement: "Mitel, in collaboration with its parent, British Telecom, is dedicated to the provision of voice and data communications systems and networks to meet the needs of business in small and medium premises and public switching in specific market segments. The corporation is committed to profitability and growth by excelling in quality, customer service, rapid product innovation, and operational resilience."

The ride hasn't always been easy, but from the mission statement it's clear, the result of the journey to date is a tougher, better Mitel with a clear business direction for the future.

STM SYSTEMS CORP.

STM Systems Corp.'s new office and computing centre is scheduled for completion in late 1989. Located in the Ottawa Business Park, this new facility affirms the company's status as Canada's leading provider of information technology services.

STM Systems Corp. is a large and growing organization offering its customers total information management solutions on a global basis.

Formed in 1988 as a result of the amalgamation of Canada Systems Group and Datacrown, STM Systems Corp. is the leading provider of information technology services in Canada, with 1988 sales of approximately $185 million. Offices are located throughout Canada and in the Far East to serve its 700 corporate and government clients.

STM's Ottawa division has a long, successful history in the national capital region dating back through its predecessor companies to 1967. Over the years STM's staff has built an enviable reputation for growth, innovation, and leadership in an industry accustomed to change. Currently more than 400 Ottawa-based employees generate more than $50 million in annual sales and occupy 100,000-plus square feet of office and computer centre space.

According to James Over, Ottawa divisional vice-president, STM has succeeded because of its ability to adapt and develop "both in business and technology. We've never limited our horizon to just one technology, and this has allowed us to be flexible. We are able to design and operate a system perfectly suited to our clients, using many different components if necessary."

With such a large presence in the nation's capital, it is natural that one of the company's largest clients is the federal government. Success has been achieved through offering a high level of service at competitive prices—introducing innovative business solutions and the latest technological advances to address changing needs.

STM introduced Facilities Management to the Ottawa marketplace. It now operates more than 20 computer environments for Ottawa clients and is the largest supplier in Canada.

An example of STM's international focus is the Careerware unit that is actively developing in Ottawa a range of micro-based packages for the education and other markets. This software series includes a group of counselling products designed to assist people in career selection and development. Careerware's Choices software is licensed to more than 1,500 customer sites worldwide. Choices Jr., a spinoff package, has been selected for distribution of nearly 3,000 copies to schools in North America, Europe, and the Pacific Rim.

STM Systems Corp. is part of the Semi-Tech Group. The parent of the group is International Semi-Tech Microelectronics Inc., a Canadian public company listed on both the Toronto and Hong Kong stock exchanges.

James Ting, president and chief executive officer of Semi-Tech, has stated that "We are enthusiastic about the future of the information management service industry in Canada and its future in the international marketplace . . . We are on the edge of our next generation in the computer industry . . . the STM Group intend to be leaders."

ATOMIC ENERGY OF CANADA LIMITED

The continuation of Canada's unique electric power option—the CANDU reactor—is AECL's main objective. Computer-aided design and drafting systems are used by CANDU operations staff Anne Haller and Al Guerrero to reproduce a three-dimensional model of the new CANDU 3 nuclear generating station.

Uniting the 4,200 men and women at Atomic Energy of Canada Limited (AECL) is a common purpose: to make available to Canadians the peaceful benefits of nuclear energy. This has been the company's mandate since it was formed as a Crown Corporation in 1952.

AECL's laboratories, engineering offices, and marketing posts are involved in a kaleidoscope of projects, developing procedures and products to solve problems and improve existing methods. AECL scientists created the nation's unique CANDU nuclear power system in cooperation with Ontario Hydro and Canadian industry, pioneered the use of radioactive cobalt-60 to treat cancer and sterilize medical products, and developed uses for new radioactive elements in medicine and industry, building their expertise into a thriving international business.

The nuclear industry, with AECL at its heart, employs 30,000 Canadians and pumps more than $4 billion into the economy annually, making it one of Canada's major industries. The nation's return on its nuclear research investment is high; Canada produces the greatest amount of electricity, per research dollar, of any country in the western world.

Rich in human and technical resources, AECL's multidisciplinary engineering, research, and commercial enterprise consists of two main divisions: CANDU Operations and the Research Company.

CANDU Operations engineers the CANDU system and provides operating support services to Canadian and overseas electrical utilities. It also operates a mechanical and hydraulic testing laboratory, which has been used as a model for similar facilities worldwide.

The Research Company's 750 scientists and engineers work in integrated teams in four major program areas: reactor development, waste management, radiation applications and isotopes, and physics and health sciences. Research, development, and demonstration work at its Chalk River Nuclear Laboratories and Whiteshell Nuclear Research Establishment supports the CANDU nuclear power system and pioneers medical, industrial, and commercial applications of nuclear science.

Well known for its work in nuclear energy, the Research Company also has an international reputation for its research into the nature of matter. In addition, it contributes to Canadian society by exploiting its scientific discoveries and spinning them off into the marketplace. Its scientists offer their expertise to the Canadian and overseas marketplaces by applying their skills to industry and governments on a commercial basis.

Through improvements to its existing products and the development of new technologies, Atomic Energy of Canada Limited aims to ensure that all Canadians enjoy a safe, clean, secure, and affordable source of energy now and in the future.

AECL's Research Company's 750 scientists and engineers work in four major program areas: reactor development, waste management, radiation applications and isotopes, and physics and health sciences. Linda Paterson, a research technologist in the Radiation Biology Branch, carries out an analysis of blood cells as part of a cancer proneness screening test.

NORDION INTERNATIONAL INC.

Nordion International Inc.'s state-of-the-art isotope-processing facility, located at the firm's head office in Kanata, Ontario. Other Nordion sites are located at the TRIUMF facility; University of British Columbia, Vancouver, British Columbia; and the Canadian Irradiation Centre, Ville de Laval, Quebec.

Many people in the industrialized world have benefited from the Canadian-developed technology of the Nordion International Inc., whether they have used a band-aid or cotton swab or had sutures, all sterilized by gamma. If they had an organ transplant or suffered from a severely depressed immunological system, the transfused blood they received was probably treated by Nordion technology. Many millions have had diagnostic medical tests using Nordion radioisotopes.

Nordion International Inc. serves the international health care industry. As a leading supplier of nuclear-based industrial and medical products, Nordion services nuclear medicine and radiation-processing markets through its Isotope and Industrial Irradiation Divisions.

Nordion products, more than 95 percent Canadian in content, are exported to countries worldwide. Company sales in 1987 totalled $87.2 million.

Nordion International Inc. is a wholly owned subsidiary of the Canadian Development Investment Corporation.

The present-day Nordion began on October 1, 1946, as Commercial Products, a division of Eldorado Mining and Refining 1944 Limited. Founder Roy Errington and two employees operated out of a temporary government building. Commercial Products' initial mandate was to market radium, then widely used in the treatment of cancer. In 1952 the government of Canada transferred Commercial Products' assets and 84 employees to the newly formed Crown Corporation, Atomic Energy of Canada Limited (AECL).

In the mid-1960s Nordion International Inc. moved to its present Kanata site, where the majority of its almost 400 employees are located. In 1979 the company was renamed the Radiochemical Company.

In 1988, recognizing the com-

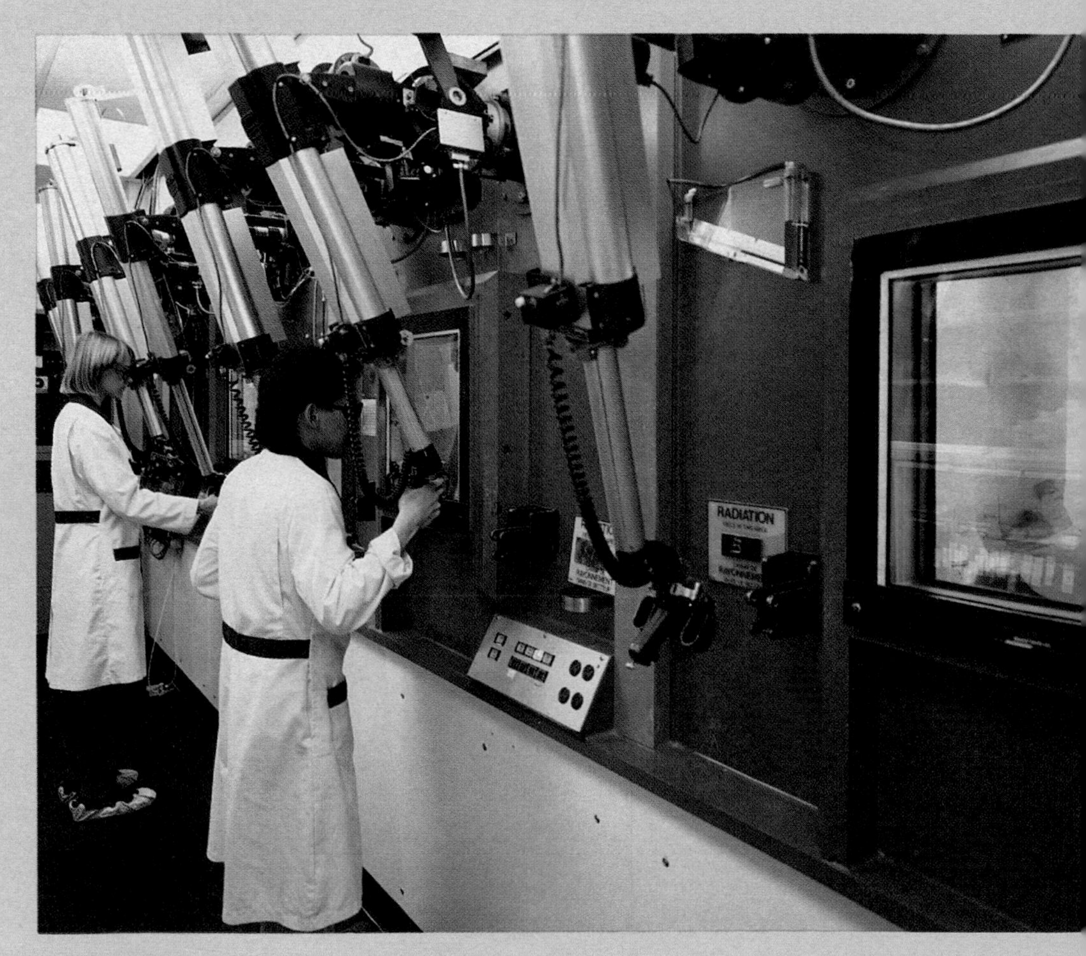

These skilled Nordion technicians are controlling manipulators that operate within the shielded "hot" cell. (The radioactivity is contained within the cell.) In this case, the end product will be Nordion's ultrapure radiopharmaceutical Iodine-123, which is used in nuclear medicine to diagnose heart, lung, and kidney problems.

pany's self-sustaining success, the government of Canada announced plans to transfer ownership of the company to the private sector. Thus, in October 1988, in preparation for privatization, the government transferred ownership of the company from AECL to the Canada Development Investment Corporation (CDIC). CDIC's mandate is to sell Crown Corporations. It was at this time that the company changed its name to Nordion International Inc.

Nordion's Isotope Division's products can be grouped into three major categories: bulk radioisotopes, radiopharmaceuticals, and miscellaneous products and services. The Isotope Division supplies roughly two-thirds of the world's bulk, reactor-produced, and cyclotron-produced isotopes, as well as a range of related technologies, equipment, and services. It also develops and produces its own finished radiopharmaceuticals; Nordion supplies more than one-half of Canada's radiopharmaceutical requirements.

The Isotope Division's products are used primarily in nuclear medicine applications such as the imaging of human organs and studying chemical processes in the body. Some radioisotopes are used in medical therapy, while others are used in research laboratories and industry to measure the level, density, and thickness of materials and determine the integrity or chemical composition of materials ranging from biological samples to mineral products.

In 1979 Nordion's Isotope Division entered the finished product market in radiopharmaceuticals—sterile, non-pyrogenic radioactive chemicals used for medical diagnosis and therapy. Full-scale production of radiopharmaceuticals began in 1984 with the completion of the company's multimillion-dollar state-of-the-art Kanata Isotope Processing Facility.

Nordion's Industrial Irradiation Division produces and supplies capital equipment and radioactive sources to international industrial, medical, and research markets. Its major products include cobalt irradiation systems, which use cobalt-60 as the gamma radiation source; research and clinical irradiators; and medical teletherapy sources. Radiation processing is used primarily to sterilize disposable medical products.

The history of the division began in 1951 with the installation, in the Victoria Hospital in London, Ontario, of the world's first Eldorado "A" cancer treatment unit, which used cobalt-60 as a radiation source. The division marked a major milestone in 1986, when total cobalt-60 shipments surpassed the 200-million-curie mark. One of the division's strengths is its ability to provide customers with total turnkey packages, including engineering consultation services, custom-designed irradiation equipment and sources, licensing documentation, manufacture testing, installation, user training, and after-sales service.

Nordion International Inc. is the winner of both the 1987 Canada Export Award and the 1987 Canada Award for Business Excellence. Both awards are sponsored by the Canadian Government. In receiving the award for outstanding export performance, the company was acclaimed for increasing exports, successfully introducing new products, and penetrating new markets. Nordion, which received the Business Excellence Award for innovation, was recognized for its outstanding achievement in the development and commercialization of high-purity Iodine-123 (used to diagnose brain, heart, and kidney diseases) for medical diagnostic application. Nordion produces this radiochemical at its Vancouver operations site, located at the University of British Columbia; 28 Isotope Division technicians work at the Vancouver site.

A typical Cobalt-60 source rack submerged in a storage pool. The bright blue/white underwater glow is known as the Cerenkov Effect. Nordion supplies 80 percent of the world's Cobalt-60 and more than half of the world's Cobalt-60 gamma-processing facilities that are used to sterilize medical and consumer products such as cotton swabs, needles, syringes, and catheters.

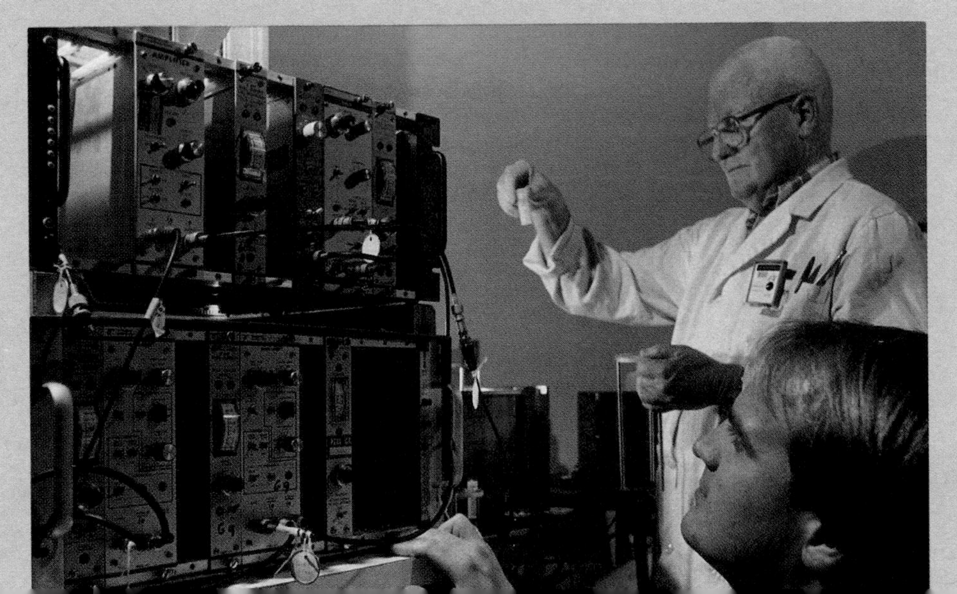

Nordion International Inc.'s quality-control technicians are shown with some of the company's quality-control equipment. The firm takes pride in its high standards of product quality and safety.

DY-4 SYSTEMS INC.

Since it was founded in 1979, DY-4 Systems Inc. has worked to become a leader in both the defence and civil-electronics sector. The company was established to design, manufacture, and market industry-standard, board-level products to system integrators. DY-4 products include boards, chassis, system-level diagnostics, application software, and real-time operating systems.

DY-4's engineering and manufacturing expertise lies in the design

The DVME-138 is a high-performance 68030-based-single-board computer with 4MBytes of memory. It includes DY-4's Advanced VMEbus Interface Chip Set (AVICS) to achieve a 30MBPS transfer rate over the VMEbus.

and manufacture of innovative hardware and software computer systems, based on the 32-bit VMEbus board-level architecture. The firm's boards have been used for a wide range of military applications, including combat systems, air-traffic control, tactical X-ray units, and short-range air defence systems.

The firm's VMEbus architecture approach has contributed a great deal to its success in developing field-proven system solutions. It offers client companies and agencies the opportunity to build a partnership between their own experts and DY-4's professionals. The result is a complete solution, designed to meet specific needs.

"Our mission is to successfully position DY-4 as a world leader in providing system solutions using industry-standard, board-level products and software to system integrators," says Garry Dool, the company's president and chief executive officer. DY-4's impressive list of customers, including British Aerospace, Rockwell, Magnavox, Unisys, Ford Aerospace, and the Canadian Department of National Defence, indicates that this mission has met with a large degree of success.

Headquartered in Nepean in the capital region, where the company's research and development activities occur, DY-4 also has offices in Los Angeles and Campbell, California; Boston, Massachusetts; Washington, D.C.; and Hammel, Denmark.

More than 35 percent of the firm's 200-person staff is involved in the engineering group. This department consists of hardware and software managers, team leaders, project engineers, technicians, technologists, design engineers, and technical writers.

DY-4's engineering expertise lies in the creation of innovative products and system solutions in board-level architecture, developed within the design constraints of ruggedized or MIL requirements. The staff

The DMV-976 is a fully compliant military chassis designed for Vetronics applications. Other chassis in the DMV family can be used in naval and airborne military systems.

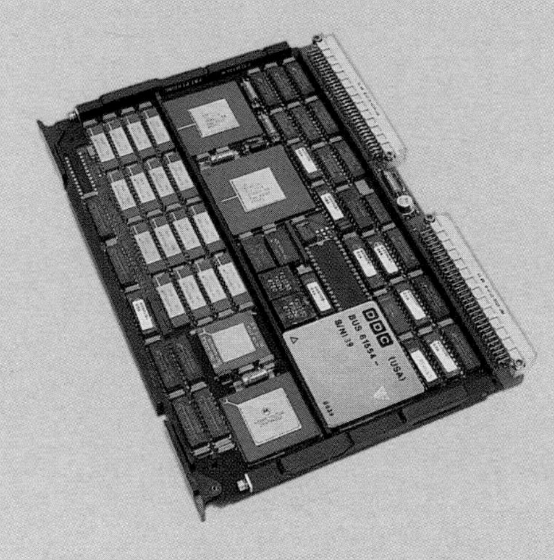

The DMV-154 is a high-performance 68020 single-board computer compliant to conduction cooled military specifications. It also includes DY-4's custom Advance VMEbus Interface Chip Set (AVICS) and a MIL-STD-1553 interface.

has significant experience with multi-processing system design.

The company's engineering capabilities in the logistical and technical aspects of large projects have been confirmed through its ongoing management of major projects such as Transport Canada's RAMP program. Detailed scheduling and project reporting mechanisms are complemented by strict enforcement of documentation standards, frequent design reviews, and functional and system testing.

DY-4's technology group is responsible for developing corporate technical strategies and managing the timely introduction of technology into the company. Working with the engineering section, this group makes sure the best-possible tools for both hardware and software are employed, assessing advances in such tools on an ongoing basis. In major programs, the technology group provides pre- and post-contract systems design support, ultimately transferring

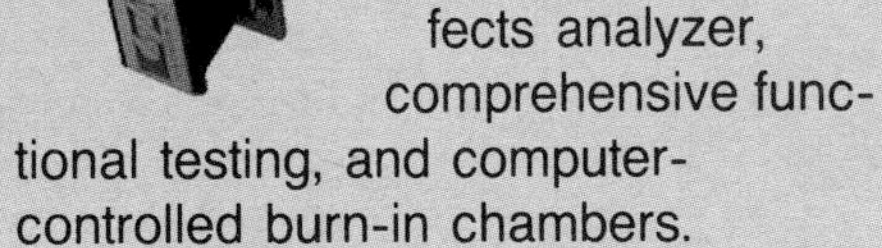

Right: DY-4 Systems manufactures ruggedized cards and chassis for use in severe environments in either land, air, or naval applications.

project responsibility to engineering as a program gets under way. This department keeps DY-4 aware of technological trends through both active membership in industry-wide working groups and regular attendance of technical conferences.

The work of the technical and engineering groups is supported by a strong program management section. Each program undertaken by DY-4 has an assigned program manager, who is responsible for carrying out both technical and administrative contractual activities.

The program manager is the liaison between the customer and the company and is responsible for ensuring that all relevant information is disseminated and acted upon appropriately. Tight scheduling and cost controls are maintained at all times, and the program manager undertakes frequent internal and contractual reviews.

The company's CAD division, Plus 1, has expertise in the design of very-high-density printed circuit boards. DY-4 has invested nearly a half-million dollars in a Cadnetix computer-aided design system for printed circuit board design and related equipment.

This division operates as a service bureau to the high-technology industry and also carries out all printed circuit board design (PCB) for DY-4. The division's current external customer base includes Bell Northern Research, Northern Telecom, Gandalf, Electrohome, and the Canadian Government Communications Research Centre.

More than 18,000 square feet of DY-4's 40,000-square-foot Nepean facility is dedicated to manufacturing. The manufacturing division is proud of its record of delivering a high-quality product at a reasonable cost. Each item produced at the plant undergoes a rigorous series of tests for defects and reliability that includes a manufacturing defects analyzer, comprehensive functional testing, and computer-controlled burn-in chambers.

DY-4 has also implemented DY-CIM, a system that integrates the company's data bases and provides the capability to collect, store, and retrieve data. This system increases productivity awareness and accuracy.

"Success at DY-4 depends on having the right technology at the right time," says Jeremy James, the firm's manager of software technology. "By anticipating appropriate technical developments, we can identify and incorporate them into new programs or products to the benefit of our customers."

With a client list that includes some of the nation's largest corporations, it is apparent that DY-4 Systems Inc. has indeed succeeded.

The DY-4 Systems Inc. facilities in Nepean, Ontario.

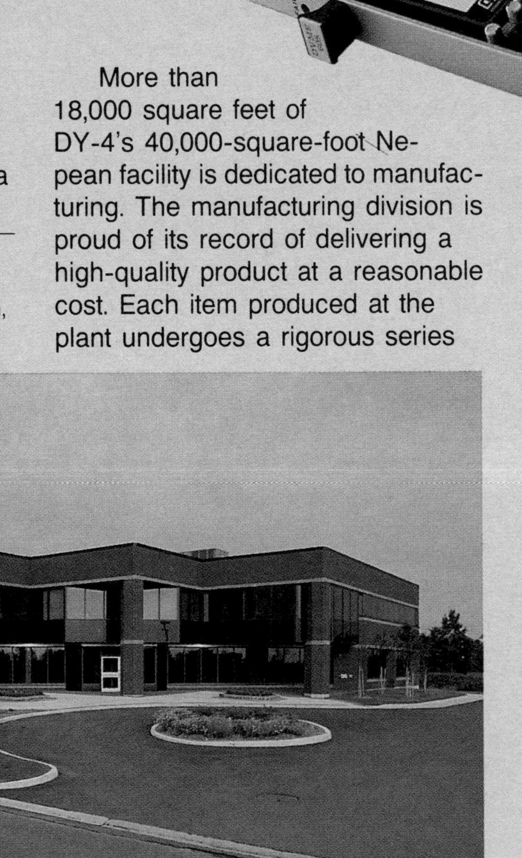

LUMONICS INC.

Lasers. The word conjures images of the twenty-first century. At Lumonics Inc. that future has already begun. The laser is very much a part of today, and the company is at the forefront of using it to create a brighter tomorrow.

Lumonics is an international technology firm that specializes in the development, manufacture, and sale of lasers and laser-based systems. It is one of the world's leading companies in the field, with products based on both gas and solid-state technologies.

Headquartered in Kanata, west of Ottawa, the operation has manufacturing facilities in four countries and worldwide sales and service support. Lumonics offers comprehensive laser-based solutions to the broadest range of customers globally, by combining laser and systems expertise to address applications in materials processing, product identification, scientific research, semiconductor processing and medicine.

Above: A Lumonics laser in use as an amplifier for ultrashort picosecond pulses.

Right: A precision cutting operation is being performed by a Lumonics laser in an industrial application.

Since pioneering laser marking technology in the 1970s, Lumonics continues to be the world's leading supplier of laser-based product-identification coding systems, with more than 2,300 installations worldwide. Among the firm's leading customers are packaging, beverage, and pharmaceutical manufacturers; electronics, automotive, and aerospace firms; and those involved in semiconductor processing.

The company offers a full array of laser technologies, including pulsed-CO_2, YAG, and Excimer, which can be combined with special-

Laser marked IC.

ized beam delivery systems to meet the broadest range of marking applications, including date and lot coding of products, part number identification, and serialization.

The marking of electronic and semiconductor components has traditionally been Lumonics' largest market area, with other areas expanding rapidly. The company offers two complementary families of marking systems, the LaserMark® and the LightWriter™.

In its Laser Products area, Lumonics specializes in the manufacture of pulsed-laser sources that are among the most sophisticated and technically advanced in the industry. The firm's current markets for these products include universities, industrial and government research laboratories, and semiconductor equipment suppliers. In addition, some remarkable breakthroughs have been accomplished in the field of medicine.

In 1988 a Lumonics excimer laser was used in the world's first live-patient coronary angioplasty operation, performed by the renowned Dr. Wilbert Keon at the University of Ottawa Heart Institute. Other important applications for lasers in surgery are constantly being explored by the company.

Lumonics is committed to maintaining a leadership position in the development and commercialization of these advanced laser technologies. It has achieved this status by delivering state-of-the-art equipment to customers, by its substantial commitment to internal research and development through cooperation with researchers in other companies and institutes, and by developing customized products to meet client needs.

Among the Lumonics laser products family is INDEX®, an industrial excimer laser for marking, materials processing, and semiconductor processing; other major products include Excimer, pulsed CO2, YAG, and Dye lasers for spectroscopy, photochemistry, and other specialized research applications.

Lumonics is also at the forefront in developing ways to apply laser technology to materials processing. The company offers the broadest commercially available range of lasers and laser-based systems for use in industries such as electronics, aerospace, and automotive manufacturing.

Offering both standard and custom systems, Lumonics scientists and technicians work closely with customers to develop cost-effective solutions for their precision machining and materials treatment requirements. Among the primary applications areas are welding, drilling, cutting, and surface treatment.

Lumonics Inc. employs 180 people in its Ottawa-area operations and more than 400 more at plants and offices in Germany, England, Japan, and the United States. In 1988 the company recorded more than $87.5 million in sales.

A Lumonics Laserdyne Beam Director™ system cutting holes in hydroformed hemisphere. The hole size and location are programmed on an off-line programming system.

IBM CANADA LTD.

The initials IBM are synonymous with business success and quality the world over, yet few people know that Canadians were the first anywhere to use those initials or the name International Business Machines.

The company's Canadian roots go back to the late 1800s, when three subsidiaries of U.S. manufacturers of tabulating machines, scales, and time recorders were in business to provide productivity solutions to their customers. These companies merged in 1911 to become the Computing-Tabulating-Recording Co., and by 1917 the firm's Canadian operations became known as International Business Machines—seven years before that name was used in the U.S. market.

At that time the company's 100 Canadian employees manufactured and sold clocks, butcher scales, and tabulating devices. Today, of course, IBM is known worldwide for providing the modern business with complete information systems and for contributing to modern business effectiveness.

IBM Canada Ltd. is a wholly owned subsidiary of the IBM World Trade Corporation, the IBM organization responsible for conducting the company's business in 130 countries outside the United States. This means that IBM Canada can offer Canadian customers the resources of one of the world's most successful enterprises. IBM Canada is proud of its autonomy. It is managed and staffed by Canadians, and decisions are made in Canada by Canadians.

The firm's 12,000 employees carry out its operations through 23 branch offices in 13 cities, 14 location offices, 2 manufacturing plants, one laboratory, 56 service locations, and computing and telecommunications facilities that link the company and its customers across the country. In Canada, the firm owns or leases 5.73 million square feet of space to house its research, manufacturing, customer support, and office facilities.

In Ottawa, where the company has operated since the 1890s, IBM Canada currently employs more than 160 people. A new Ottawa office was opened in the fall of 1987 at 55 Metcalfe Street. One of the most advanced of IBM Canada's facilities, it employs IBM's own cabling systems for combined telephone and computer communications, and uses the latest audiovisual and satellite technology in support of customer education activities.

Along with providing advanced job opportunities for a great number of Canadians and contributing to the country's growing high-technology community, IBM Canada is also a leader in the field of education, with an education budget equal to that of a medium-size university.

In 1987 alone the firm spent $42.5 million on 153,300 teaching days for both staff and customers; that is $171,000 per working day. In

The satellite receiver atop the new IBM building receives live broadcasts of customer education courses.

IBM's new high-tech home at 55 Metcalfe Street.

The Customer Support Centre computers provide hands-on training and testing.

addition, IBM Canada actively participates in four-month co-operative education programs and annually creates hundreds of jobs for students across the country. This commitment to education has ensured the company's role as a leader in the information technology industry.

Beyond IBM Canada's contributions through its own payroll and development programs, the firm is also a major purchaser of Canadian goods and services. Each year manufacturing procurement totals more than $140 million, creating more than 2,300 spin-off jobs. As well, IBM Canada assists Canadian suppliers in exporting more than $18 million in products and services annually to IBM plants and laboratories worldwide.

Outside of direct procurement and job creation, IBM Canada's manufacturing and development programs also make a major contribution through active participation in university research programs, enhancing both the facilities and expertise made available to Canadian students and the research community. The manufacturing and development facilities consist of plants in Toronto and Bromont, Quebec, and a laboratory in Toronto. The two plants manufacture leading-edge computer components and high-quality products for distribution worldwide.

IBM Canada's activity as an exporter earned it the rank of 16th-largest Canadian exporter in 1987, according to the *Financial Post* 500. Export income that year totalled $993 million, accounting for 32 percent of total sales. Domestic sales income for the year was $2.1 billion.

The company's contributions to the Canadian economy are also felt in other ways. In 1987 IBM Canada paid $424 million in taxes and duties, spent $434 million on obtaining supplies and services from other Canadian companies, and invested $264 million in plant, machinery, rental, and other property. Payroll and benefits for the year exceeded $650 million.

The reason for IBM's growth and for its continued success is commitment to quality and dedication to customers. Inherent to the IBM Canada philosophy is a desire to be the leader in products and services—excelling in quality and innovation.

This philosophy is felt through all aspects of the IBM family and is exemplified by its "fair deal for the business associate" tenet, an ongoing commitment from the firm to deal with suppliers, shareholders, customers, and others "with care and ethical concern."

IBM Canada is an exemplary company in many respects. It has a proven track record of success and yet has maintained the same spirit of progressive adventure that was displayed by its founders at the turn of the century. It is a major member of Canada's business community, while at the same time driving to be one of the country's leading corporate citizens.

Earlier successes offer no guarantee of continuing leadership. It is a prize that must be earned over and over again.

Advanced technology audiovisual techniques improve speed and quality of learning for IBMers and customers.

Photo by Wayne Eardley/Burke Communications Photography

The changing of the Guard is always an impressive sight on Parliament Hill. Photo by Jessie Parker/First Light

Cossack dancers show their exceptional prowess at a national cultural festival. Photo by Wayne Eardley/ Burke Communications Photography

5

CULTURE AND THE ARTS

ABOVE: Balloons are released into the skies at the opening of the National Gallery of Canada in May 1988. Photo by William P. McElligott

ABOVE RIGHT: Visitors to the National Gallery of Canada await the beginning of an outdoor concert in the amphitheatre. Photo by Jessie Parker/ First Light

Culture is a difficult word for Canadians. Most people find identifying the culture of ancient nations or peoples an easy task—we have all enjoyed the delicate beauty of ancient Chinese porcelain, the wonder of gold artifacts from Peru, the intricacies of Ojibway beadwork—but it is a far more difficult thing to identify characteristics of a culture that is uniquely Canadian. Many have gone so far as to say that Canadians really haven't a culture; they say that Canadian culture, like so many other aspects of Canadian life, is really a *mélange* of features borrowed from other countries.

But that's not true, as anyone who has looked at a Group of Seven painting knows: Canadians have used their unique physical and political environment to develop a characteristic approach to art, and to the world.

A teen's summer job in the capital is selling these frosty treats to passersby. Photo by Wayne Eardley/ Burke Communications Photography

Internationally acclaimed Canadian architect Moshe Safdie shares his delight with Her Excellency Jeanne Sauve, Governor General of Canada, Communications Minister Flora MacDonald, and Prime Minister Brian Mulroney with his two sons, at the opening of the National Gallery of Canada. Photo by Jessie Parker/ First Light

A piece of contemporary sculpture in Confederation Park serves not only as a stimulus for conversation, but also as a play structure for children. Photo by Jessie Parker/ First Light.

FACING PAGE: A bejewelled Egyptian dancer hides coyly behind her veil during a Canada Day performance. Photo by Jessie Parker/ First Light

Ottawa plays a dual role in Canadian culture. First, as the capital, this city is where the national museums, the National Arts Centre, and the National Gallery of Canada are located, institutions that serve as showcases for Canada's culture, past and present.

Ottawa plays another role, however; as the largest city in eastern Ontario, an area that has its own history and culture (especially the Ottawa Valley), Ottawa and surrounding municipalities have another function in the development of culture: to express the thoughts, needs, and experiences of the local people.

Ottawa is a city with a myriad of theatres and art galleries, large and small; it's a place where people can see a world-class musical production, or a local theatre group re-interpreting Little Red Riding Hood for children. It's a city where one can sit outdoors in a sidewalk cafe and enjoy an Italian ice in summer, or discuss politics (an ever-present topic of conversation!) over Swiss hot chocolate and Viennese pastry in a European-style café in winter. All the municipalities take to the outdoors in wintertime and celebrate the season with festivals where theatre groups perform to passersby, and public parks are turned into fairylands of ice sculpture.

While Ottawa apparently offers a wealth of cultural opportunities, the fact is that, like many capital cities, the local activities tend to be overshadowed somewhat by the higher profile, national ones. Artists, musicians, and drama groups do not always have the venue for their work as do their confrères in Toronto or Montreal, for example, but community groups are working hard to remedy this inequitable situation, specifically through a project called Artscourt.

Artscourt is to be a centre for the visual, literary, and performing arts in Ottawa and the surrounding region. It is to serve as a showplace for all the arts, but at the regional level; located in the old provincial courthouse downtown, Artcourt, as proposed by the Ottawa Arts Centre Foundation, will have a theatre, a cinema, various

ABOVE: The Victoria Museum, now the home of the National Museum of Natural Sciences, is one of the grand old battlement style government buildings. Photo by Wayne Eardley/ Burke Communications Photography

BELOW: Shriners add music and exotic costumes to a parade. Photo by Wayne Eardley/Burke Communications Photography

galleries for art, crafts, and sculpture as well as dance studios, an art rental service, and a resource centre. Scheduled to open all its facilities in 1990, Artcourt will not only serve a community need as a showplace for local artists, it will also provide artists the chance to gain national recognition within their own community.

"Culture," wrote French novelist André Malraux, "is the sum of all forms of art, of love and of thought." Ottawa, as both a regional centre and the country's capital, demonstrates clearly the sum of all that is Canadian culture as no other city can.

MUSEUMS

Gone forever are the days when museums were dark, stuffy places with the requisite Egyptian mummy, populated merely by busloads of schoolchildren grateful for an escape from the classroom. The museums of today are vibrant and bustling, attracting not only tourists but also members of the community; a visitor to one of Ottawa's many museums is as likely to attend a film, a play, or a lecture, or perhaps a special theme workshop for children, as he is to look at an exhibit.

The National Museum of Natural Sciences, for example, is a favorite spot for Ottawa area schoolchildren and tourists alike because of its marvellous permanent exhibits, such as the tropical dinosaur hall and the splendid geological collection. Actually geology was the science from which the museum originally grew. Sir William Logan undertook a geological survey of parts of Ontario and Quebec, beginning in 1841. The rocks, minerals, and fossils he collected were first exhibited in a warehouse in Montreal; these exhibits were the foundation of the present-day museum.

After Logan's death, the government decided to move the Geological Survey and Natural History Museum to Ottawa; Mont-

realers protested, saying that the capital city was "a poor, puny place" for a great national museum. Nevertheless, nearly 10,000 people visited the museum during its first year in Ottawa, in 1881, 10 times the number who visited annually in Montreal.

In 1912 the museum moved again, to the very grand Victoria Memorial Museum building, at Elgin and McLeod streets. One of the first exhibits was the skeleton of the magnificent dinosaur, Edmontosaurus, who still resides in the museum's dinosaur hall.

Far from being a repository for old bones and rock samples, the museum today is an exciting place—perhaps the first clue to this is the family of woolly mammoths who gambol on the front lawn. Inside is a wide variety of permanent exhibits as well as special exhibits that may last for several months. For example, one show called *Birds, Birds, Birds* featured a stunning display of hand-carved decoys, a computer quiz that asked visitors to identify bird calls, and a special workshop area where children could sit near specimens of birds and then duplicate them using pieces of colourful felt—or they could create a whole new bird!

Not all the displays rely on the research undertaken by staff members—for the museum is primarily a research facility—many of the shows in any given year are exhibitions of the talents of local people. During the year when the museum highlighted birds, a competition was held for the makers of birdhouses. Some of the entries were simply amazing, such as a huge bamboo pagoda, or a rustic log birdhouse . . . or the house that was a likeness of the Prime Minister. More recently, an exhibit of art with an Arctic theme was displayed, contributions having come from high school students in the National Capital Region.

"Museums," Director Dr. Alan Emery has said, "are not simply reflections of what we already know—they are places

A marble statue of Queen Victoria overlooks the calm of the richly panelled reading room in the Library of Parliament. Photo by Paul von Baich/ First Light

One of a family of giant prehistoric wooly mammoths trumpets a welcome to the National Museum of Natural Sciences. Photo by Wayne Eardley/ Burke Communications Photography

The gently undulating walls of the National Museum of Civilization imitate the gently rolling seas that have so shaped the civilizations of Canada. Photo by William P. McElligott

where we find out about new things."

While the National Museum of Natural Sciences is housed in the venerable old Victoria Museum with its ornate carved stonework depicting Canada's animal and plant life, the Canadian Museum of Civilization is in a spectacular building that has been described as "state-of-the-art," a monument to life in our times.

Indeed, the architecture of the new museum is itself a remarkable statement of the advances in civilization. Situated in Hull on the banks of the Ottawa River along the Ottawa-Hull Ceremonial Route, it lies directly across the river from the Parliament Buildings. From the outside the building seems almost like a sculpture, with curved lines that echo the landscape of Canada. The main entrance on Laurier Street in Hull presents a formal plaza with interesting landscape architecture, but the rear of the building folds out toward the river, embracing the museum's natural setting.

Inside, the museum offers a stimulating environment where visitors are able not only to view, but also to experience, the physical and social environments of this land, as far back as the Ice Age. For

Workers survey the enormous curved entry hall of the National Museum of Civilization. Photo by William P. McElligott

Workers install the new copper roof on the National Museum of Civilization in Hull; the roof will oxidize like those on buildings in the Parliamentary precinct. Photo by Jessie Parker/ First Light

example, in the Grand Hall, with its curved windows looking out onto the Ottawa River, there is a replica of a complete Pacific Coast Indian village as such a habitation might have looked a hundred years ago; as visitors walk along a boardwalk connecting six Indian longhouses, they are surrounded by the sounds—even the scents—of a living village.

On a much larger scale is the History Hall, a space which is larger than a football field, and stands three storeys high. Visitors to the hall can wander through full-scale reproductions of period settings, in which every detail has been duplicated and furnished with artifacts from the museum's collections. The exhibits range from the period when the first Norse ships touched the shores of Newfoundland, to the age of New France, to today's Arctic explorations.

The Mediatheque offers even more innovative opportunities for learning and experiencing. Visitors are encouraged to learn more about the collections in the museum, using different information technology and multi-media learning programs. And visitors don't have to leave their town; a sophisticated electronic information network, including a two-way satellite link, makes possible the transmission of activities at the museum across Canada.

Information is the name of the game at the Museum of Civilization, and the new building is the first government structure to be equipped with fibre optic cables, so

A light shower does not deter a visitor to the Ornamental Gardens at the Central Experimental Farm. Photo by Justine Hill

A native dancer in traditional dress takes part in a cultural festival. Photo by Wayne Eardley/ Burke Communications Photography

that information is transmitted by photonic signals rather than through conventional electronics. The result is enhanced quality of the video images that are the backdrop for many of the museum's dramatic exhibits.

State-of-the-art technology is present throughout the museum: visitors are able to get up-to-the-minute information about all its activities by consulting video screens, and, in the exhibition halls, to interact with computer terminals for more details on the displays. And people don't have to try to remember all they have seen and learned at the museum; they can take home copies of texts, and even photographs, by using printers and the computer terminals. Visitors seeking in-depth information can access layered data bases on the museum's collections that answer the needs of students and researchers as well as of private collectors.

Participation is another important part of the Museum of Civilization; animators who are dressed in period costume perform vignettes of Canadian history, and the public is encouraged to take part—perhaps by beating a drum as a participant in an Haida Indian ceremony, or dancing at an eighteenth-century wedding, or dealing for furs with a nineteenth-century trader.

Canadian technology is showcased at the Museum in the IMAX/OMNIMAX Theatre, which is the only one of its kind in the world. The IMAX technique was first demonstrated to the world in Montreal at Expo 67—a technology which allows clear images to be presented on screen as high as 21 meters. OMNIMAX goes a step further, surrounding viewers with a semi-spherical screen. The result is a breathtaking presentation of images and motion so lifelike, the experience seems real. Films shown at the museum deal with a wide range of human endeavours, such as underwater exploration and space travel; in fact, astronauts who have viewed their own adventures on IMAX/OMNIMAX have said they've felt they were in space once again.

The activities at the Canadian Museum of Civilization change focus when the sun goes down; educational by day, events become recreational in the evening. At night the museum offers multimedia presentations, interactive theatre performances, and concerts in both the Grand Hall and in the exhibition halls.

The National Museum of Science and Technology also varies its schedule of events according to the time of day. In the daytime hours it plays host to dozens of school groups and visitors, and offers demonstrations and practical activities related to the items on display. In the evening the museum offers an astronomy program with audiovisual presentations for families and organizations, including observation of heavenly bodies through the 15-inch telescope, which is the largest refracting telescope in Canada.

The theme of the museum is said to be the "artful observation of things". Scientific discoveries, the scientists believe, always begin with observation, and the museum has plenty of things to look at and use. There are satellites, boats, fire engines, computers, films, periscopes, locomotives, and baby chickens hatching before your eyes. But more than observation must be analysis of what has been observed; exhibits at the museum provide an opportunity for observers to test principles of science, conduct their own experiments, and otherwise toss ideas about.

In the Physics Hall there are dozens of experiments to attract the curious: an Archimedes screw activated with the touch of a button, a 50-pound weight lifted by tugging hard on a pulley, and power brought to a television screen by pedalling a bicycle.

The main exhibit areas in the museum serve as showcases for various technologies, such as marine and ground transportation, communications and space exploration, astronomy, physics, agriculture, printing, and computer technology.

Children cannot believe their eyes when they enter the "room" full of vintage locomotives. It is one thing to see a picture of these magnificent and mighty engines, but it is quite another to stand beside one, noting that the top of its wheels rise above your head, and still another to climb up into the cab, listening to a simulation of the sound of the monstrous engine as it chuffed down the track.

The computer room is another popular exhibit. The displays trace the development of computer technology from early inventions, such as the Jacquard loom and Pascal's calculator—and of course, a Chinese abacus—to a mainframe computer and microcomputers. There are several terminals available for use; one of the programs offered is a health and fitness quiz developed by Health and Welfare Canada, which rates the participant's level of health. Another terminal allows the visitor to interact with a devilishly clever program called Psychiatrist (which, like the real thing, seems always to answer a question with a question).

The museum grounds also have several interesting exhibits, including the Cape North lighthouse, at the corner of St. Laurent Boulevard and Lancaster Road,

Exotic species of flora grow under glass at the Central Experimental Farm. Photo by Wayne Eardley/ Burke Communications Photography

that has become an Ottawa landmark. The lighthouse was retired after 72 years of service in Cape Breton and brought to Ottawa, its delicate lamp dismantled and handled with extreme care. The lighthouse is fully operational and contains a small display of artifacts and photographs which illustrate the rich history of Canada's lighthouses.

Under the direction of the National Museum of Science and Technology are two other museums which are nothing short of fascinating. The Canadian Agricultural Museum is a few kilometers away at the Central Experimental Farm, and consists of a wonderfully vivid re-creation of a 1920s barn where early agricultural implements are displayed. There is even an old-style telephone one can pick up and seem to eavesdrop on others on the party line!

One of the world's best collections of vintage aircraft is the centre of the National Aviation Museum, in the eastern part of the city. Aviation technology has played a dramatic role in Canada's history; in fact, no other country on earth has relied more on exploring the sky than has Canada. The "flying machine" has been crucial to the investigation of natural resources and the connection of distant settlements. Among the more than 100 aircraft displayed are such classics as the Junkers W-34, the German-made aluminum plane that served Canadians well as a bush plane; the Lockheed CF-104, one of Canada's early fighter jets; and the Sopwith Camel.

Ah, beautiful, you may say, but can they fly? And the answer is yes: this collection of airplanes is constantly maintained, and many of the planes have been restored to "flight trim" —not with modern-day replacement parts or engines, but with their own engines and instruments. And they don't stay in the hangar at Ottawa all the time, either—the Sopwith Pup, Nieuport 17, and Avro 504K frequently perform at air shows across the country to the delight of onlookers.

In Ottawa there are as many museums as there are areas of human endeavour; the National Postal Museum has a collection of Canadian stamps worth more than $8 million, which represents the history of Canada's postal system.

Everyone is intrigued by the sight of money, and the National Currency Museum has at least one example of every coin circulated in Canada since the first French settlement, as well as an extensive collection of bank notes. Some of the forms of foreign currency also displayed are quite unusual, such as ancient Chinese knife money, currency made from cowrie shell, and an enormous Yap stone from the Pacific Islands. The museum is located in the marvellous Bank of Canada building in Ottawa, where there is also a reference library containing more than 7,000 books, periodicals, and auction catalogues, all available to the general public.

Besides the wealth of national museums in Ottawa, there are three fascinating local museums: the Bytown Fire Brigade Museum with its antique firefighting equipment, the Bytown Museum maintained by the Ottawa Historical Society, and the Billings Estate Museum, which depicts life in Ottawa before the turn of the century.

THEATRE

There is no "theatre district" in Ottawa. Theatre is everywhere in the Capital Region: at the grand National Arts Centre, at small local theatres, in restaurants and cafes, in high schools—in short, anywhere people are likely to gather, theatre in Ottawa is there too. Children in Ottawa grow up accustomed to watching puppet shows at school or in the public library's special reading rooms for children, and to seeing small theatre groups perform at the many festivals held in the region throughout the year.

Theatre in Ottawa is a part of everyone's life; there are theatres for large national and international productions, and there are plenty of little theatres too, offering local playwrights and performers their chance to be seen.

The National Arts Centre enjoys a high public profile; the huge complex, which cost $46 million to build, sits on the banks of the Rideau Canal in downtown Ottawa and is as much a part of the cityscape as are the Parliament Buildings. Fondly known as "The NAC," the centre was conceived as the federal government's centennial project for the Capital Region; it was intended to provide facilities for all the performing arts and to serve as a showcase for the development of the arts in Canada.

The NAC hosts a continuous program of visiting performers and productions, and regular series of presentations are offered by its orchestra as well as English and French theatre companies. The arts complex contains four halls, the 2,300-seat Opera, the 967-seat Theatre, and the Studio and Salon which seat 350 and 150 people, respectively. In addition, there are full backstage and workshop facilities, and a charming restaurant, Le Café, which in summer spills out onto the sidewalk overlooking the canal. Many visitors to the capital arrive by boat; they simply tie up near The NAC, and enjoy a show and dinner, or perhaps a cool drink while they watch other boaters go by.

The NAC is unique in North America—not just because the stage in the Opera is the second-largest in the continent, or because the centre's acoustic and technical systems are among the most sophisticated in the world, but also because of the range of activities held at The NAC, year round. Other performing arts centres do not spend as much of their resources on visiting companies as does The NAC, nor does every large arts complex operate its own performing companies.

The NAC is also unique in that it is a government agency, reporting to Parliament through the Minister of Communications. Funding for The NAC comes in part from an annual grant from both the federal government and the Regional Municipality of Ottawa-Carleton, as well as from earned revenues.

The National Arts Centre has earned an international reputation as Canada's top presenter of dance. The annual Dance Showcase series offers a wide variety of performances that not only showcase the best of Canadian dance, but also sample the most important international trends. Each year are the appearances by Canada's three principal dance companies: the National Ballet of Canada, the Royal Winnipeg Ballet, and Les Grands Ballets Canadiens. The program is complemented by the "hottest" of contemporary dance troupes, such as the bold Danny Grossman Dance Company, along with distinguished international visitors, such as the Central Ballet of China.

While The NAC offers a glittering season of theatre, music, and dance presentations which enhance Canada's international artistic reputation, Ottawa has another distinction in the world of theatre—that of supporting the oldest, continuing community theatre in the country. In fact, Ottawa has a long history of amateur theatrics; early Governors-General often sponsored grand balls for Ottawa society, which highlighted skits that made light of politics and social mores of the day.

The Ottawa Little Theatre began in 1913 when the Ottawa Women's University Club founded the Society for the Study and Production of Dramatic Art, which became known later as the Ottawa Drama League. In its early years the league won many awards at the annual Dominion Drama Festival; in 1936 a workshop group was formed to train and encourage inexperienced actors and directors, and to produce experimental plays. The league offered the first national playwriting competition and a number of now well-known writers, such as Robertson Davies,

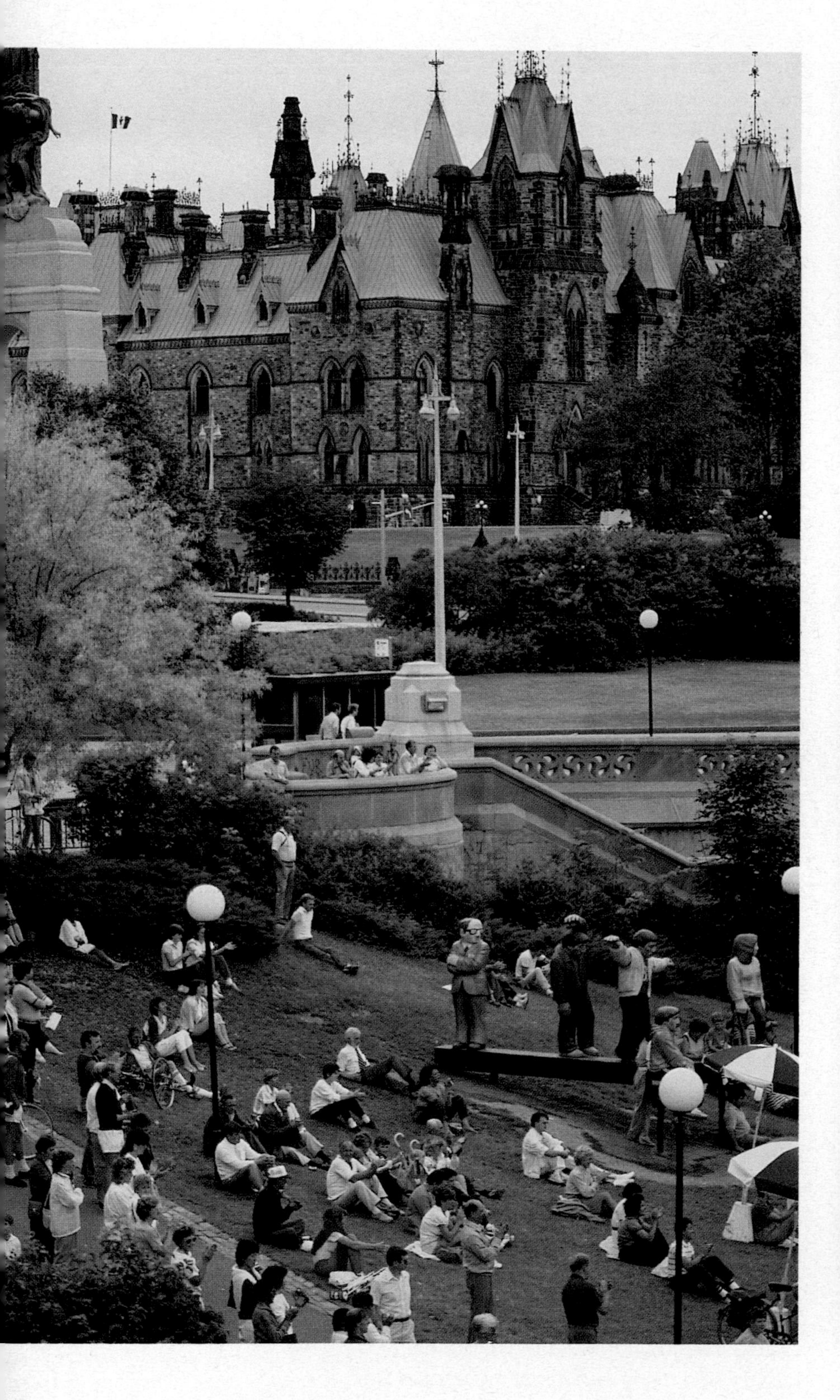

LEFT: The National Arts Centre is mirrored in the Rideau Canal. Photo by Cosmo Condina/ The Stock-Market

FACING PAGE: The Parliament Buildings with throngs of tourists can be seen from the National Arts Centre. Photo by Bruce Rutherford/ The Stock-Market

saw their plays first produced on the Little Theatre's stage.

In 1952 the Drama League changed its name to Ottawa Little Theatre, and in 1972 the theatre moved into its own new building, constructed with money raised from a tremendously successful public fund-raising campaign.

Today, the Ottawa Little Theatre produces seven plays in its winter season, each production running about 18 nights, and another three plays in the summer season. Each year more than 600 volunteers are involved in the productions, and the theatre has the support of more than 9,000 subscribers. In fact, the theatre is so popular in Ottawa that it has never needed a grant from any level of government.

Renowned Canadian poet Duncan Campbell Scott, who was president of the amateur theatre during the 1920s, said that the Ottawa Little Theatre was "built on something better than bricks and mortar—a love of the theatre for its own sake."

It is a love of Canadian theatre in particular that drives the people behind the Great Canadian Theatre Company (known as GCTC in a city that adores acronyms). Founded in the mid-1970s by a group of professors from Carleton University, the theatre's mandate is to produce *only* Canadian works that have some social or political relevance to present-day society. As well, the GCTC is known for its commitment to encouraging new work, and many a local playwright has had his or her first production staged by the company.

The brand new Centrepointe Theatre is the jewel in the cultural scene in Nepean, and part of the new civic complex. Photo by Jessie Parker/ First Light

The Great Canadian Theatre Company offers a six-play season which includes four of the company's own productions as well as two touring shows. In addition, the theatre sponsors a six-concert series, and again, all the material is Canadian. The building, when not the site of a GCTC production or concert, is rented out to other local theatre and music groups, and is home to the Ottawa Film League.

There is a myriad of other theatre groups in the capital region, including the popular Nepean Little Theatre, the New Edinburgh Players, the Orpheus Operatic Society of Ottawa, and the Kanata Theatre, to name a few.

Although the majority of large theatres are located in the City of Ottawa, the City of Nepean recently completed its own centre for the performing arts, as part of the city's Civic Square development. Included in the complex is an auditorium that seats more than 900. Notable features are the orchestra shell that can be raised or lowered mechanically, and a special hearing-loop system designed for use by the hearing impaired. The Nepean Centrepointe Theatre is home to the Nepean Symphony Orchestra, the Nepean Little Theatre, the Nepean Concert Band, Les Petites Ballets, and the city choir.

Dinner theatre has become especially popular in the city, and the l'Avant-Garde on Elgin Street in the heart of Centretown features regular productions ranging from a musical review of the career of famous composers to light comedy.

Canadians are known the world over for their gift of comedy. Many of the world's most popular comedy writers in the United States and Britain are Canadian: people such as Dan Akroyd, Lorne

Michaels, Rich Little, and John Candy. Ottawa has its own resident comedy troupe that has a devoted following; whenever Skit Row puts on a show at a dinner theatre, or during their annual summer sojourn at The NAC, tickets are a hot item in town. The troupe lampoons the jargon of civil servants, notorious for the acronyms that signify government departments and jobs (only an Ottawan would understand what it is to be a CR2 who used to work at F&O but got seconded to the JMB at TP) and draw on the distinctive accents of the Ottawa Valley for their scandalous characterizations.

Adult productions are just one part of the theatre scene in the capital region; people in Ottawa spend a great deal of time entertaining their children, and so children's theatre groups are much in demand. There are several puppet theatre groups, and companies that produce plays just for children. Just For Kids puts on old favourites like Red Riding Hood at local high schools, while the Salt'N' Pepper Theatre Company produces original plays for radio and festivals such as Winterlude.

DANCE

Although The NAC has the reputation as host to national and international dance troupes, Ottawa has two professional dance companies of its own: Le Groupe de la Place Royale and the Theatre Ballet of Canada.

Le Groupe de la Place Royale is known in the city for its amazing variety of performances, which are given in the troupe's Sparks Street studio. Many of the works presented by the group are original, and are enhanced by video and original music.

Theatre Ballet of Canada specializes in modern ballet presentations, which it brings not only to the City of Ottawa but also to the other municipalities in the Capital Region. The repertoire is usually varied each year, featuring new work by prominent Canadian choreographers.

Besides these major dance groups, Ottawa is also home to a number of smaller performing arts groups, such as the Ballet Russe d'Ottawa, the Anabarrach Highland Dancers, Anjali Classic Dances from India, and the International Folk Dancers of Ottawa, to name just a few. Many of these dance groups, reflecting the rich cultural heritage of Ottawa, bring the traditions of more than a dozen countries, such as

LEFT AND BELOW: The brilliance and gaiety of a Caribbean dance brightens the Cultures Canada Festival. Photos by Wayne Eardley/Burke Communications Photography

ABOVE: Wee lassies perform traditional Highland dances on Canada Day. Photo by Jessie Parker/ First Light

FACING PAGE BELOW: A crystal entrance hall welcomes visitors to the National Gallery. Photo by Wayne Eardley/ Burke Communications Photography

Egypt, Lebanon, Poland, the Philippines, Ireland, and Holland, to the stage. Young people especially enjoy the more recent forms of dance, as practised by the Canadian Floor Masters, a group of Ottawa breakdancers.

Very much a part of the world of dance locally are several excellent training facilities, such as The School of Dance, where classical ballet is taught to children from the age of three, and the Margaret Morris Method school.

ART

Like most other facets of the cultural scene in Ottawa, there are opportunities for artists to present their work at both the national and local levels. Ottawa boasts not only the glittering new National Gallery of Canada, the regional Artscourt centre, but also a collection of intriguing, small galleries.

The National Gallery opened in the spring of 1988, an extraordinary building designed by internationally known Canadian architect Moshe Safdie. Finally the gallery found its home, after having been in temporary lodgings for more than a century. Resting on a parcel of land overlooking the Ottawa River, its neighbours are the Parliament Buildings, the Royal Canadian Mint, the Museum of Civilization, and the Byward Market. A work of art in itself, the gallery has been described as a stately glass pavilion, a giant "candelabrum" in the heart of the community. Inside, the sparkling glass is contrasted by the warmth of the pink granite walls and the flooring of Canadian oak and maple. Unique are its skylights, which introduce natural light to both the upper and lower levels of the galleries.

Inside the National Gallery are approximately 40,000 works of art. The showcase is in the Special Exhibition Galleries where exhibits of international standing, such as those featuring Edgar Degas, the French Masters Drawings, and William

FAR LEFT: Wide open spaces and a peaceful room in which to enjoy the beauty of art can be found at the National Gallery of Canada. Photo by Wayne Eardley/ Burke Communications Photography

LEFT: The glass spire of the National Gallery of Canada echoes the majesty of both the Peace Tower and the twin spires of the Notre Dame Basilica, nearby. Photo by Wayne Eardley/ Burke Communications Photography

Berczy, are shown.

Other areas of the gallery include the Historic Canadian Art section, which features the nineteenth-century Rideau Street Convent Chapel, and the Birks Silver Collection. In a two-storey wing the gallery houses the Contemporary Art collection, which features works from Canada, the United States, and Europe, and represents major artistic movements since the 1960s.

The European and American Art collection offers examples of painting, sculpture, and the decorative arts in vaulted rooms with skylights. As well, there will be rooms dedicated to Asian art, with a special collection of Indian sculpture. Exhibitions of the collections from the Canadian and European Prints, Drawings and Photographs are shown on a rotating basis in the gallery; this collection of 12,000 pieces includes work by Canadians William Berczy and Michael Snow, as well as by international artists such as Picasso, Cezanne, Matisse, Chagall, and Escher.

The National Gallery of Canada is unusual among galleries in that it offers exhibitions of video art, and all the programming comes from tapes in its own collection. In fact, the National Gallery is one of the few North American galleries to have embarked on an extensive collection of videotapes; the collection now numbers about 300 tapes, most of which are Canadian, but which also include work from Japan,

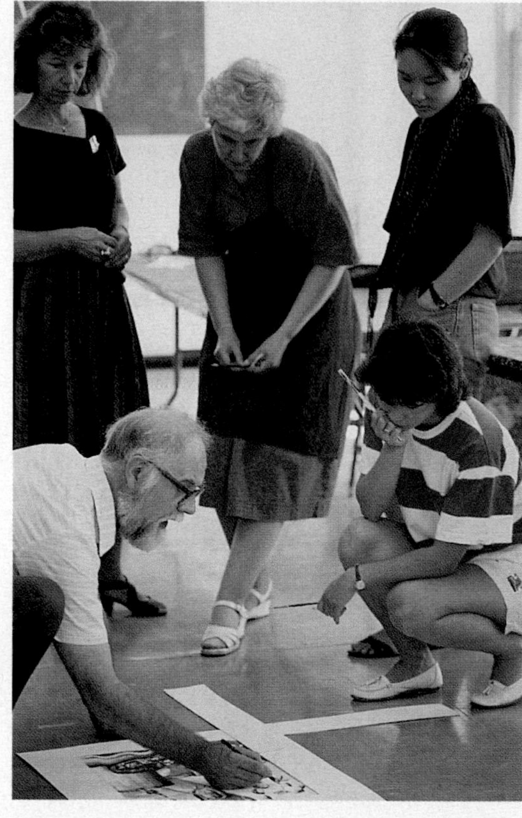

ABOVE: An outdoor concert enhances a visit to the National Gallery of Canada. Photo by Wayne Eardley/ Burke Communications Photography

ABOVE RIGHT: A class is in progress at the Ottawa School of Art. Photo by Wayne Eardley/ Burke Communications Photography

RIGHT: Opening-day ceremonies for the new National Gallery of Canada were by a throng of dignitaries. Photo by William P. McElligott

LEFT: Children await their parents after a Saturday morning art class at the Ottawa School of Art. Photo by Wayne Eardley/ Burke Communications Photography

BELOW: The view upwards in the National Gallery of Canada is as though looking through a kaleidoscope; complex, intriguing, and always full of light. Photo by William P. McElligott

Great Britain, France, Brazil, and the United States.

Ottawans regularly visit not only the National Gallery with its tremendous collection and its varying visiting exhibitions, but they also rely on smaller, local galleries for a look at the work of local artists. Two of the most prominent are Gallery 101 and the SAW Gallery, though many others exist throughout the city. Best of all, if not in the mood to buy, Ottawans can rent art from the Art Bank, funded by the Canada Council, which in fact is Canada's largest collection of Canadian contemporary art.

People are encouraged to take an even more active role in artistic pursuits through the Ottawa School of Art. Located in a renovated heritage stone building in the Byward Market, the School of Art is a nonprofit organization that has a broad membership of students (including children as young as five), faculty, and interested members of the public. The school offers instruction, in both French and English, to people of all ages in a variety of disciplines, including painting, printmaking, drawing, and sculpture. Although classes are offered as general interest courses, a profession-oriented, three-year diploma program is also available.

Education is more than reading and writing: it's learning to appreciate the arts too. Photo by Wayne Eardley/ Burke Communications Photography

FILM

Like most Canadians, Ottawans love a good film. The city is liberally sprinkled with movie theatres from east to west, in shopping centres or alone on city thoroughfares. Most of the theatres of course offer first-run films, but there are two theatres, the Mayfair and the Towne, which are repertory houses regularly offering old classics, or "theme" nights and festivals.

The Canadian Film Institute (CFI) has made its home in Ottawa, promoting film as vigorously as the National Gallery promotes art, for more than five decades. The CFI holds regular showings of films in the National Library and Public Archives Building, often with special guests. Presentations may be serious, such as a retrospective look at women's films, or lighthearted, as in children's films or comedy from around the world.

MUSIC

Critics have praised the National Arts Centre Orchestra (NACO) as nothing less than a "national treasure," a not inconsiderable accolade given the orchestra's size. Guest conductors have raved about the NACO, saying it ranks among the greatest chamber orchestras in the world; although with just 46 members the NACO is not a full symphony orchestra, its quality is unmistakable. Director Gabriel Chmura rates all 46 musicians as first-class.

The NACO's season includes recitals by world-renowned pianists in the "Grand Piano" series. It also offers a chamber music series, performances by Canadian artists in the "Debut" series, and special appearances by leading Canadian and international orchestras.

The city has another orchestra, the Ottawa Symphony, which recently has specialized in light classical music, encouraging whole families to attend its regular appearances.

Besides the classical music of the two symphony orchestras, the music scene in Ottawa is as varied as one could imagine. From Berlioz to the blues, Ottawans have it all.

There are a number of choral groups, for instance, such as the Ottawa Choral Society, which often appears jointly with the Ottawa Symphony, the Cantata Singers of Ottawa, and the Ottawa Jazz

Chorale—to name just three out of dozens.

Ottawa is reputed to be one of the North American cities most devoted to the blues, regularly attracting such big-name performers as Son Seals, James Cotton, and Stevie Ray Vaughn, as well as local blues bands.

Hard-core rockers frequent Barrymore's, Ottawa's historic rock showpalace, built in 1812. Seating more than 400 at full capacity, Barrymore's hosts live music every night. Huge concerts are also held at the stadium at Lansdowne Park in Ottawa's south end, particularly during the SuperEx, when artists such as Tina Turner or David Bowie pull in crowds of 25,000 or more. Because Ottawa has three universities, and the student population of the city at any given moment is more than 30,000, rock and pop concerts are frequent in the capital.

But Ottawa is a jazz town too, aided in no small way by the annual Ottawa Jazz Festival, held each July. Most of the Jazz Festival events are held in the National Arts Centre, often outside, but others may be scheduled for the Sparks Street Mall, in the Byward Market, or in one of the city's jazz or blues clubs.

Barrymore's is the rock music emporium on Bank Street, where Tina Turner played on her comeback tour in 1984. Photo by Paul von Baich/ First Light

FESTIVALS

The Ottawa social calendar is dotted with annual festivals, many of which attract tourists from all over North America and Europe. Perhaps the biggest and the best-known is Winterlude, Ottawa's annual celebration of the season of winter. Now with a budget of more than $1 million, Winterlude, which is organized primarily by the National Capital Commission, attracts over half a million visitors to the region, and more than $10 million in revenues.

Held during the second week of February, Winterlude centres on the Rideau Canal, which in winter is the world's longest maintained skating rink and a significant tourist attraction. Events include a trotting race, barrel-jumping and skating demonstrations, the Great Canadian Bed Race on ice, and visits by the Winterlude mascots, Mr. and Mrs. Ice Hog. Every year a competition of ice sculptures is on view on Dow's Lake; the entries are often astonishing in their ability both to amuse and to provoke thought.

Other municipalities in the region participate in Winterlude by hosting sporting events or concerts; the first world championship in marathon speed skating to be held in North America took place recently in Ottawa, as well as an ice carving competition that brought entries from Japan and the United States.

While Winterlude celebrates how Ottawans are undaunted by winter, the Festival of Spring welcomes the return of warmer days. Visitors come from all over the world to see the splendid beds of tulips on Parliament Hill and along the canal on the Queen Elizabeth Driveway, and to hear the romantic story of Ottawa and tulips. Queen Juliana of The Netherlands took refuge in Ottawa during World War II

ABOVE: Winterlude mascots Mr. and Mrs. Ice Hog and their offspring wave to skaters on the Rideau Canal. Photo by Jessie Parker/ First Light

ABOVE RIGHT: An earmuffed entertainer juggles for the crowd at Winterlude. Photo by Jessie Parker/ First Light

RIGHT: Braving the cool spring waters of the Rideau Canal, 50,000 ducks race to the finish line in a charity race for the Children's Hospital of Eastern Ontario. Photo by Jessie Parker/ First Light

(her daughter Margarethe was born in Ottawa, in fact), and to show gratitude for sheltering their queen, the people of Holland to this day send tulip bulbs. In the early weeks of May these tulips, and others planted by the National Captial Commission, transform the city into a beacon of springtime.

A few weeks later is the annual Franco-Ontarien festival, usually held in the centre of the city in Confederation Park, near the Rideau Canal. The festival lasts almost a week, featuring songs, dances, and drama from noted Franco-Ontarien performers. More dance is presented in June at the Canada Dance Festival, held at the National Arts Centre.

The first of July of course is Canada Day, and there simply is no better place to be on Canada's national holiday than in the capital city. Hundreds of thousands gather downtown on Parliament Hill and on the streets nearby to watch a stage presentation and a breathtaking display of fireworks. Thousands more citizens take to boats to view the display from sailboats and yachts on the Ottawa River, taking pride in the splendour of the lights on The Hill.

Later in July is the annual Ottawa Jazz Festival, as well as the International

LEFT: A fire-eater demonstrates one way to keep warm during Winterlude festivities. Photo by Jessie Parker/ First Light

BELOW: A bed of tulips beautifies the south bank of the Rideau Canal during the Festival of Spring. Photo by Jessie Parker/ First Light

ABOVE: Let us entertain you! These song-and-dance men are ready to go at SuperEx. Photo by Wayne Eardley/ Burke Communications Photography

ABOVE RIGHT: Miss Ottawa Rough Rider shows her winning smile. Photo by Wayne Eardley/ Burke Communications Photography

RIGHT: Face-painting is always a delightful part of festival activities for children. Photo by Wayne Eardley/ Burke Communications Photography

Cycling Festival in Hull. The hot days of August bring Festivoile, a celebration of the history and beauty of the Ottawa River, held in Aylmer. The SuperEx heats up the days and nights with exhibits, agricultural competitions, a midway, and rock concerts at Lansdowne Park.

In September, as the leaves on city trees and in the not too distant Gatineau Hills begin to turn colours, Fall Rhapsody begins, as does a spate of agricultural fairs in towns around the region, such as Richmond, Spencerville, and Almonte. The Festival of the Arts begins in September and lasts into October, hearkening a new opening of Ottawa's winter-long arts season.

At Christmas is the Festival of the Lights, when city and federal governments both plan special displays of lights for the

ABOVE: There is something for everyone in this convenience store, from East Indian specialty foods to Ontario lottery tickets, as well as the daily papers. Photo by Jessie Parker/ First Light

LEFT: Filipino dancers, in butterfly-sleeved traditional dress, perform at Canada Day celebrations. Photo by Jessie Parker/ First Light

The Ukrainian Catholic Church, in its spectacular canal-side setting, is another reminder of the diverse cultural background of the Ottawa-Carleton area. Photo by Jessie Parker/ First Light

Although modern in design, the mosque on the community Islamic temple is clearly a representation of centuries-old beliefs. Photo by Jessie Parker/ First Light

holidays, and Ottawans decorate their homes with coloured lights.

There is more to the definition of *culture,* however, than museum and art gallery displays, and demonstrations of dancing and song. Culture is, after all, how people live—the things they do that make up their daily lives, and which distinguish their life-styles from those of other countries and places.

Ottawa is like many other Canadian cities in that it has long been a destination for immigrants to Canada. As a result, the people of Ottawa today represent many cultures, not just the English-speaking immigrants from England, Ireland, and Scotland, nor the French-speaking descendants of the settlers of New France. Today in Ottawa there is a very visible and important Italian community, a Lebanese community, a Vietnamese community, and Chinese, Greek, and East Indian communities. There is even a small and very close-knit contingent of families from Peru.

All these groups influence the quality of life in the capital city, whether through full-fledged festivals such as the Italian community holds in the summer of each year, or through smaller scale activities such as presentations of traditional performing arts. Everyone benefits from the cosmopolitan nature of the city, particularly when it comes to dining out (a pastime of which Ottawans are extremely fond). It is possible to have an elegant dinner prepared in the Continental European fashion, or a casual lunch of Lebanese *shawarma,* or a breakfast of Chinese *dim sum,* not to mention meals prepared by cooks from Afghanistan, India, and Ecuador—all in Ottawa.

As the nation's capital, Ottawa presents the best of all cultural worlds—great national treasures and the pleasures of a vibrant and historically rich region of Ontario.

A piper brings to life the music and traditions of Scotland. Photo by Jessie Parker/ First Light

The swinging chairs ride at the SuperEx never fails to thrill. Photo by Jessie Parker/ First Light

6

RECREATION AND SPORTS

Visitors to the National Capital Region often ask what is the favourite sport of people who live in the area. The answer is, there isn't one. There are dozens!

The first thing most Canadians plan to do when they visit Ottawa is to tour the Parliament Buildings and other sights in downtown, but the second thing (at least in winter) is to skate on the Rideau Canal. Most people who live in Ottawa make a point of skating on the canal during the two months it's usually open during the winter. (The fact that the canal is sometimes only open for six weeks is an accurate measure of how long Ottawa's winter *actually* lasts. Although Ottawans like to tell tall tales about how cold the temperature gets or how many meters of snow are plummeted upon us, the truth is that the weather stays relatively mild up until Christmas, and then winter lasts until mid-March. Summer begins delightfully with a

LEFT: The water is cool and fresh at the Prince of Wales Falls, at Hog's Back. Photo by Justine Hill

FACING PAGE TOP: Trotters run a quick pace to the finish line in the Molson's Ice Trotting Classic at Winterlude. Photo by Jessie Parker/ First Light

FACING PAGE BOTTOM: Everyone's for tennis on a sunny summer day. Photo by Wayne Eardley/ Burke Communications Photography

spring fragrant with lilac blossoms, and spans the months from June until September. Autumn, with its spectacular colours, offers crisp, clear days until well into November.)

The image of skaters on the canal is not merely a romantic depiction of one aspect of the city; in fact, it tells a great deal about how Ottawans feel about sport and recreation—that is, to get out there and have a great time!

Nevertheless, skating remains one of the most visible sports in the region, whether recreational or professional. For many years, early in the twentieth century, Ottawa was known as the best in the land for its sports teams: the Capitals in lacrosse, the Rough Riders in football, and the Silver Sevens in hockey. Other celebrated hockey players were the Ottawa Senators, and in all, Ottawa hockey teams won the coveted Stanley Cup nine times, last in 1927.

Today, Ottawa has no contenders in the National Hockey League (NHL), but popular support for its junior league team, the Ottawa 67s, is enthusiastic. The 67s' first season was in Canada's Centennial year, 1967, and since then the team has entertained Ottawans with thrilling hockey. Many of the team's players have gone on to NHL glory, such as Denis Potvin, Bobby Smith, and Doug Wilson.

Amateur hockey players—some of them as young as four or five—can be found any weekend in the region's hockey rinks. Children, both boys and girls, develop an interest in the sport at an early age; they participate in competition at one of five levels of play, vying against other teams on a local, regional, and provincial basis. Watching the youngest players is

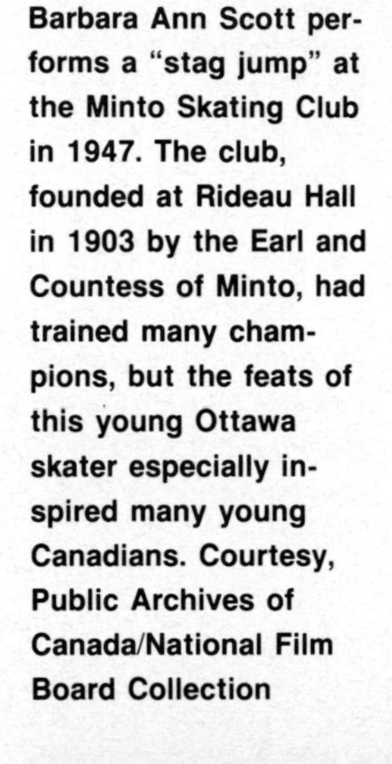

Barbara Ann Scott performs a "stag jump" at the Minto Skating Club in 1947. The club, founded at Rideau Hall in 1903 by the Earl and Countess of Minto, had trained many champions, but the feats of this young Ottawa skater especially inspired many young Canadians. Courtesy, Public Archives of Canada/National Film Board Collection

one of the finest forms of entertainment to be had, claim hockey aficionados; nothing, not even rudimentary skating skills, stands in the way of the players' enjoyment of the game!

After the 1988 Winter Olympics in Calgary, all the world recognized Ottawa as a city that fosters figure skating champions. Barbara Ann Scott was a role model for Elizabeth Manley (nicknamed "the little blonde Rocky"), who won a silver medal in a truly memorable competition.

Many other Olympic champions have come from Ottawa, athletes such as skiiers Anne Heggtveit, Betsy Clifford, and Horst Bulau, as well as sailor Bruce Kirby, known to Canadians as the man who designed the ships *Canada One* and *Two.* Ottawa native Linda Thom won a gold medal at the 1984 Olympics in the sport pistol category, setting an Olympic record as she did so. Other champions, such as water skiier Pat Messner and kayaker Sue Holloway, give an indication of the incredible range of athletic opportunities available.

One of the things about Ottawa that appeals to so many of the people born in other cities who have chosen to live here is that one can step out of a downtown office complex at 5, and then be on the golf course, at the top of the ski slope, or tall in the saddle, just half an hour later. Only the season determines which activity one might choose.

Autumn in Canada means one thing—football. And for some, there's no better place to be on a sunny Saturday afternoon than in the stadium at Lansdowne Park . . . especially if the Riders are winning! Although football is an important part of the sports scene, there has been a general decline in the popularity of attending football games. People seem to want to stay home and watch games on TV rather than turn out to watch their team play. This is perhaps understandable when one considers that the football season can go on until late in the fall. "What would you rather do?" says one Ottawa sports fan. "Go to Lansdowne Park and freeze, if it's that kind of a day, or stay home and watch the Miami Dolphins running around where it's warm?"

Does this trend mean the Canadian Football League is losing the battle for popularity to the American Football League, or is it a wider trend away from spectator sports? The Ottawa Roughriders have had difficulty attracting more than 25,000 fans to a game in recent years, and when the Montreal Alouettes folded in 1987, many predicted that the Riders' days were numbered too. But diehard fans of Canadian football in Ottawa were determined not to let their club die; the Roughrider Rooters got together and planned special program evenings, prizes, and campaigns that did a great deal to boost interest in the Riders' games. That, plus a shift in attitude about what a "successful" football club is, had dulled the mumblings about the Roughriders' demise. "We just have to look at the facts, at what's going on across Canada," said football great Russ Jackson at a Roughrider Rooter dinner, "and realize that getting 25,000 people out to a game is pretty good."

Looking at the Riders' story may make one wonder whether people in the capital

The Ottawa Rough Riders thrill the crowd with the last touchdown in their winning game. Photo by Wayne Eardley/ Burke Communications Photography

50
45

61
78
35
76

aren't a bunch of couch potatoes, who give a Pierre Trudeau-like shrug when asked if they care about the fate of their football club. Not so! What makes this city different from many others (and defies the image of a sleepy, civil service town) is that the people here like to get out and do things, rather than sit and watch.

People in Ottawa cycle, jog, water ski, cross-country ski, and ski downhill; they canoe, they sail, they ride horses or motorcycles, they golf, and they curl. Ottawa may have the distinction of being the only capital city in the world where it is a regular occurrence to look up from one's backyard on a summer weekend morning, having heard the distinctive *hussssh* sound of a huge, colourful hot air balloon. There are at least a dozen places to go hot air ballooning in the capital region.

Because much of Ottawa's history is linked to immigrants from the British Isles, certain sports tend to be very popular today. Golf is a common pastime all over North America, but Ottawa is rumoured to have more golf courses on a per capita

LEFT: More than 20,000 fans throng to Lansdowne Park on a bright, crisp autumn day. Photo by Wayne Eardley/ Burke Communications Photography

FACING PAGE LEFT AND BELOW: Excitement builds as fans await the Riders' return to the field at Lansdowne Park. Photos by Wayne Eardley/ Burke Communications Photography

Since 1890, many Ottawa citizens have displayed football mania. Their ardent support has mostly been for the Ottawa Rough Riders, established in 1890 as the Ottawa Football Club. Lacking only the padded uniforms and helmets of today, these fifteen men of the charter 1890 team look confident enough to defeat any team. Courtesy, Public Archives of Canada

Hot air balloon enthusiasts gather for a day of exploring the beauty of the countryside from the skies. Photo by Jessie Parker/ First Light

basis than any other city on the continent. This happy situation is due no doubt to the fact that although Ottawa is a busy metropolis, the city is situated in the midst of beautiful "greenbelt" land, with the scenic Gatineau Hills just to the north of the Ottawa River.

Some of the clubs are historic and have exclusive membership, such as the Royal Ottawa Golf Club, which presides majestically over the Aylmer Road in Aylmer, and the Rivermead and Hunt Club facilities. Others are public golf clubs that attract a wide range of players, including the younger generation who seem to have caught the golf "bug." One of the most challenging courses is known affectionately as "The Dome," a public facility in the Gatineau Hills, just 10 minutes from downtown Ottawa. At the Kingsway Park Golf and Country Club is Canada's only golf museum, featuring a feather-stuffed golf ball from 1830, as well as woods and irons used by some very famous golfers.

A tell-tale "whoosh" sound causes one to look up and see a huge colourful hot air balloon overhead. Photo by Jessie Parker/ First Light

Curling, which, like golf, was invented by the Scots, is extremely popular in Ottawa, played by men and women of all ages. The appeal of curling, players say, is its very social nature; while it can be a very competitive game, there is still plenty of time for conversation, and of course, there is the time-honoured tradition that the winners must buy the losers a round of drinks after the game.

Rugby too came to Ottawa with the scores of British immigrants, and to this day the sport remains a focus of social life for many in the capital region. Rugby clubs or unions may have several hundred members, of whom a small portion actually play the game; the majority come out to support the players and gather at regular intervals for special dinner celebrations or just a casual evening at the "pub."

Come summer, the Ottawa River, Mooney's Bay, and Britannia Bay are dotted with the bright sails of small boats and windsurfers. Sailors head down to their crafts every evening after work, staying out on the water until the last light. Many are casual boaters, though the various sailing and yacht clubs in the capital region do hold regular competitions as well as demonstrations such as the Nepean Sailpast held each year, and season's end regattas.

The Britannia Yacht Club holds a treasured place in the history of Ottawa; formed in 1887 as the Britannia Aquatic Club when Britannia was a cottage colony at the end of the tram line from downtown Ottawa, the Yacht Club sits on the edge of the Ottawa River at the point where the river widens into beautiful Lake Deschenes.

The Rideau Canoe Club is another venerable Ottawa institution, now housed in a

RIGHT: Teeing off at the Pineview Golf Course means summer fun for thousands in the capital region. Photo by Wayne Eardley/ Burke Communications Photography

FAR RIGHT: A Saturday afternoon soccer game is played in a park near the scenic Ottawa River Parkway. Photo by Wayne Eardley/ Burke Communications Photography

modern building on the Rideau River. Canoers and kayakers call the club home, and a number of exciting events begin at the Canoe Club every year, including several triathalon competitions. The annual Colonel By triathalon inspires a whole range of citizens to come out and try their stamina; local corporations usually send representatives, and at least one canoe full of weekend athletes gets dumped, without fail.

Running was popular in Ottawa long before it caught on in other parts of Canada, and no wonder, with such scenic routes as the bicycle/jogging paths along the Rideau Canal and the Ottawa and Rideau rivers. Moreover, downtown Ottawa is rife with health clubs, and local hotels offer health club or locker facilities to lunchtime runners, who haven't far to go before they're running along a waterway, or through residential neighbourhoods under the shade of mature trees. A familiar sight in downtown Ottawa is the Ottawa YM/ YWCA bus that makes stops at all the major office complexes and street intersections, picking up people for their lunchtime exercise break.

The National Capital Marathon, now an event that attracts hundreds of runners from across Canada as well as their countries, is held in May of each year. Its route winds along the canal, past the Parliament Buildings and through the city and Experimental Farm back to the starting point at Carleton University. Crowds line every inch of the route, shouting encouragement to the participants.

Another world-class sporting event held in the capital region each year is the Gatineau 55, a Worldloppet cross-country skiing event. The route for this race traces through the Gatineau Hills and finishes in Hull, Quebec, to the delight of a huge and enthusiastic crowd.

A recent development in Ottawa is the formation of the National Capital Polo Team. The team has more than 20 members, of whom half are women, and has attracted players from all strata of local society, including professionals such as doctors and lawyers. The team com-

petes regularly against polo players from Montreal and Toronto, and as the popularity of the sport grows in Canada, will likely go farther afield for competitions. If polo continues to catch on here as it has, perhaps we'll one day see the Prince of Wales in town to compete for a cup.

Ottawa could not have encouraged so many people to get involved in athletics—and developed so many champions in such a variety of endeavours—without the high quality sports and recreation facilities that are so accessible throughout the region. Each municipality plans programs at the local community and recreation centres, whether learn-to-skate and learn-to-swim programs for the tiniest athletes, or opportunities for practised players to get together for badminton and baseball. Other clubs and complexes—such as the Minto Skating Club and the R.A. Centre—have done much to promote both interest and professional skills in sports.

LEFT: What better way to spend a warm summer day than by windsurfing in Britannia Bay? Photo by Wayne Eardley/ Burke Communications Photography

BELOW: A pleasure boat on the Rideau Canal passes buildings of the University of Ottawa, and the Nicholas Street Transitway station. Photo by Jessie Parker/ First Light

ABOVE: Sunbathers make the most of a spring day . . . and of the flat top on the fence of a nearby church. Photo by Wayne Eardley/ Burke Communications Photography

RIGHT: A sunbather is oblivious to both passing cyclists and the nearby waters of the Rideau Canal. Photo by Wayne Eardley/ Burke Communications Photography

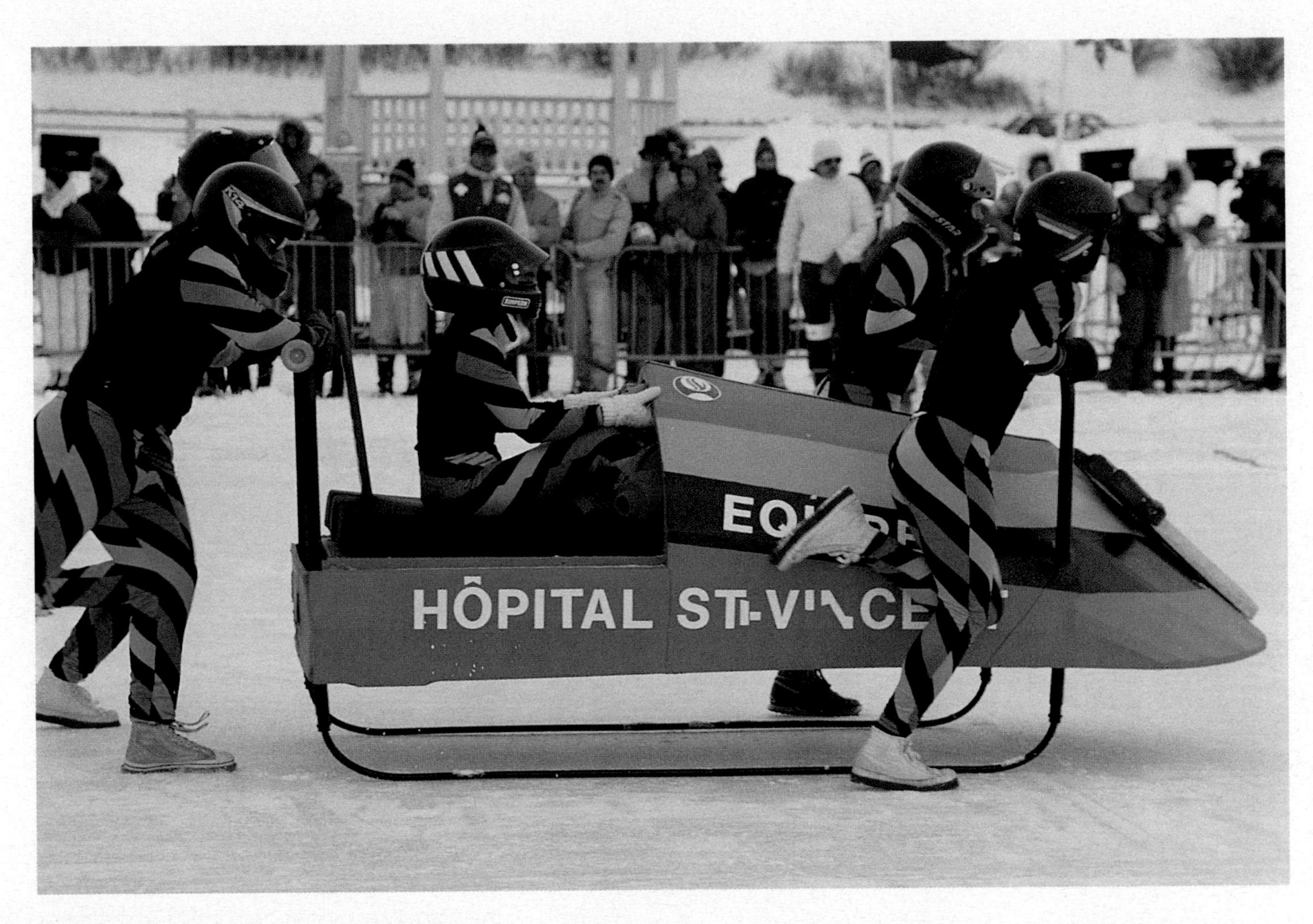

The Minto Skating Club is not merely a part of Ottawa's history; it is one of the pioneer skating clubs in North America. Founded in 1903 by the Earl of Minto and Lady Minto, the then Governor-General of Canada and his wife who contributed so much to Ottawa during their tenure, the Minto Skating Club was the home of many champion skaters, including Olympian Barbara Ann Scott. The quality of instruction at the Minto is, and has always been, high, and the parents and people involved in the club have made the difference between skating as a casual pastime and as a fascinating pursuit.

The Minto Skating Club had several homes over the years but finally lodged in the world-class facility on Lancaster Road in the southeast of Ottawa, where it has three ice surfaces—an Olympic-sized arena, a North American standard arena, and a studio training rink. According to

ABOVE: A sledding team from St. Vincent's Hospital stands poised for take-off. Photo by Jessie Parker/ First Light

LEFT: Corporate-sponsored teams launch their fibreglass canoes into the icy water for the Winterlude canoe race. Photo by Jessie Parker/ First Light

ABOVE: Running is not merely a sport in Ottawa: it's a full-fledged passion for many. Photo by Wayne Eardley/ Burke Communications Photography

TOP RIGHT: There are two levels of pathways along the Rideau Canal: one for cyclists and another for those out for a stroll. Photo by Wayne Eardley/ Burke Communications Photography

Donald Jackson, famed figure-skater and an alumnus of the Minto Club, skating lessons are regarded as an important part of the club today. "You can't build a successful club if you don't get tomorrow's stars as soon as they're able to stand on skates."

While the Minto Skating Club has established a distinguished reputation for developing skaters' skills, the Ottawa Civil Service Recreation Association has done much to foster an interest in all sports. Known simply as "the R.A.," the association is one of the largest recreation associations in North America, with a membership of more than 45,000. The R.A. began in 1938 principally to amalgamate the various athletic leagues that had been formed by government workers and to provide recreational facilities, then a scarce commodity in the city, which would be accessible to all civil servants, especially low-income earners.

In 1955 the federal government gave a parcel of 40 acres of land along the Rideau River, near Billings Bridge, along

with a low-interest loan for construction of a huge, multi-purpose recreation centre. Although the R.A. began as an association of civil servants, today membership is open to others. The present centre, constructed in the 1970s at a cost of $5 million, includes badminton, squash, and racquetball courts; lighted outdoor playing fields; tennis courts; a pool; lounges; and the Ray Kinsella Arena. Kinsella served several terms as president of the R.A., and was instrumental in developing the facilities and getting support for new programs and construction.

Just to give a final idea of how important sports are to people in the capital, it must be said that one of the most beloved—and despised—columnists in Ottawa is Earl McRae, the sportswriter for *The Ottawa Citizen.* Nobody who reads McRae would ever accuse the man of being lukewarm; although a certain amount of his writing amounts to the age-old columnist's trick of being outrageous just to attract attention, McRae in fact has stimulated a great deal of interest in local sports, and in the Rough Rider dilemma particularly. The end result is that people who have no interest in sports at all end up arguing with others about the subject of McRae's latest column—a new form of recreation for Ottawa!

TOP LEFT: Hundreds of skaters take to the ice on the world's longest maintained ice skating surface, the Rideau Canal. Photo by Lorraine C. Parow/ First Light

ABOVE: Worth lining up for is a slide in the Piruvik ice village, where snow and ice have been sculptured into fascinating structures. Photo by Jessie Parker/ First Light

A young family enjoys a crisp sunlit day on the Rideau Canal. Photo by Devries Mikkelsen/ First Light

CFRA/CFMO-FM A DIVISION OF CHUM LIMITED

CFRA and CFMO have recently moved to a spacious new, technologically advanced, 21,000-square-foot facility in the City of Ottawa Business Park, at Walkley Road and Don Reid Drive, built by R.J. Nicol Construction Ltd.

Radio station 580 CFRA has been pleasing listeners since it was licensed in 1947. Its first owner, Frank Ryan, recognized the need for an independent station, and CFRA became the third radio station in Ottawa during the postwar period, introducing an imaginative approach to broadcasting.

A crowd of 10,000 people jammed into the Ottawa Auditorium on May 3, 1947, to hear the Percy Faith Orchestra launch CFRA's first broadcast. "We opened with a bang," recalls vice-president J. Terry Kielty, who has been with the station since it opened. "And we never looked back."

The winning formula was based on a family-type format emphasizing community involvement, news, special events, and play-by-play sports. This success paved the way for another popular radio voice in the capital, CFMO-FM.

Allan Waters bought the stations for CHUM Limited in 1967 and, while continuing with a policy of solid news, information, sports, and special events, also developed an adult-contemporary style around CFRA and CFMO's fundamental broadcast personalities. CFRA proudly responds to the sobriquet "The news voice of Canada's capital." CFRA's information programming revolves around a commitment to credibility, and listeners depend on the station for local news as well as an independent slant on national news. "We have the largest news staff in the city," says Kielty, "and we co-produce the noon CHUM national newscast, fed to CHUM Group stations coast to coast in Canada by satellite."

The strong news and information element is complemented by CFRA's adult-contemporary sound, targeted at age 25 and up listeners. "CFRA was the forerunner of the adult-contemporary stations," says Kielty. "We're unique in our appeal for the traditional, yet with an up-to-date entertaining sound."

The station is noted for its personalities, including morning show host Ken "The General" Grant, who has marshalled the morning team for more than 25 years.

CFRA-FM introduced frequency modulation broadcasting to Ottawa in 1948. Eleven years later it sparked development of FM interest with new call letters, CFMO, and a different music format that has evolved into an easy listening style. CFMO's show business personality is reflected in the great support offered to music and drama groups in the national capital area. CFMO also partners with the *Ottawa Citizen* annually for a spectacular radio appeal in support of the Christmas Exchange. The loyal following of CFMO's easy listening format, combined with CFRA's strong image as the information station, creates a dynamic broadcast team. The two stations have distinct sounds, operate separately, but exhibit a real sense of sharing.

From an original staff of 20 in 1947, CFRA/CFMO has grown to almost 100 employees, including full-time staffs of 65 at CFRA and 25 at CFMO.

The company recently moved to its fourth home, a more spacious technologically advanced building on Walkley Road at Don Reid Drive, in the City of Ottawa Hi-Tech Business Park. CFRA operated out of the Ottawa Auditorium for its first 10 years. From there it moved to Isabella Street, and again into a new complex at virtually the same location. The Business Park building increased the stations' space from 14,000 to 21,000 square feet.

CJOH-TV

CJOH-TV, Ottawa's first private, English-language television station, has come a long way since it went on the air on March 12, 1961, broadcasting from a small building at the corner of Bayswater and Somerset. In its early years the station had a staff of 80, a single studio and control room in the basement, and a 600-foot transmitter 11 miles away, in Hazeldean. Today CJOH-TV is at 1500 Merivale Road in Nepean, boasts a staff of more than 300, and is the fourth-largest station in the CTV network.

The driving force behind this new operation was Ernest L. Bushnell, one of the pioneers in Canadian broadcasting and the creator of the first singing radio commercial. Bushnell, who resigned as acting president of CBC to build CJOH, joined with N.A. Taylor, president of Twentieth Century Theatres, and his associate, Dave Griesdorf, to establish E.L. Bushnell Television Company Ltd., predecessor to Bushnell Communications Limited and CJOH-TV (Channel 13).

In 1961 the station also became a founding member of CTV, the new private network. In November 1962 CJOH was chosen to be the originating station for the CTV National News, with Peter Jennings in Ottawa as co-anchor. In 1967 the station was among the first in Canada to broadcast in color. An $800,000 mobile-color unit designed by CJOH engineers for live, on-the-spot telecasts was the first of its kind in the country.

The company went public in 1969, changing its name to Bushnell Communications. In 1975 Standard Broadcasting Corporation Limited of Toronto assumed control of the firm. Ten years later Allan Slaight bought Standard Broadcasting. In 1988, another ownership change saw CJOH-TV become part of the Baton Broadcasting group.

Community involvement is important to CJOH, which has held telethons for the Ottawa Civic, the Children's Hospital of Eastern Ontario, and Participation House. The station has also dedicated time to and produced specials on the drinking/driving issue and alcohol abuse as well as its support of organ transplants.

"Every night almost a quarter-million people invite us into their homes," says Max Keeping, vice-president/news and anchorman since 1972. "Commitment to news excellence has been the CJOH tradition since the station first went to air." Keeping, the focal point of the station's community effort, makes about 200 personal appearances each year on behalf of community events, charitable groups, and organizations.

"Our challenge," says general manager Bryn Matthews, "is to make sure CJOH takes advantage of developments within the industry to remain a vibrant, creative force in the broadcasting system and expand our efforts to be a good neighbor to the people of Ottawa and eastern Ontario."

CKBY-FM/W1310-AM

In 1977 Canadian-owned Maclean Hunter Limited acquired Ottawa radio stations CKBY-FM and CKOY-AM (now W1310). The corporation's strength was well documented through its print successes, but it had yet to earn recognition as a major force in the broadcast industry.

Today CKBY-FM is Canada's most-listened-to FM country music radio station. The former CKOY, now the popular W1310, has taken a well-researched, highly targeted classic hits format and turned it into a success any broadcaster would envy.

Hal Blackadar, vice-president and general manager of Key Radio Ottawa (the Maclean Hunter subsidiary made up by the two radio stations), willingly acknowledges his pleasure with the audience share the two stations enjoy in the Ottawa market.

"Maclean Hunter resources are definitely a benefit," he says, "but the biggest benefit MH offers comes from what can only be considered a corporate philosophy. First of all, Maclean Hunter allows us the necessary autonomy to be sensitive to the needs of this community. Ottawa is not Toronto or Edmonton," Blackadar emphasizes.

"Secondly, we get the right people to do the job—pro-active professionals who pride themselves on staying a step ahead of the competition. We place a special value on human resources," Blackadar continues.

Both CKBY-FM and CIWW (W1310) are full-service radio stations, providing the community with complete news, weather, sports, and traffic reports. Information and entertainment is coupled with the best in country music (CKBY) and classic hits of the 1960s, 1970s, and 1980s (W1310). In 1987 alone the two stations both singularly and collectively raised more than $200,000 for local charities.

These two radio stations, along with its other radio and TV properties, have assured Maclean Hunter's place at the top of the Canadian broadcast industry.

INDUSTRIAL TRADE & CONSUMER SHOWS INC.

The Canadian trade show industry has grown to the multibillion-dollar level because exhibitors know that well-managed shows, with specific audiences, sell product. The shows bring the buyer and seller together; when the product or service meets the need, a sale is made.

Many exhibitors return year after year, selling more product during the few brief days at the show than at any other time. For most repeat exhibitors it is the single most important selling opportunity of the year.

Industrial Trade & Consumer Shows Inc. (I.T.C.S.) is a subsidiary of Maclean Hunter Limited, Canada's largest communications conglomerate. It is involved in the production of 26 shows annually, in a wide variety of industries.

its

The company also offers professional show and conference management services to more than 30 industry associations across the country.

In Ottawa, Ontario, I.T.C.S. Inc. owns and manages The Ottawa Spring Home Show; The Ottawa Fall Home Show; The Ottawa Christmas Craft Sale; "Renovations," A Kitchen, Bath & Window Show; "Originals," A Spring Craft Sale; and The Ottawa Business & Government Computer Show. More than 1,500 companies use the six Ottawa shows as an important part of their overall marketing plan. In excess of 175,000 visitors will spend time comparing products and making buying decisions at these shows, generating millions of dollars in the local economy. After more than 12 years in the nation's capital, I.T.C.S.'s shows are truly an integral part of the Ottawa business community.

OTTAWA CONGRESS CENTRE

Adjacent to Rideau Canal and Parliament Hill, the world-class Ottawa Congress Centre has gained distinction for its fine facilities, service, and attention to detail.

The Ottawa Congress Centre, overlooking the Rideau Canal, is a place for people. Just down the street from Parliament Hill, the centre is designed with a view to history.

The meeting facilities, food and beverage services, spacious reception area, lighting, and rooftop terraces all make up a convention centre that works. Completed in 1983, the centre has proven itself to be a world-class facility, hosting major conferences and industry shows. Most important, its attention to service is finely tuned, with a staff of hospitality experts who add that special touch by ensuring that every detail is perfect and anticipating every need. The centre's key players have been with the facility since its opening.

Located in the heart of Ottawa, the centre acts as a vortex of culture, business, and international affairs, having been the site of a national economic conference, major federal party conferences, musicals, fashion events, consumer and trade shows, as well as hundreds of major banquets and receptions.

The main Congress Hall, a free span space with a 26-foot ceiling, accommodates up to 5,000 delegates in a plenary session and 3,500 for dining. The lower Capital Hall level can be arranged into nine rooms for groups of 50 or more.

One of the centre's main attractions is its flexibility. The staff is equally skilled in presentation for large delegations as they are for

The Ottawa Congress Centre plays host to numerous conferences and industry shows throughout the year.

sales seminars. The versatile hospitality experts, with years of catering and hospitality experience, prepare memorable dinners for 1,200 and cater small receptions for a few distinguished guests.

The Congress Centre's flexible meeting space can handle diverse needs of trade shows, conventions of 2,000, or meetings for 50. The executive boardroom accommodates anything from the smallest function to a head table reception for 100. Extensive catering facilities include a full array of food services, and the centre's director of food and beverage and executive chef prepare menus in consultation with clients. Skylights lend a sense of warmth and openness to the reception area adjacent to the main Congress Hall. Overlooking the canal is the centre's 8,000-square-foot rooftop terrace, the perfect setting for alfresco cocktail parties and barbecues.

The expansive Congress Hall features a 26-foot ceiling and accommodates up to 5,000 delegates in a plenary session (above) and 3,500 for dining (left).

The Congress Centre focuses on the most important criteria for communications facilities: reliability, flexibility, and convenience. It offers technical facilities and equipment unmatched in Canada. Bilingual, multilingual, and top security conferences receive one of three types of simultaneous interpretation systems, available in all meeting rooms and in the reception area. Meeting rooms are also equipped for video and multi-image slide presentations.

The centre is a five-minute walk from Parliament Hill, the National Arts Centre, and some of the nation's finest dining and liveliest night life in the Byward Market area. The new National Gallery of Canada is 10 minutes away, and just east are Rideau Hall—the governor general's official residence—and 24 Sussex Drive, home of the Prime Minister.

Across the canal from the National Arts Centre, adjacent to the Rideau Canal, The Westin, Novotel, and the Château Laurier, the centre offers easy access by car or public transit. The parking garage, operated by Citipark, can accommodate 1,500 cars.

The Congress Centre makes up part of the uniquely designed Rideau Centre shopping complex, which incorporates three major department stores, 200 shops, restaurants, galleries, and cinemas, and affords indoor access to The Westin Hotel.

The Westin, Château Laurier, and the new Novotel combined comprise 1,200 rooms bordering the Ottawa Congress Centre and more than 5,000 rooms within the downtown core.

RADISSON HOTEL OTTAWA CENTRE

It has been a long time since Pierre Esprit Radisson travelled these parts. Back in the seventeenth century, as one of the original voyageurs, his efforts were instrumental in developing the largest commercial enterprise of the age—the great fur trade.

These days the Radisson name is connected to another venture altogether: luxury business hotels. But the determined spirit that led Pierre Esprit through New World frontiers is still very much alive at the corner of Kent and Queen streets.

The Radisson Hotel Ottawa Centre is one of the latest additions to the fastest-growing chain in the industry—jumping from 23 properties worldwide in 1983 to more than 160 in 1988.

"We bring Radisson's excellent worldwide reputation to Canada's capital," exalts hotel general manager Robert Perrin, who was trained in Lausanne, Switzerland. "Ours is a first-class hotel with a promise to service and quality at a price to please the national and international traveller."

A key aspect of the promise is Radisson's unique "Yes I Can" service. Based on a staff attitude and commitment to service, the program was implemented to ensure that guests receive the finest hospitality available.

The 27-storey Radisson tower, open since February 4, 1988, offers more than 500 elegantly appointed rooms. Of these, 46 have been designated to Radisson's Plaza Club for executive business travellers. The exclusive service provides a concierge and hostess, as well as several thoughtful touches, such as complimentary Continental breakfast, hors d'oeuvres, milk and cookies in the evening, and a copy of the *Globe and Mail*—the businessman's daily.

Overseeing the hotel's dining experience is award-winning executive chef Frits Marechal. Trained in Amsterdam, Marechal was selected in 1986 for the Maurie Carp Award—the highest standard of excellence in the national capital region. That same year he captured five gold medals at Expogast in Luxembourg and won top honors for table presentation at the 1984 Culinary Olympics in Germany.

Marechal's gastronomic delights can be sampled in any of the fine din-

Below and right: Radisson Hotel Ottawa Centre, at Kent and Queen streets, provides the finest hospitality available for the tourist or the business traveller.

Above: Award-winning chef Frits Marechal ensures a dining experience at any of the Radisson restaurants. Shown here is the beautifully appointed all-day dining room, Café Toulouse, featuring casual dining in a bistro-style atmosphere.

Left: Guests enjoy the conviviality of Lautrec's Piano Bar.

ing facilities found in the hotel or if preferred in the privacy of the guest's room. The hotel suggests visiting La Ronde, Ottawa's only revolving rooftop restaurant, if not just for the food, then for the view. If a more relaxed atmosphere is desired, guests may try Café Toulouse—a touch of France—offering bistro-style dining.

Guests are invited to indulge themselves at the hotel's executive leisure club facilities. The Kent Club offers both club members and executive travellers the very best in health and fitness amenities. It is equipped with state-of-the-art exercise equipment, indoor pool, sauna, whirlpool, tanning beds, and a fitness testing clinic. The health specialists are ready to put guests through their paces.

After a workout Radisson personnel suggests one of many services offered at the club such as massage therapy, reflexology, shiatsu, and acupuncture—then retiring to the club lounge to enjoy a healthy repast while pondering strategy in the billiards room.

In recognition of the hotel's predominant business clientele, Radisson has created the Business Centre. An office away from the office, the centre is fully equipped with administrative assistants, word processing, photocopying, telex, fax, even furnished office and boardrooms.

The Radisson name has come a long way over the years and interestingly, it is starting to mean as much to Ottawa today as it did in the seventeenth century.

Graduates of Carleton University have had the choice of studies in social sciences, science and engineering, architecture, industrial design, computer science and business disciplines, among others. Courtesy, Carleton University

7

EDUCATION AND HEALTH CARE

RIGHT: The University of Ottawa is a highly visible fixture in the Sandy Hill area. Photo by Wayne Eardley/ Burke Communications Photography

One of the effects of the postwar boom on Ottawa's growth was a concurrent increase in the number of educational and health care facilities, and the expansion of services offered by existing ones.

EDUCATION

It would not be for long that the city, which attracted so many highly educated people to positions in the civil service and in the growing commercial sector, had only one university, the University of Ottawa. Today, in fact, Ottawa has three universities and one community college, and the quality of their programs is known throughout Canada.

The University of Ottawa, meanwhile, remains unique among Canadian universities in that almost every facet of its operation takes place in both of Canada's official languages. Having been founded in 1848, the University of Ottawa is also one of Canada's oldest universities, though in many ways, it's among the newest as well.

The university was originally established when Joseph-Bruno Guigues, the Roman Catholic Bishop in Bytown, observed the lack of available educational facilities, and the fledgling college was placed under the direction of the Oblate Fathers. In 1861, after Bytown adopted its new name, the college changed its name from the College of Bytown to the College of Ottawa, and 17 years later the college received a pontifical charter, the second in Canada after Université Laval.

The college moved several times after its birth, to settle finally in its location in the Sandy Hill area of Ottawa, in 1855. Once ensconced there, the college began to grow, and attracted as much as one-third of its students from the New England states.

Today the University of Ottawa—so named when it changed from a church-run institution to a secular university by an act of provincial government in 1965—is a highly visible and integral part of Sandy Hill. As one walks along Laurier Avenue, or proceeds north along King Edward, the blue Gatineau Hills distant across the city, one can't help but overhear university students chatter as they travel from class to class. Old Victorian houses have been

BELOW: Ottawa's Teacher's College is just one of the many institutes of higher education in the area. Photo by Wayne Eardley/ Burke Communications Photography

painted gray and white and bear signs of various university departments and offices, and a truly charming development of student residences lines King Edward, made striking by the use of traditional architectural elements combined with modern pipe rail detailing.

Some of the city's most interesting restaurants are located within the informal boundaries of the university district too. One of Ottawa's best Mexican restaurants, for instance, is haunted nightly by students eager for burritos and nachos, and a whole range of intimate cafés are invitingly cosy on winter evenings, or spill out onto sidewalks with umbrella-covered patio tables in summer.

The university's oldest building is the Visual Arts Building, constructed in 1893, and the second oldest, the Academic Hall, was once home to a museum, science

The buildings of the Carleton University Campus can be seen in the background of this winter skating scene. Courtesy, Carleton University

Tabaret Hall, at the heart of the campus, is the recognized landmark and symbol of the University of Ottawa. Courtesy, University of Ottawa

laboratories, and a model bank where students practised accounting and banking. Today it houses classrooms as well as a theatre that is among the oldest in the National Capital region, where troupes put on productions in both English and French.

The university's history as a Catholic college is its cornerstone; its role today, as a university situated in Ottawa at the point where the English and French cultures meet, is to offer students a place to encounter the best of the intellectual and scientific traditions of the Western world.

The institution saw incredible growth after 1945, particularly after the 1960s. The School of Medicine was established in 1945, and the School of Pure and Applied Science (now the Faculties of Science and Engineering) a year later. Now the School of Human Kinetics, the Institute of Physical Education was created in 1949, and in 1953, the Faculty of Law was reestablished. The latter faculty is unique in Canada in that it teaches both the Civil Law of Quebec and the Common Law, which stems from Canada's British heritage and which is practised in all other provinces.

Bilingualism and an integration of two cultures is just one of the unique features at the University of Ottawa; in addition, there are several departments and centres within the university that make it truly a distinctive institution. The Child Study Centre, for example, which is part of the School of Psychology, is a training centre for students whose career goal is to work with children who have psychological problems. And the Human Rights Research and Education Centre is a one-of-a-kind resource centre that promotes the study of issues in human rights, both domestic and international. The Research Centre in French-Canadian Civilization features a collection of documentation on the history and culture of French Canada that is among the largest in the world.

Perhaps the newest among the University of Ottawa's facilities is Canada's first-ever school for judges. Doubtless because of the university's reputation, its fine law library, and its tradition of teaching both types of law practised in Canada, the University of Ottawa was chosen in 1988 as the location of the Canadian Judicial Centre. The centre will co-ordinate and design educational materials for 1,700 Canadian judges, at all levels. Prior to its establishment, there had been no national body to coordinate judicial activities and resources.

The university, although encompassing several large city blocks, with an average student population of more than 22,000, nevertheless does not exist as a city in itself; it has combined its graduate programs in several areas of science and engineering specialization with those at Carleton University. The net effect has been the creation of one of the strongest, most diverse resource and research centres in North America. This arrangement also offers graduate students an enviable opportunity to work with teams of researchers in laboratories providing first-class facilities.

The story of how Carleton University began is quite an interesting one, and says a great deal about the entrepreneurial community spirit that exists in Ottawa. In 1942, while the nation was embroiled in a world war, people at the local YMCA were talking of providing night school for the hundreds of civil servants who had come to Ottawa. Henry Marshall Tory, former president of the University of Alberta and then president of the National Research Council, was 77 at the time, but he had no shortage of energy; he recognized the acute need for additional educational facilities in the area, and within that year formed Carleton College, without government grants or assistance of any kind. In the fall of 1942 first-year university courses were offered, to be taught evenings in local high school classrooms. Tory had expected perhaps a hundred

LEFT: Carleton University has 150 acres of land for students to roam on their way to classes in any of the 24 buildings on campus. Courtesy, Carleton University

FACING PAGE TOP: One interesting feature of the Carleton University Campus is the network of tunnels that protect students from the coldest winter temperatures, an option that this student on a crisp but beautiful day chooses not to use. Courtesy, Carleton University

FACING PAGE BOTTOM: Many forms of transportation are available to the student wishing to commute to Carleton University. Courtesy, Carleton University

students to enroll—more than 700 registered!

For several years Carleton College, as it was then known, operated out of rented facilities about town, but when the war ended and thousands of returning veterans were encouraged to upgrade their education, Tory saw the opportunity to establish a full-time college. By the time he died in 1947 the college was well on its way; with the support of various community members—including H.S. Southam, publisher of *The Ottawa Citizen*—the college soon had its own space and was offering degrees in arts and science, as well as public administration and journalism. As the veterans graduated, enrollment began to decline; some Ottawans questioned whether a second institute for higher learning could survive in the city, but as the trend for more and more high school graduates to continue their education grew, enrollment at Carleton rose from a low of 410 in 1952 to 850 just eight years later.

Today, visitors arriving in Ottawa at the Ottawa International Airport, who travel to downtown by Colonel By Drive, cannot fail to notice the splendid university that sits on high land adjacent to the Rideau Canal. The three original buildings, which were all finished in 1959, are situated around a quadrangle. One of the architects in the consortium of designers was the world-renowned Hart Massey; the style of these three, highly visible buildings, has been described as the International Style. Carleton has 150 acres of land for students to roam, between the 24 buildings on campus; a noteworthy feature is the network of tunnels that keep students from having to brave the elements in winter. Rumour has it that a student from Nigeria, who simply could not bear the cold at all, managed to attend an entire winter term without ever venturing outside!

Carleton's early programs in the arts and sciences grew into respected and reputable programs in Social Sciences,

Carleton University students can rise to new heights in academic achievement during off-campus activities, like this earth sciences field trip. Courtesy, Carleton University

Science, and Engineering, as well as architecture, industrial design, computer science, and business. Carleton was the first university in Ontario to offer a combined program in biotechnology and biochemistry. Putting the university in the forefront of educational institutions in Canada is Carleton's pair of parallel processing computers, which are able to break down complicated mathematical calculations into fragments that can then be fed to other computers and worked on simultaneously.

A new Master of Management Studies program at Carleton combines research skills with learning about the special problems of business, another "first" for the University.

Carleton is the home of the Ottawa Carleton Research Institute, a non-profit corporation that was established in 1983 to promote collaboration in research conducted by both industry and educational institutions. At any time, several major projects are ongoing, funded by millions of dollars from external sources. Indeed, research is such an important activity at Carleton, and so much of the National Research Council's high energy physics research was being done there, that the council moved its physics division to the campus.

The university made news again in 1988 when it combined forces with the federal government and a dozen major corporations to form Canada's first, university-run centre for research into the use of illegal drugs. The new Canadian Illicit Drug Abuse Research Centre will conduct studies which in turn will be used by government and law enforcement agencies to fight, and prevent, the problem. The centre is funded entirely by private industry.

News and the people who report it is an important concern at Carleton's School of Journalism, from which many of Canada's print and TV media stars have graduated. The Carleton Journalism Poll, conducted by the students, gleans information on a variety of topics for private companies; journalism students can also be seen often on local cable TV stations, as well as heard on broadcasts by Carleton's Radio CKCU, which is supported by donations from the public.

Although the city's two large universities may be better known to the public because of their visibility and their numerous distinctive features, there is yet another university in the city. This one counts its students in the hundreds, not thousands, and occupies a quiet space in a residential neighborhood. When the University of Ottawa was granted a provincial government charter, the Oblate fathers who had run it since its inception gave up their holdings, and created St. Paul's University, which today holds both a civil and a pontifical charter. The two universities are now autonomous but federated; for example, there is an exchange of professors in such faculties as Philosophy. Full-time students at St. Paul's are in fact automatically registered at the University of Ottawa, and certificates, diplomas, and degrees are jointly conferred by both universities.

About a thousand students, all told, attend St. Paul's, half of whom come from Ontario, a quarter from Quebec, and others from elsewhere in Canada or from foreign countries. Like the University of Ottawa, St. Paul's is a bilingual institution. The largest faculty is that of Theology, not surprisingly; a program in Anglican Studies has recently been added. Linked with Theology is the Institute of Mission Studies, which prepares qualified people to embark on "mission-evangelization"; the program offers either a certificate or a Master of Arts in Missiology.

St. Paul's has one feature that makes it truly unique in Canada, its Faculty of Canon Law. The only other university with such a faculty, which studies the legal system governing the Roman Catholic Church, is in Washington, D.C. This program manages to attract students from all over the world, including Europe and Australia.

Not all of St. Paul's activities are concerned with religion and philosophy, however. The Institute of Social Communications offer programs in animation and communication; the institute features a modern media centre complete with TV and sound studios, a closed circuit TV system, and a darkroom for photographers.

The newest baby on the block in Ottawa is Algonquin College, which at its birth was Canada's largest bilingual community college. Properly called the Algonquin College of Applied Arts and Technology, Algonquin was founded in 1967 on two existing educational institutions: the Ontario Vocational Centre and the Eastern Ontario Institute. The original mandate was to train high school students for employment, and in 1967 the Ottawa Board of Education transferred all Adult Training programs to Algonquin; in 1970 it assumed responsibility for all the diploma programs in nursing in the area, as nursing was phased out of the domain of hospital-based schools of nursing.

Besides being known as Canada's largest bilingual college, Algonquin is famous for several of its distinctive programs, such as the Women's Program and the several French programs that cannot be found or duplicated elsewhere in Canada. Algonquin offers full-time training in health sciences, business, trades, technology, and applied arts. Part-time studies offer an incredible array of options; students can enroll to upgrade professional certificates or to pursue non-academic subjects such as Chinese cooking, photography, or gardening with perennials.

Like so many other ventures and institutions in Ottawa, Algonquin is a showcase of sorts for modern technology. By 1984 the college had more than a thousand telephone lines, scattered across the various campuses located throughout the city. What was needed was a network that would allow administration more control over use of the telephones, and would

FACING PAGE TOP: The right of their children to learn and be taught in French was defended by these 19 Ottawa mothers in January 1916. Courtesy, City of Ottawa Archives

also lower costs. What they got was a complex communications network that has a few other tricks up its sleeve: if classroom temperature rises beyond a certain level, for instance, the system triggers an alarm.

The 50,000 students at Algonquin attend classes at one of eight schools throughout the Regional Municipality of Ottawa-Carleton. Algonquin is not involved in high-level research or government activities; it simply trains people for work. The college, it's been said, is run more like a corporation than an "Ivy League" institution, which befits its main goal. One of the college's mottos for instance is, "Be an Algonquin Graduate . . . Or Be Prepared to Compete With One."

Such is the state of higher education in Ottawa and the surrounding region. But what about the basics, the elementary and secondary school education? Just as the rest of the world has gone beyond the rudiments of readin' and writin,' so too has so-called "basic" education in Ottawa.

As throughout Canada, both the public and separate school systems offer schooling for children from the junior kindergarten level. What distinguishes Ottawa is that every child in the city is offered a number of opportunities to begin learning French. All the elementary students in the public system are eligible to begin French immersion at three different levels at the junior or four-year-old kindergarten level, at Grade Four and Grade Six. Students not enrolled in French Immersion take daily instruction in French as a core program beginning with five-year-old kindergarten. Similarly, in the separate school system, a partial French immersion program is available in all schools.

Now, in other Canadian cities, French immersion is seen as something that concerns only the "Yuppie" generation, and it isn't as accessible a public school option as it is in Ottawa. The difference between Ottawa and other cities is that, being a French-English community, as well as the capital city in a country that recognizes two official languages, the reality of life in Ottawa is bilingualism. And Ottawa parents are aware of that fact. They want their children to have every advantage when it comes to choosing a career in later years.

Another reality that Ottawa educators have noticed is that not all children are the same, neither do they all progress at the same rate in school, which is why the Board of Education developed the Alternative programme. Students from Junior

The 50,000 students at Algonquin College, Canada's largest bilingual college, attend classes at one of eight schools throughout the Regional Municipality of Ottawa-Carleton. Courtesy, Algonquin College

BELOW: In 1869, the Ottawa City Directory ran this advertisement for the Convent of Ottawa, later known as the Rideau Street Convent. With several large additions in the 1880s, the beautiful stone convent dominated the south side of Rideau Street between Waller and Cumberland. It was sold in 1971 and, after much discussion, was demolished in 1973. Public Archives of Canada

Kindergarten to Grade Four are allowed to progress both socially and academically at their own rates; furthermore, there are no rigid grade levels, and parents take an active role in the program.

There are special facilities available for the use of all schoolchildren in the region, one of which is the MacSkimming Natural Science School. Every child has an opportunity for a field trip to the school, which is usually reported to parents as, "I went to the science farm today!" Students there explore nature, agriculture, outdoor living, and pioneer living.

Children in most cities are taught safety, but in Ottawa, the word *safety* has an extra dimension. Although we in Canada feel fortunate that, for the most part, our society is relatively free of violent crime, nevertheless every parent worries about some danger befalling a child. Abductions of small children by strangers is a horrifying part of life, but the abuse of children by people they know—an uncle, a family friend, a stepfather—is a very real and surprisingly commonplace situation. The Ottawa Board of Education developed a program in 1986, first implemented in

CONVENT OF OTTAWA.

Boarding School for Young Ladies,

UNDER THE DIRECTION OF

THE GREY SISTERS.

THIS INSTITUTION, established about twenty-five years ago, affords the greatest facilities for acquiring a complete knowledge of the English and French languages. Nothing has been neglected that will promote this object; and the testimony invariably borne in favor of the Institution, shows that the effort has been successful.

To cultivate the intellect, and impart a taste for literary pursuits, the young ladies are afforded the opportunity of managing a Post Office and a Monthly Newspaper.

During recreation hours, on certain days, conversation is held in French for such pupils as are learning that language, and in English, for such as desire to acquire proficiency in it.

Every facility is given for the study of Music, so that students can rapidly attain the highest degree of success therein. Musical Instruments in use are the Harp, Piano, Guitar, Melodeon, Organ, &c.

Oil Paintings, Pastel, Water Colors, &c., together with the various kinds of Drawing, Embroidery, Wax-Work, Artificial Flowers, &c., are taught. The ornamental is not, however, allowed to supersede the useful, all the Pupils being obliged to learn the theory and practice of Domestic Economy.

TERMS:

Board and Tuition, per year,	$80 00
Half Board,	40 00
Quarter Board,	16 00
Piano,	30 00
Harp,	50 00
Organ,	40 00
Guitar,	30 00
Drawing and Painting,	10 00
Oil Painting,	12 00
Rent of Bed, Wash-Stand, &c.,	2 00
Bed and Bedding furnished,	8 00
Vacation, (if spent in Convent),	15 00

Washing, Doctor's Fees, Books and Stationery, form extra charges, payable in every case in advance.

No distinction of Religion is made in the admission of pupils. Children of different denominations, though obliged to conform to the order of the House, are not required to attend the religious exercises of the Institution, and special care is taken that all pupils attend the Churches of their own persuasion.

Quarterly Reports of the health, progress, and conduct of the Pupils are sent to the Parents.

In 1874, Lord Dufferin laid the cornerstone for Ottawa's first public high school, Lisgar Collegiate. W.J. Topley took this photograph of students outside the Gothic stone school sometime between 1875 and 1880. Courtesy, Public Archives of Canada

1987, that was designed to use the basic assertiveness skills to teach children how to protect themselves from abuse. The program, called the Personal Safety program, was based on the highly acclaimed National Film Board production *Feeling Yes, Feeling No,* but because the original production was somewhat sophisticated for very young children, it was adapted in a unique way. So unique, in fact, that educators from across the country have travelled to Ottawa to learn more about it.

One would expect that children living in Ottawa, one of the major advanced technology centres on the continent, would be exposed to computers—and micro-computers are available to all students, in both school systems—but children in the capital also engage in an innovative social studies program designed to stimulate their imaginations and involve them in classroom discussion. Called "Lost Island," the program was introduced to Grades Four, Five, and Six in 1988. It is centred on the story of a family marooned in the Atlantic Ocean, on a "lost" desert island. The story is not meant to be studied as literature, however. Instead, the family's travails serve as a springboard for discussion about such issues as problem-solving, the concept of family, and what it means to be part of a community. In the first year more than one student who previously thought Social Studies was nothing short of a drag actually began to enjoy the subject, even going to the library to do further reading on related themes.

HEALTH CARE

One tends to separate education from health care, looking at universities as places for the young and at hospitals as places for the ill, but the truth today is that the functions of these two types of institutions are not so very different. For one thing, education is very much a part of health care, as a significant proportion of the care that is delivered in Canada is done so by people who are learning, and learning is a process that never stops. Moreover, as the concept of health care changes from the old medical model—in which "health care" really meant the cure and treatment of disease—to the new model, in which illness is prevented and people are helped to maximize their potential for health, education plays an ever-increasing role.

The relationship between Ottawa's hospitals and health centres and its universities and community college is therefore a strong one, constantly renewing itself and accepting new challenges.

Challenges by the dozen is what Mother Elisabeth Bruyère encountered when she first set foot in Bytown; the 27-year-old nun had travelled from Montreal with two other members of the Grey Sisters order to begin ministering to the sick. Plenty of disease plagued Bytown; built on swampy land, surrounded by the stagnant water of the Rideau Canal, the little lumber town was frequently buffeted by epidemics of fever, such as that of 1828 that killed hundreds of workers. In 1832 cholera accompanied a shipful of Irish immigrants, and caused 1,500 people to die throughout Upper Canada. Until 1840 the sole medical care in Bytown was a 20-bed military hospital, and it was only available to the citizens of the settlement as long as a military doctor was not required for care.

Finally, following these epidemics, a Board of Health was formed under Dr. Alexander Christie, and a rather primitive isolation hospital set up on Sussex Drive. The

A sister walks with small friends through Ottawa East, a historic Ottawa neighbourhood. Photo by Wayne Eardley/ Burke Communications Photography

Named after the pioneer in health care in Bytown, the Elisabeth-Bruyère Health Centre offers a contemporary approach to the health care needs of the community. Photo by Wayne Eardley/ Burke Communications Photography

Grey Nuns were called upon to establish a permanent hospital, which led to Mother Bruyère's journey to Ottawa.

The Grey Nuns' tiny hospital eventually grew into Ottawa General Hospital, today one of Ottawa's two major hospitals. The Grey Nuns managed the hospital until 1980, when "the General" moved to a new building on Smyth Road, and the old hospital building became the Elisabeth Bruyère Health Centre.

The Ottawa General today is recognized as one of the most advanced hospitals in North America; its computer systems serve as a model for other health care institutions in both Canada and the United States, and its businesslike approach to hospital administration has helped hospital accountants be able to write the books in black ink, not red. Recently the Ottawa General has taken a hard look at its operations and services,

The Ottawa General Hospital is the location for the new Eye Institute and a specialized cancer research centre. Photo by Jessie Parker/ First Light

and subsequently realized that there was a market for services outside hospital walls. Now on the ground floor is a bakery, a pizzeria, and a dry cleaner, among other services, which are available not only to patients and staff, but to members of the community as well. Staff members and visitors can pick up a loaf of fresh bread on their way home, and members of the community can call the hospital to have a party catered—the end result is that the hospital has made the maximum use of its services and facilities.

The Ottawa General has had a longstanding relationship with the University of Ottawa's Faculty of Health Sciences; the hospital has a large number of staff physicians and surgeons who also hold appointments with the university, and the General's halls are well-known to medical and nursing students.

In 1988 the Ottawa General was chosen to be the site of the regional High Risk Pregnancy Unit, which offers comprehensive monitoring to women whose pregnancies may be complicated by other health factors. Specialists in perinatology, respiratory diseases, hematology, and rheumatology are available to the health care team.

In addition, the first pre-pregnancy counselling clinic in Canada was established at the General, and women have travelled from as far away as Australia to use the clinic's resources. The clinic was intended to help women contemplating a pregnancy who have a history of medical or obstetrical problems; through counselling and diagnostic testing, physicians can do what they must before the pregnancy begins, so that both mother and baby do well.

St. Vincent's Hospital is where the chronically ill, the disabled, and those convalescing after surgery go for care. Photo by Wayne Eardley/ Burke Communications Photography

Originally dubbed "Fisher's Folly," the Ottawa Civic Hospital today is a centre for a diverse range of health care services. Photo by Wayne Eardley/ Burke Communications Photography

At nursing stations in the University of Ottawa Heart Institute at the Ottawa Civic Hospital, nurses employ sophisticated equipment to monitor their patients' progress. Photo by Wayne Eardley/ Burke Communications Photography

Meanwhile, expectant fathers don't walk the halls anymore; now they're right there in the labour rooms. Family contact is encouraged at the General, where the doctors and nurses are proud of the very healthy rate of spontaneous deliveries (relative to Cesarean births) and in the proportion of mothers who choose to breastfeed.

The Ottawa General is also home to The Eye Institute of the National Capital, which isn't a surprising fact given that the General has seen a number of firsts in opthalmology over the years, and remains a referral centre for patients from all over the world. The Eye Institute features an investigative centre to aid in the diagnosis and treatment of "difficult" conditions affecting vision, as well as a laboratory research centre. Another innovation is the Day Surgery Unit, which enables patients who have had eye surgery to stay in hospital for as little time as possible, meaning greater comfort for them and lowered health care costs for the community.

One of the top priorities at The Eye Institute will be the study of cataracts. Dr. Brian Leonard, who is the institute's director, has said that cataract surgery is the most frequently performed of all operations in North America, and that finding a way to eliminate the need for cataract surgery would save the health care system millions of dollars.

Health care, and most certainly surgery, has come a long way from Mother Elisabeth Bruyère's day; no one could have foreseen the advances in surgical technique and other specialties of medicine that are today practised at the Ottawa Civic Hospital.

It's interesting to note that the Civic was at first considered by many to be a bad idea. In 1919 the mayor of Ottawa, Harold Fisher, had thought it a smart idea to amalgamate the three hospitals built since the General opened—a general hospital, a maternity hospital, and the County of Carleton Protestant—and relocate them as a unit to a site close by the city limits, in the middle of farmland. Needless to say, there were detractors, and for a time the new Ottawa Civic Hospital was called "Fisher's Folly." In our time, Mayor Fisher's foresight is obvious: the Ottawa Civic Hospital is now in the centre of a highly populated area, although still pleasantly adjacent to the green fields of the Central Experimental Farm.

If you asked Ottawans what was the one thing that makes the Civic special, though some might say that comedian Rich Little was born there, they're more likely to name the University of Ottawa Heart Institute. Formerly the hospital's cardiac unit, the specialized Heart Institute opened in 1983 and now includes more than 100 beds for cardiac patients, a day-surgery unit, and clinic space. The expertise offered at the institute goes beyond surgery; it also features a unique cardiac disease prevention centre and rehabilitation facility. But surgery at the Heart Institute certainly grabs the headlines: the

Ottawa Civic was the first hospital in Canada to use the Jarvik artificial heart—which was used as a stopgap solution for a patient while a donor heart could be found—and the first in the world to incorporate laser surgery into a common procedure to remove plaque from arteries.

Cardiac surgery hasn't been the only area in which Ottawa Civic surgeons have excelled; recently the hospital saw Canada's first surgical implant of adrenal tissue as a treatment for Parkinson's Disease. Not to exclude the world of medicine, the Civic was also the first hospital to use a nonsurgical procedure to treat retinal detachment.

Research is an important activity at both the Heart Institute and the Loeb Institute for Medical Research. The latter facility conducts studies into molecular endocrinology, reproductive biology, neurobiology, and clinical epidemiology, among other areas. The Loeb Institute, with its 17 laboratories, is regarded as the finest diagnostic research facility in Canada. Together the two research facilities have several hundred studies ongoing at any moment.

Having a baby is an exciting moment for any family, and at the Civic, as at the General, family-centred care is the philosophy in the obstetrical areas. The hospital was among the first in Canada to have a special "birthing room," where women could undergo labour and delivery in a less clinical environment. It also followed a trend in progressive nursing by allowing one nurse to look after both mother and child for more consistent, comprehensive care.

The Ottawa Civic Hospital has had a high-risk pregnancy unit since the late 1970s, much in advance of most other hospitals. The hospital's record in the successful delivery of twins and the children of diabetic mothers is today among the best in the world.

Children are the business, the only business, at the Children's Hospital of Eastern Ontario (CHEO), the large pediatric facility located on Smyth Road near the Ottawa General. Before CHEO opened in 1974, residents of Ottawa had to take their children, if they needed specialist care, to pediatric hospitals in Montreal or Toronto. A group of citizens decided that Ottawa was a big enough city to have its own children's hospital, and so CHEO was born. The hospital serves not only as a community hospital, with a variety of outpatient services and clinics, but also as a central referral point for eastern Ontario, and is the location of the regional Poison Control Centre. About 11,000 children are admitted to CHEO each year, passing by the huge, stuffed Winnie the Pooh bear in the lobby in admitting, or by the gigantic Papa Smurf near the Emergency department.

The Children's Hospital is the treatment centre for the specialized care of premature or ill newborns, who are admitted to the Neonatal Intensive Care Unit. Physicians from Neonatology have recently begun teaching area physicians emergency care for deliveries, and within months the new program received high praise from doctors who had occasion to appreciate what they'd learned.

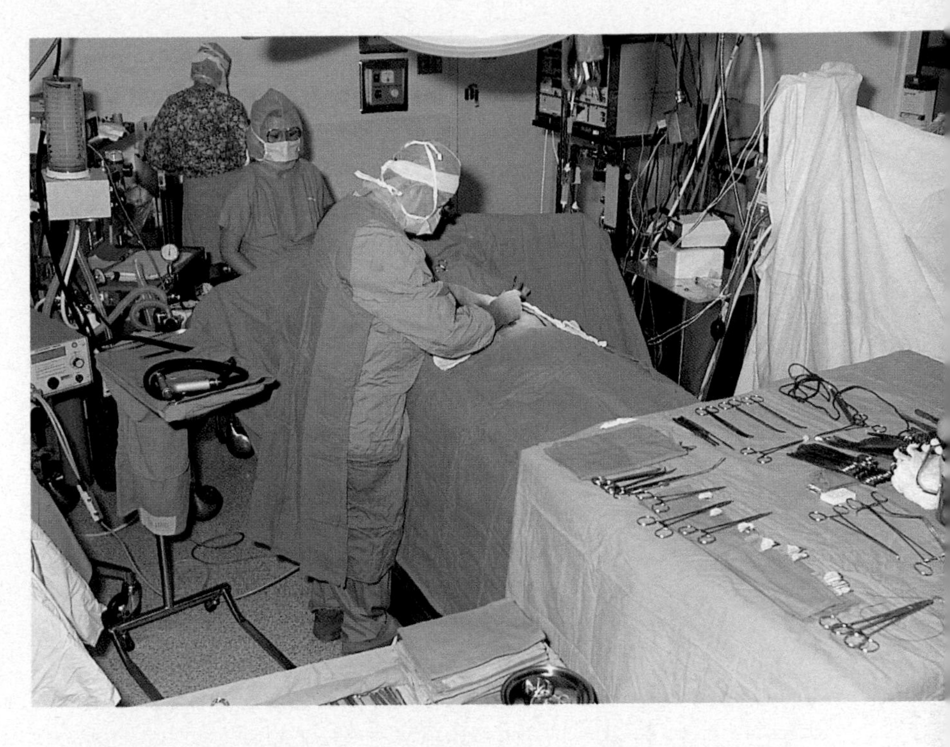

Medical history has been made repeatedly in the operating rooms at the Heart Institute. Photo by Wayne Eardley/ Burke Communications Photography

The outreach work at CHEO goes beyond the region and the Ottawa Valley, however; in 1988 the hospital began a twinning project with Bustamente Hospital for Children in Kingston, Jamaica. Using equipment developed at the University of Ottawa, staff can transmit and receive high resolution pictures by telephone lines, a technological advance that aids in the training of physicians, diagnosis of problems, and for consultation between doctors in the two countries.

Decades ago, infectious diseases were a major cause of death—diseases we now neither think nor worry about, such as smallpox and tuberculosis. In 1901 Ottawa, which had a population of just under 60,000, counted 125 deaths from what was then called "consumption." The fight against tuberculosis was taken up by a number of community groups, particularly women's groups in Ottawa such as the May Court and the International Order of the Daughters of the Empire. Just after the turn of the century, citizens realized that a special hospital for TB victims was much needed, and after a great deal of searching for a suitable site, the Lady Grey Hospital—named after the wife of the current Governor General, Earl Grey, who had done so much work for TB patients—opened in 1910.

Located on Carling Avenue, just east of the site where the Ottawa Civic stands, the Lady Grey Hospital had plenty of acreage surrounding it, which was fortunate because in the following years the hospital expanded greatly. It became the Royal Ottawa Sanitorium and offered a pleasant place for TB patients to receive treatment.

Fifty years later the scourge of tuberculosis had all but disappeared, and although the Royal Ottawa still served as the main treatment centre for the disease in eastern Ontario, the hospital moved on to assume a new and larger role, that of the treatment of people with psychiatric disorders or with any kind of physical disability.

The newest addition to the Royal Ottawa Hospital has allowed for an expansion of health care services. Photo by Wayne Eardley/ Burke Communications Photography

The City of Ottawa's own Riverside Hospital offers medical and surgical care to the community from its beautiful location on a hill beside the Rideau River. Photo by Wayne Eardley/ Burke Communications Photography

Today, the Royal Ottawa's many services are grouped under the name, the Royal Ottawa Health Care Group. These services include the adult mental health services at the Royal Ottawa Hospital, which feature inpatient and day units as well as assessment clinics and the regional forensic centre, and children's mental health services. The Royal Ottawa Rehabilitation Centre, which is located near the Ottawa General and Children's Hospital on Smyth Road, has a comprehensive range of services, including special programs for new amputees and for people who have suffered head or spinal cord injuries.

Any city has hospitals other than the large, general teaching hospitals, and Ottawa is no exception—except perhaps in the quality of care and in the affection that citizens have for their community hospitals. The Perley Hospital, for example, was first opened in 1897 as a "home for incurables." Today health care professionals take a somewhat more positive approach, and the Perley has assumed responsibility for people who are chronically ill or disabled, and for those who require a short term of convalescence. In the early 1990s the Perley will move to a new home on Smyth Road—another addition to Hospital Row—and will incorporate the Perley's own residents with the present Veterans' Home, and veteran residents at the National Defence Medical Centre.

The Riverside is truly a community hospital, owned by the Corporation of the City of Ottawa. Situated on the banks of the Rideau River, not far from Braddish Billings' old mansion, the Riverside offers the bread-and-butter of health care: medical, surgical, and obstetrical services, as well as complementary services such as palliative care. As Chairman of the Board Eleanor Dunn has said, "We're not like the Civic—we don't have any glamorous stuff like the Heart Institute, but we have community spirit."

Serving the western portion of the region—Nepean, Kanata, Stittsville, and West Carleton and Rideau Townships—is the Queensway-Carleton Hospital, an acute-care, general hospital which provides both emergency and limited-term health care services. It has an unusual emergency facility that features several separate units as opposed to one large department; among the 160 or more patients seen in Emergency every day are children, but those who require very specialized care are transferred to CHEO, which is minutes away by ambulance. As the western portion of the capital region grows—which it has done, dramatically, in recent years—the need for more beds at the Queensway-Carleton has increased, and the hospital has plans for a significant expansion.

On the grow too is the Salvation Army's Grace Hospital, established in 1904. The Grace's maternity services are known far and wide, but recent expansions have enabled it to include comprehensive services in a new Ambulatory Care Unit as well.

The name of Elisabeth Bruyère lives on in the hospital community and in the city of Ottawa through the Elisabeth Bruyère Health Centre, which is located downtown in the buildings that used to house the Ottawa General. Today the Bruyère offers a range of services; it is the regional Palliative Care Unit, and it boasts a variety of very specialized clinics, such as the Camouflage Clinic, where people who have been disfigured by skin defects, illness, or tattoos are referred by physicians for treatment. The Bruyère Centre also has a geriatric day hospital and a nursing home. In fact, administrators believe that what has been created at the Bruyère is not an institution or a hospital *per se,* but a health-oriented community.

Community health concerns are the focus of the work done by the Ottawa-Carleton Regional Health Unit, which oversees everything from the vaccination of children, to home support of the elderly or the disabled, to inspection of restaurants and food facilities, to monitoring trends in communicable diseases, to . . . well, you get the picture.

A perfect example of how the Health Unit works is its approach to one goal in community health care: reducing the incidence of heart disease in the region. Nurses and other staff have attended health fairs, and set up blood pressure and counselling clinics in shopping centres, in order to get as close to people in their day-to-day lives as possible. Other members of the Health Unit professional team have worked closely with businesses to develop in-house no-smoking policies, thus providing support for employees through smoking cessation programs.

And, of course, the members of the community that is Ottawa-Carleton have helped each other. Local service clubs have made a tremendous difference, by raising funds for much-needed facilities and by sponsoring innovative projects, like the Ronald McDonald House near CHEO, where the families of young cancer patients can stay together in a home-like atmosphere during treatment, or like the low-cost Rotel Motel near the General. One of the things that marks Ottawa as a truly caring community is the extremely active volunteer movement; people in Ottawa extend a helping hand whenever they're called upon, whether to deliver hot suppers for Meals on Wheels or to canvass for various research funds.

"Only the modern city," wrote Georg Wilhelm Hegel in the eighteenth century, "offers the mind the grounds on which it can achieve awareness of itself."

ABOVE: St. Vincent's Hospital is where the chronically ill, the disabled, and those convalescing after surgery go for care. Photo by Wayne Eardley/ Burke Communications Photography

LEFT: A splendid atrium makes for a dramatic entrance to the centre for health and social services administration in the Regional Municipality of Ottawa-Carleton. Photo by Wayne Eardley/ Burke Communications Photography

THE UNIVERSITY OF OTTAWA

Colonel By Hall is University of Ottawa's centre for a multimillion-dollar research investment by academics, government, and industry in advanced engineering and geological studies.

By its tradition and character, the University of Ottawa reflects Canada in an academic setting.

Located in the heart of Ottawa, it is North America's oldest and largest bilingual university, where students and staff find an exceptional meeting ground for two of the intellectual and scientific traditions of the western world. Proximity to government agencies and laboratories and to business and industry enables it to advance Canadian scholarship and technology worldwide.

Established by the Oblate Fathers as the College of Bytown in 1848, the university, secular since 1965, comprises a staff of 2,400 and a student body of 20,000. The capital's eighth-largest employer, it generates more than $200 million annually for the local economy and conducts sponsored research of close to $40 million per year.

Academic and professional programs, most of them to the doctorate, are offered in eight faculties—administration, arts, education, engineering, health sciences, law, science, and social sciences—and through the School of Graduate Studies and Research.

The University of Ottawa Second-Language Institute attracts students from on and off campus who wish to become bilingual. The Centre de Recherche en Civilisation Canadienne-Française houses one of the world's largest collections on the history and culture of the French in Canada and North America.

The Faculty of Law is unique, offering degree programs in both civil and common law, the latter available in both official languages. Associated with the Faculty of Law is the Human Rights Research and Education Centre, the only university-related institution of its type in Canada.

Medicine (established in 1945) and Nursing (1933) are part of the Ottawa Health Sciences Centre. The Ottawa Civic Hospital, Ottawa General Hospital, the Children's Hospital of Eastern Ontario, the Royal Ottawa Health Care Group, and the National Defense Medical Centre are the major teaching hospitals. Ottawa Civic also is home to the University of Ottawa Heart Institute, internationally acclaimed for its advanced work in coronary surgery and research. New bilingual programs have been established in physiotherapy and occupational therapy.

Excellence is also the focus in the basic medical science research at the University of Ottawa, where one of many major studies seeks to discover a vaccine that will control a number of communicable diseases, including hepatitis B.

In science and engineering, the university shares in substantial research initiatives with several corporate partners. Among them are the Alcan/NSERC Industrial Research Chair in Basic and Applied Electrochemistry and the BNR/NSERC Industrial Research Chair in Signal Transmission Technology. The Electrochemical Science and Technology Centre (ESTCO) is investigating a number of areas of interest in science, engineering, and the health sciences, in particular those dealing with battery longevity and miniaturization.

The university's Departments of Biochemistry, Biology, and Chemistry are internationally recognized in a range of specializations that includes pesticides, nutrients, mass spectrometry, and several areas of biotechnology. Research activities in physics, mathematics, and computer science focus on several threshold areas such as semiconductors and computer protocols.

Nuclear magnetic resonance studies are just one area with exciting long-term biotechnological implications, in which the university is assuming leadership en route to the twenty-first century.

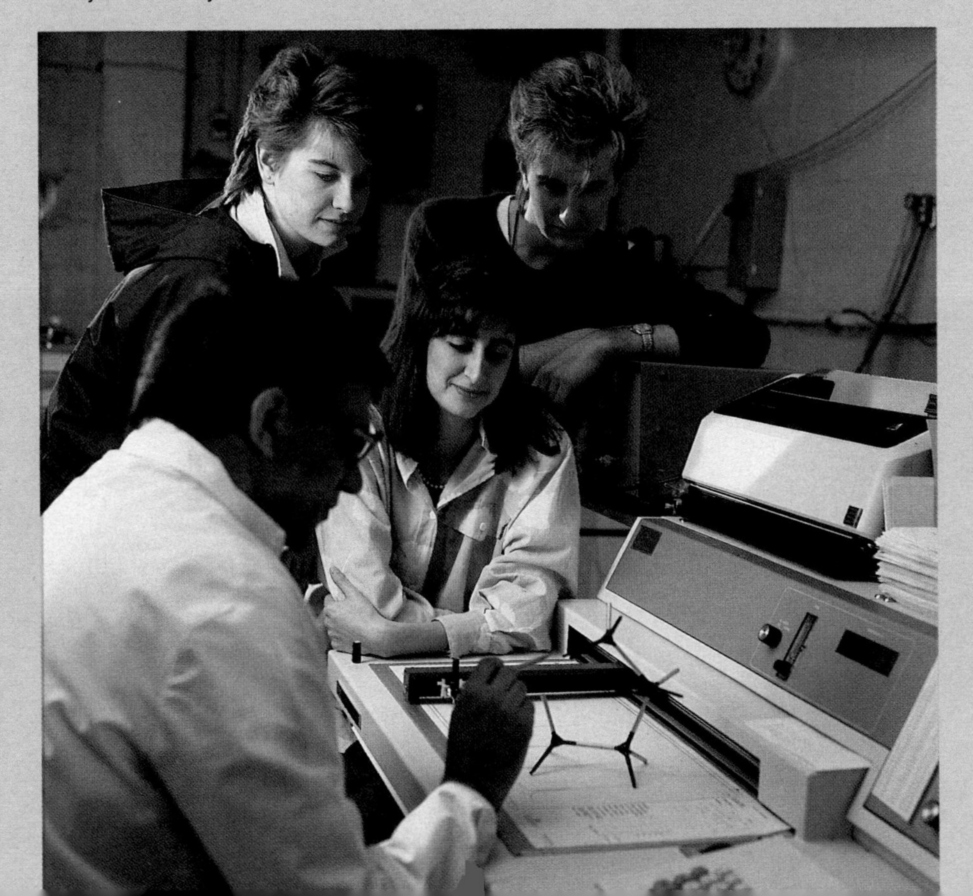

The university is active in the Ottawa Carleton Research Institute, which seeks to strengthen financial and research links among Ottawa's two universities, Algonquin College, and the government and corporate world. The university's Innovation Centre provides support to local inventors, and the university also operates a Small Business Consulting Service.

The university's Co-operative Education programs, alternating periods of work and study, are in high demand. Its Master of Health Administration students twice have proven tops among 60 other North American universities in annual American College of Health Care Executives' hospital simulation competitions.

The Child Study Centre of the School of Psychology trains graduate students in managing childhood psychological problems and learning disabilities.

The Institute for International Development and Co-operation offers programs for Canadian and third world government officials, administrators, and planners. The Department of Modern Languages and Literatures, with the Department of External Affairs, offers courses in Russian, Arabic, Chinese, and Japanese for Canada's diplomatic corps.

Many University of Ottawa alumni and researchers excel in areas as diverse as the concert stage and international and national academic organizations. Among these achievers are a recent Molson Prize recipient, a president of the Royal Society of Canada (the country's highest academic organization), and several winners of Steacie and Killam Fellowships (the most distinguished research awards in Canada). The university also boasts two recent Rhodes Scholars and the first female vice-president at a major Canadian university.

The recently completed Brooks Residence Complex, 17 four-storey apartment buildings that include 12 units especially designed for the disabled, has increased on-campus residence accommodation to almost 1,800.

The University of Ottawa is closely linked with the community. Thousands of youngsters enjoy the school's Christmas Science Lectures for Children, and high school students take part in mini-courses, an annual week in which professors from several departments provide instruction to bright and curious minds. The university's Continuing Education program, which offers credit courses in Ottawa, Pembroke, Cornwall, and Hawkesbury, as well as on the main campus, is a pioneer in distance education by telephone. A thriving Seniors Resource Centre organizes a range of activities and events for those who believe that learning enriches the lives of people of all ages. The new Women's Studies Centre is a recent example of initiatives to promote women in all aspects of university life.

Traditional in its pursuit of excellence, yet contemporary in its academic and research commitments, the University of Ottawa meets many needs.

OTTAWA BOARD OF EDUCATION

For more than 100 years the Ottawa Board of Education (OBE) and its predecessors have been teaching the people of Ottawa-Carleton how to learn.

The OBE, one of five area school boards, provides public education to residents of Ottawa, Vanier, and Rockcliffe Park. Its pledge has always been to ensure that each student is afforded the opportunity to develop his or her skills to full potential. This responsibility is shared on the elementary and secondary levels with the Ontario Ministry of Education.

In the 1987-1988 school year the OBE served more than 32,000 students in both English and French through 81 different learning centres. In addition, more than 85,000 registrations were recorded for the board's extensive list of continuing education courses.

The ammunition behind the OBE's rocketing success is its 2,400-member teaching force, which is bolstered by a strong educational support staff.

The board is comprised of 18 elected trustees whose mandate runs three years. The board meets twice a month to debate and set OBE policy. These meetings are open to the general public, and the board welcomes the input.

As a matter of necessity and convenience it was decided in 1970 that a properly regulated and administered kindergarten to grade 13 system should be the responsibility of a single board of trustees. The OBE is actually the amalgamation of the Ottawa, Vanier, and Rockcliffe school boards.

OBE programs are "child centred." With the lowest teacher/pupil ratio of any major school board in the province, the board is able to offer high-quality alternative school programs, French Immersion programs, and English/Core French programs.

OBE psychologists, social workers, and visiting teachers are available for students experiencing social, emotional, behavioral, or serious medical problems. Busing is provided for students living beyond a defined walking distance.

Several special secondary programs are available for students interested in extensive arts training—programs in drama, visual arts, music, and dance.

Bilingual secondary programs are seen by the OBE as the logical continuation of its excellent elementary school French immersion.

A special commercial program is featured at the High School of Commerce on Rochester Street for students who will be entering the work force immediately following graduation.

Many students take advantage of co-operative education programs that allow high school credits to be earned by a combination of in-school training and practical work experience.

Three OBE schools offer the convenience of semestered programming. This system enables the student to take four different courses in each of two semesters to accommodate different learning styles.

Technical specialization is another area in which the OBE is a leader. Ottawa Technical High School offers pre-engineering courses for students who intend to pursue higher scientific training. A supervised learning alternative of life and work skills is available for transitional students who have either dropped out or are having difficulty coping with the regular system. Three OBE high schools have been equipped to prepare students for careers in areas such as food services, horticulture, merchandising, and woodworking. These vocational programs are taught in the classroom and through work experience.

OBE high schools conform to their own individual code of student discipline, as well as to the OBE's Drug and Alcohol Policy and Race and Ethnic Relations Policy.

The OBE provides for the needs of exceptional children in both elementary and secondary schools by offering regular classes, withdrawal classes, and segregated special classes.

Through its massive continuing-education program, the OBE has given the community a unique supplementary learning opportunity. In 1988 more than 85,000 registrations were recorded. Many of them were from residents applying to either English or French adult day schools. Adult basic education has seen rapid growth in the areas of literacy and numeracy.

The OBE is one of the leading boards in the province in terms of community use of schools during the day and at night. These "lighthouse schools" make maximum use of all available resources.

More than 57,000 registrations were recorded in 1987 for noncredit courses ranging from belly dancing to badminton and from chess to calligraphy.

It is this sort of community interest that has allowed the Ottawa Board of Education to maintain the standard of excellence that it has always strived for.

Facing page: Welcome to Learning! Ottawa's public schools provide students with inviting, stimulating learning environments.

Ottawa Board of Education **Conseil scolaire d'Ottawa**

OTTAWA GENERAL HOSPITAL

Left: The Ottawa General Hospital is a model for other technology-oriented health care institutions.

The Ottawa General Hospital combines the most modern of facilities with the most modern way of thinking. Founded in 1845, the hospital moved to its present location at the Ottawa Health Sciences Centre on Smyth Road in 1980, taking the opportunity to reorganize and re-equip.

Most important for any hospital is its patient care, its research, and its facilities. The General has significantly increased its medical research and developed innovative patient care programs.

A model for modern technology-oriented hospitals, this 529-bed, bilingual institution is known for its referral centre for the neurosciences, its transplant programs, high-risk perinatal unit, regional home dialysis program, and burn unit. It is also recognized for its research-oriented kidney programs, AIDS clinic, and its research on sleep and memory disorders. The memory disorder program, established in September 1986, offers a unique team approach to helping those with diseases such as Alzheimer's, while also being committed to active research in brain-related diseases.

The General is the first Ontario hospital east of Toronto to acquire, at a cost of $3 million, a Magnetic Resonance Imaging Unit, a diagnostic device that permits exceptionally clear visualization of the body's soft tissues and organs.

The General's most famous recent success story, originally code-named Operation Rainbow, is the birth of the Forgie quintuplets. The Forgies are Canada's first set of quints in 50 years to survive since

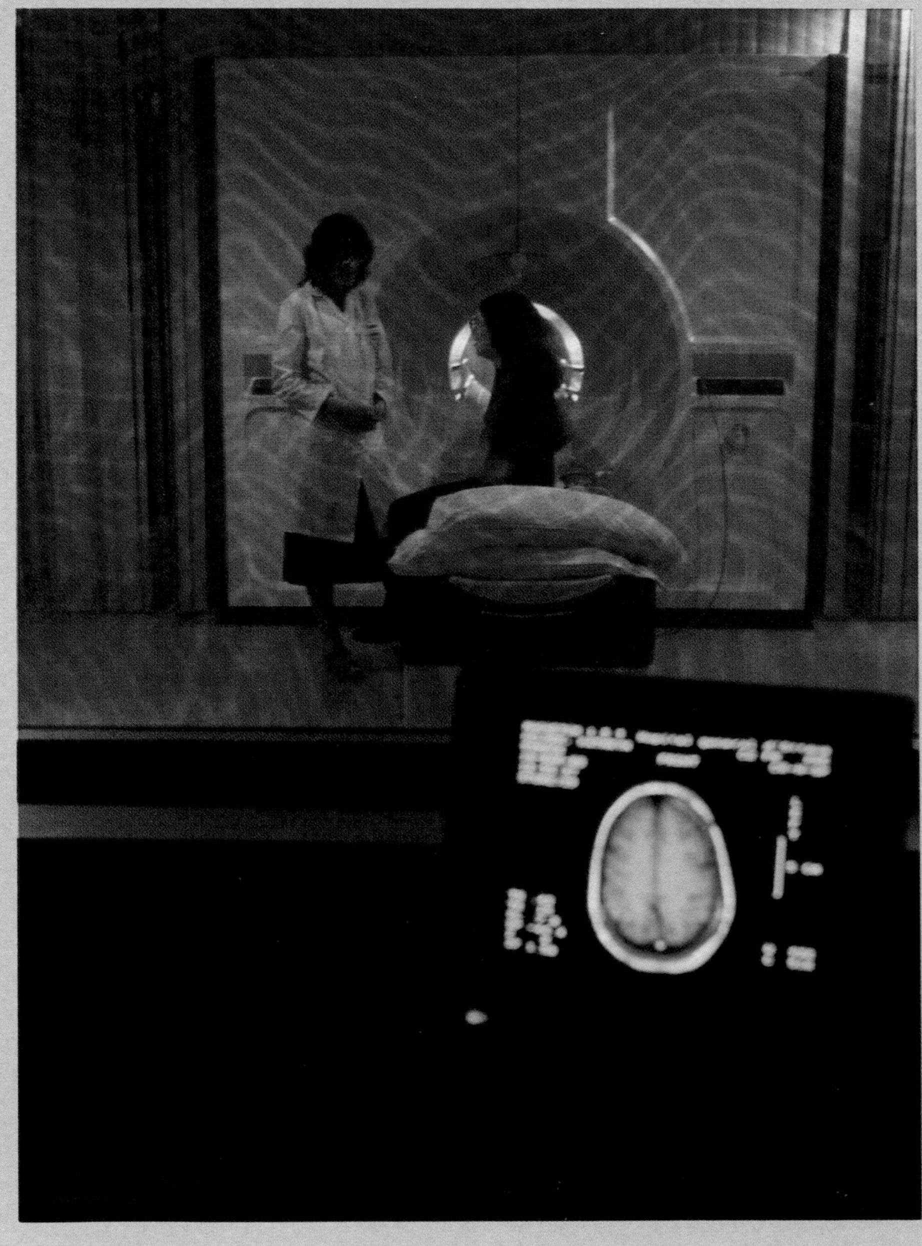

Below: The Ottawa General Hospital's magnetic resonance imaging unit, one of nine such machines in Canada, allows exceptionally clear visualization of the body's soft tissues and organs.

the Dionne sisters. The General's perinatal service features a unique high-risk maternal/fetal team of consulting perinatologists and neonatologists, available around the clock.

A leader in ophthalmology, the General recently established the University of Ottawa Eye Institute Ottawa General Hospital, a centre dedicated to diagnostic and clinical work and research in ophthalmology. The institute makes full use of the resources in the Ottawa region, operating in collaboration with the University of Ottawa School of Medicine, local high-technology industries, and the National Research Council.

The General is a bilingual teaching hospital primarily dedicated to medical education, but it also brings in students from a wide variety of fields, including nursing, physiotherapy, social work, pharmacy, neuropsychology, and biomedical engineering.

While the research, technology, and teaching programs speak of the future, the spirit of the hospital is rooted in its earliest history, which dates back to 1845, the year of the hospital's founding. Responding to the needs of the prosperous lumber centre then known as Bytown, four Grey Nuns of the Cross opened the first institution and with them grew a tradition—a dedication to caring and, since 1980, a sense of entrepreneurship.

Dr. Edward van Courtland, a surgeon, donated his services for one year to the seven-bed facility. From this staff of one physician in 1845, the institution (now a public corporation with 25 board members) has grown to a medical staff of more than 400 doctors and 850 full-time nurses.

Throughout the progress and expansion, however, the tradition of dedication and determination shown by the Sisters was preserved. An example of that spirit is seen today in the many yellow smocks brightening up the hospital and identifying the Friends of the Ottawa General Hospital, a force of 364 volunteers. The friends work in many departments and are responsible for the gift shop, tea garden, beauty salon, and library and convenience carts—and bring in more than $400,000 per year for equipment and projects.

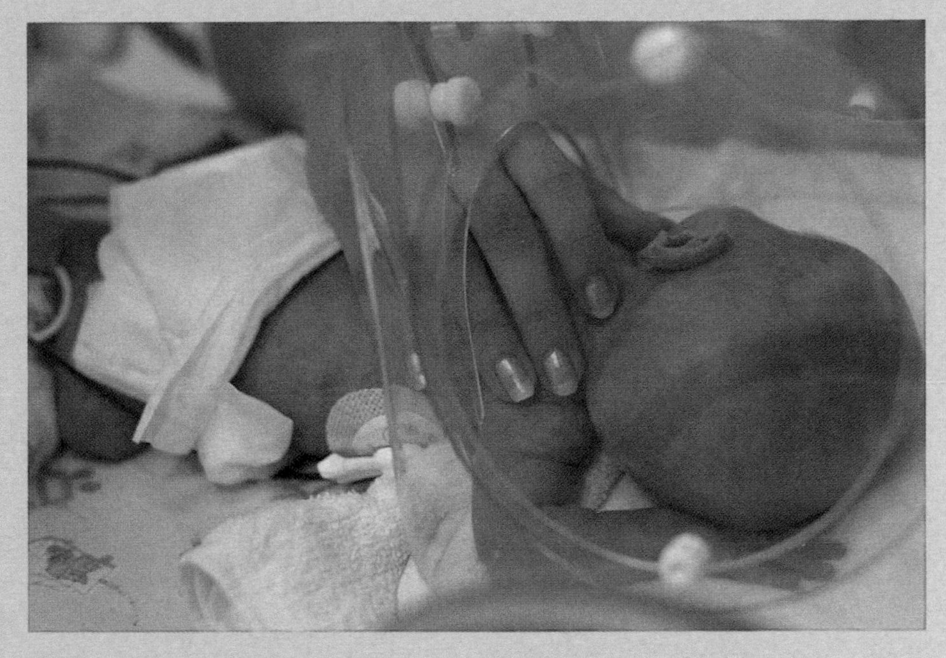

The Eastern Ontario Level III Regional Perinatal Unit, located at the Ottawa General Hospital, offers high-level care to mothers with high-risk pregnancies and to their newborns.

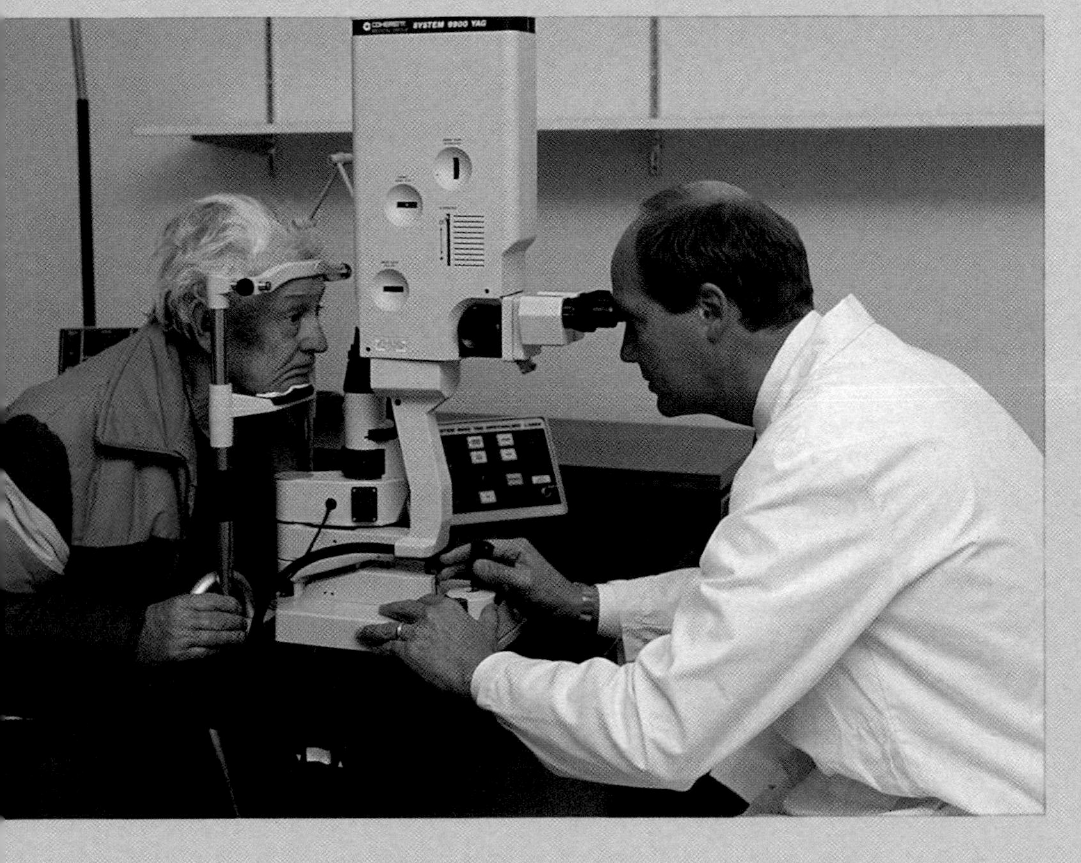

The General, a leader in the field of ophthalmology, has established the University of Ottawa Eye Institute, Ottawa General Hospital.

"Like many health facilities, we had to face a new reality in the 1980s: higher costs and greater community needs," explains hospital president Jacques Labelle. "We had to find new ways to make the hospital more efficient and to take full control over its destiny."

When the hospital opened in its new location, then-hospital chairman Pierre Richard began to revitalize the hospital's finances completely.

The board of trustees adopted a plan to reduce expenditures drastically while introducing new revenue-producing services. Within a year the hospital had banked a surplus of more than one million dollars, and this was just the beginning. "We needed imaginative cost-efficiency, matched with ambitious revenue-generating projects," says Harry Rogers, the current chairman.

The General introduced an innovative, sophisticated computerized system to manage its affairs, and now markets its computer services to other hospitals. "More and more, technology will be closely linked," says the chairman. "In the future, the best hospitals will be characterized by their quest for excellence. This includes managerial excellence, which will be essential to provide the funding hospitals will need to organize the ever more sophisticated equipment and human skills required to be at the forefront of medicine."

The hospital has recently completed many building and developmental initiatives. In 1987 the 80-bed addition to the General's North Tower was officially opened. The second phase, to begin at the end of the decade, includes the construction of the North Tower's final wing (along with 80 beds), the new quarters for the perinatal unit, and the Eye Institute.

The hospital's share in funding these projects, at 75 percent, is unparalleled and concretely demonstrates its determination to secure the resources needed to meet its goals.

The rationale for such dramatic growth within just a decade of its opening is underlined by patient volume statistics. Inpatient occupancy at 95 percent is higher than anywhere else in the province—while outpatient activity is 50 percent higher than the year the hospital opened. The institution's Cancer Clinic has also seen an unprecedented growth in patient activity. It is also slated for expansion.

The Ottawa General Hospital offers a unique combination of caring, tradition, modern technology, and efficiency.

The Ottawa General, founded in 1845, is the oldest hospital in the region and the second oldest in the province.

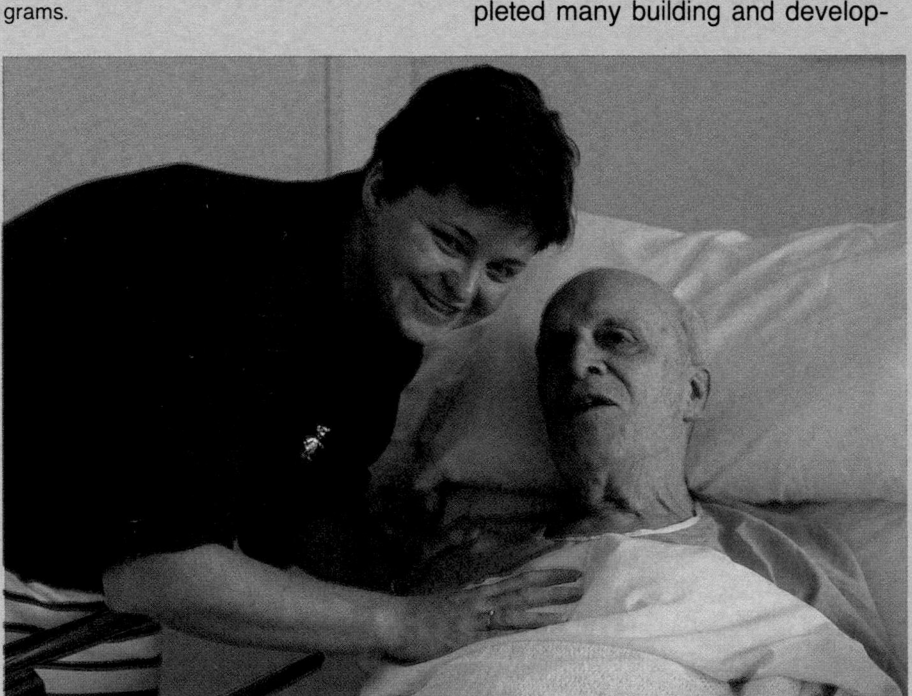

Most important to the Ottawa General is its patients; to that end, the hospital has significantly increased its medical research and developed more innovative patient care programs.

CHILDREN'S HOSPITAL OF EASTERN ONTARIO

The caring atmosphere provided by the bilingual medical, nonmedical, and volunteer staff at Children's Hospital of Eastern Ontario helps to reassure the 200,000 youngsters who visit each year.

The Children's Hospital of Eastern Ontario is committed to the special needs of eastern Ontario's roughly 600,000 youngsters, and it does so bilingually.

Infants, pre-schoolers, and school-age children are grouped together by age in medical and surgical units; adolescent patients have their own units. The Neonatal Intensive Care Unit specializes in the care of premature or ill newborns, with CHEO professionals providing the expert care.

Dozens of outpatient clinics also offer specialized care. The original 1974 plans anticipated 40,000 outpatient visits per year. There are now more than three times that many, thanks to a day-care surgical program. CHEO encourages families to take part in the patients' health care. Overnight stays can be arranged for parents. Special rooms on each floor are set aside for them, and they can visit their children any time. CHEO also provides orientation tours for both patients and parents.

CHEO applies a multidisciplinary team approach. The hospital is part of the Ottawa Health Sciences Centre, which includes the Ottawa General Hospital, Royal Regional Rehabilitation Centre, National Defence Medical Centre, University of Ottawa Faculty of Health Sciences, and the Rideau Veterans' Home. CHEO shares physiotherapy, occupational therapy, and orthopaedic surgery services with the adjacent Ottawa Children's Treatment Centre.

The Child Life Department oversees an extensive children's library, staffed by volunteers, and, with the help of schoolteachers, helps long-term patients keep up their studies. The department also supervises playrooms and activity rooms. In good weather children can use outdoor and open-air facilities. Adolescents have their own lounge.

There is a separate unit for adolescents in psychiatric care. The hospital's Department of Psychiatry also offers outpatient services and is involved in the McHugh School day treatment program.

CHEO is home to regional facilities for adults as well, including the Eastern Ontario Regional Poison Information Centre, one of only two such centres in Ontario; the Regional Virology Laboratory, which specializes in the diagnosis and treatment of infectious diseases; and the Regional Genetic Counselling Service, which offers prenatal counselling to couples whose children could inherit conditions such as Down's Syndrome or spina bifida.

The CHEO Foundation is a separate charitable organization registered with the Ministry of Consumer and Corporate Affairs. Foundation staff are constantly organizing fund-raising events in co-operation with generous service, social, business, and private groups. Community events range from neighborhood garage sales, community dances, and bingo, to the annual Teddy Bears' Picnic in Vincent Massey Park and the Duck Race, which featured 50,000 plastic yellow ducks racing down the Rideau Canal, to the annual telethon.

CHEO's dedicated medical and nonmedical staff give that required extra effort to make sure the 200,000 youngsters who visit CHEO each year have as pleasant an experience as possible. The auxiliary's more than 500 volunteers provide extra service and care.

The Children's Hospital of Eastern Ontario is responsive to the opinions and suggestions of the community, carefully examining its own day-to-day operations to fulfil its mandate of service, education, and research. Facilities, community support, and dedicated people allow CHEO to help make Ottawa more than just another capital.

OTTAWA CIVIC HOSPITAL

From a small hospital occupying a single building, the Civic has matured into a multifaceted facility and a leader among Canadian health care institutions in its ability to draw upon research and educational expertise in providing quality patient care.

The Ottawa Civic is more than a hospital. With 4,000 full-time and part-time employees—and more than 1,000 volunteers—it is a bustling community within a community, complete with state-of-the-art research facilities, specialized clinics, dedicated staff and volunteers, and even an entire indoor shopping mall.

Founded in 1924, the hospital provides excellent care to more than 100,000 patients who come to the Civic each year from eastern Ontario and western Quebec. The 922-bed facility treats patients referred to its many specialized clinics by family doctors and smaller hospitals. Its areas of expertise include heart bypasses and transplants, a geriatric assessment unit, a high-risk pregnancy unit and special care nursery, an eating disorders clinic, a large echocardiology lab, and a large cancer clinic.

The Ottawa Civic strives to find solutions to today's major medical questions with sound research and practical applications. The hospital is currently home to more than 250 active research projects, with the major emphasis on cardiac vascular disease, neurology, immunology, endocrinology, and reproductive biology.

A special feature of the re-

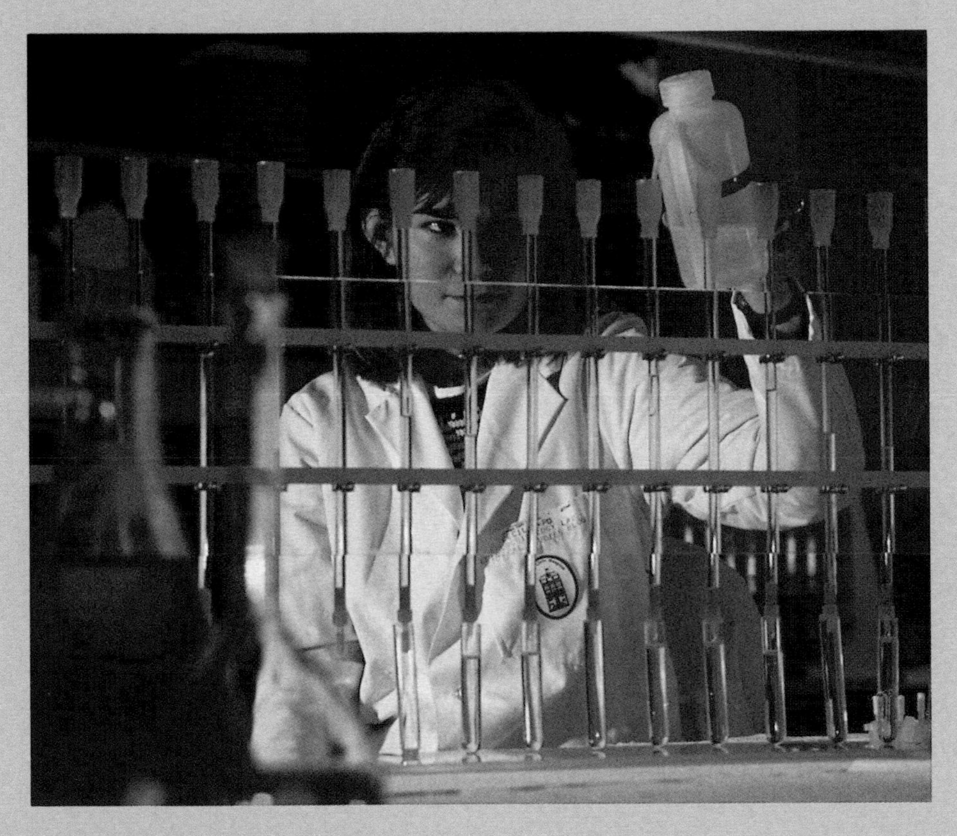

search at the Civic is its commitment to cross-fertilizing basic science and clinical medicine. Research is closely linked to improvements in patient care—while close contact with patients serves as a springboard for directed research studies. One present focus on research is aimed at developing improved medical procedures and the continuing development of professional skills.

"We encourage research that is driven by innovation and curiosity, with the aim of bringing national and international recognition to the hospital," says Dr. J. David Grimes, vice-president of clinical and research administration. One major research facility on campus is the University of Ottawa Heart Institute Research Centre, at the Ottawa Civic Hospital. It is a unique cardiac facility, integrating state-of-the-art research, patient care, and education. Sophisticated laser technology is applied to the treatment of coronary artery disease. World-class research is conducted on the artificial heart. There are joint ventures involving Canadian biotechnology companies, pharmaceutical industries, and academics.

Patients from the Ottawa region, other parts of Canada, and from outside the country have benefited since the institute's inception in 1969 and the completion of its patient care facilities in 1976. "With the completion of the research component of the Heart Institute, we have built the foundations for cardiac care in the twenty-first century," says Dr. Wilbert Keon, director general of the Heart Institute, who has received national attention as leader of the team responsible for Canada's first artificial heart transplant.

The Research Centre brings basic and clinical scientists and existing staff together under one roof. It is the first institution in the world to combine patient treatment, rehabilitation, original research, and education, all integrated within a major university hospital.

In 1980 Dr. Adolfo de Bold, the institute's director of research, capped 15 years of research with the discovery of cardionatrin, a natural diuretic produced by the heart itself. "The discovery of cardionatrin should be used to benefit the Canadian economy . . . to build something for Canada," says de Bold. Cardionatrin is expected to comprise a major part of the $5 billion worth of drugs now consumed globally for high blood pressure and heart disease. In Canada alone the current market for diuretic and antihyperten-

Left: Integrating research with the medical setting, the Moses and Rose Loeb Institute for Medical Research provides the opportunity and facilities for researchers and clinicians to benefit quickly and fully from each other's insights and discoveries.

Below: In 1952 Her Majesty Queen Juliana of the Netherlands visited the Ottawa Civic Hospital. Here the Queen is shown the pink bassinet used by her daughter, Princess Margriet, who was born at the Civic on January 19, 1943. Accompanying Her Majesty (centre) were Maternity Ward Supervisor Mary Thompson (left) and nurse Gladys Moorhead, who was the private nurse on duty at the birth.

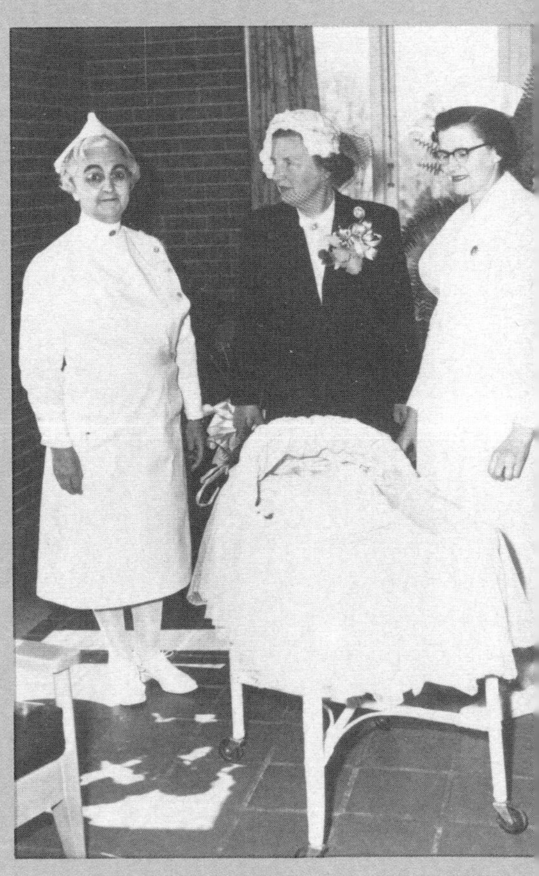

sive drugs is at least $100 million per year.

"The benefits to Canada in terms of licensing alone are inestimable," says Ottawa Civic Hospital president Peter Carruthers. "This research centre will attract the pharmaceutical industry to Canada and, in so doing, will put Canada in the forefront of biotechnology research."

Other areas of research at the Civic include the Parkinson's Disease Research Laboratory and the Endocrinology and Metabolism Unit.

Recent expansion at the hospital includes both the Moses and Rose Loeb Institute of Medical Research and the Heart Institute Research Centre. Construction of the Loeb Institute adds 35,000 square feet of dedicated research space. The institute's principal fields of research are endocrinology/metabolism; reproductive biology, especially in the field of in vitro fertilization; neurobiology/pharmacology; and clinical epidemiology. The Civic's multilevel geriatric care development project, the Woodroffe Centre, is about to become a reality.

The Ottawa Civic's research initiatives place the hospital at the forefront of medical research, realizing its goal of bringing research from the laboratory directly to clinical care.

Traditionally, most basic research has been carried out in universities. One of the advantages of research in a hospital setting is that it can focus on patient care problems and allow for new knowledge to be transferred effectively and directly from the laboratory to the clinical situation. Experience has shown that high-quality research results in high-quality patient care.

Together the thousands of skilled professionals contribute to making the Civic an exceptionally well-rounded health care institution. The skills and caring approach of hospital employees, associates, and volunteers have helped to create a high public regard for the Civic Hospital. The extraordinary difference that committed people can make is reflected in the hospital's reputation for excellence in research and teaching, for innovation in medical treatment, and for the quality of its nursing care.

The 1,200 nurses, the core of the Civic's professional staff, contribute enormously to the hospital's reputation for excellent patient care, while making a significant contribution to hospital improvements through involvement in hospital-wide committees and participation in the development and testing of innovations.

Another major advantage of having academic and scientific activities on the hospital campus is that dynamic programs attract the very

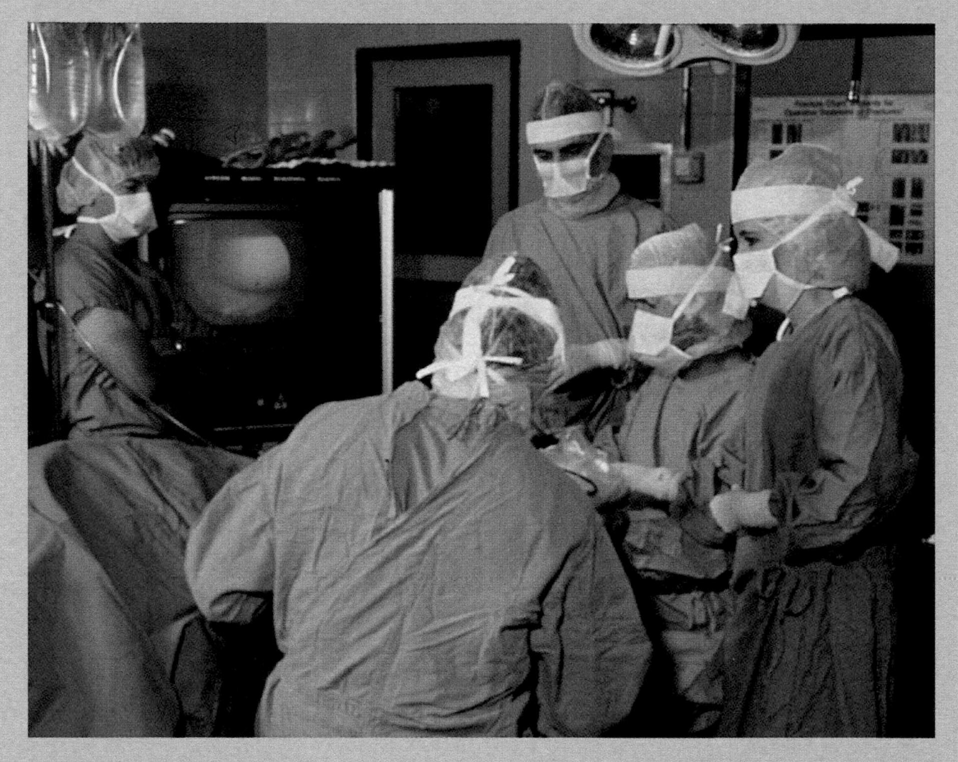

The Civic combines the finest in state-of-the-art medical technology with that special caring touch of dedicated health care professionals.

The Cardiac Rehabilitation Program at the Heart Institute is more than just an exercise program. Nutrition, lifestyle, and psychological health also play a key role in the care of the patients.

The hospital's Geriatric Assessment Unit and the Woodroffe Centre, a multilevel care facility for seniors, provides a supportive environment in which a person may continue with those aspects of his lifestyle that he is still able to enjoy as well as an opportunity to interrelate with persons of his same age.

best health care workers and physicians to the institution. Such research programs enhance the traditional university links and develop important co-operative ventures between outside agencies and government laboratories.

The Civic's medical staff consists of nearly 600 doctors. Many are recognized as the leaders in their respective fields.

With almost 50 nursing units, ranging from a Special Care Nursery to the Geriatric Assessment Unit, the Ottawa Civic provides new nursing graduates and experienced nursing staff with many opportunities to enhance their clinical abilities. Orientation programs and retraining courses introduce nursing staff to specialized-care facilities and keep them up to date on recent advances in care and treatment. Nursing education also is supported at the Civic through bursaries, educational leaves of absence, and tuition payback programs.

The Civic is committed to the education of tomorrow's doctors and nurses. One of the major teaching hospitals in Canada, the Civic provides clinical education to more than 900 medical students and graduate physicians each year, continuing education for family doctors, and educational programs for doctors and nurses from the People's Republic of China (sponsored by the federal government).

The hospital is a publicly funded health care teaching institution affiliated with the University of Ottawa Faculty of Health Sciences and Algonquin College. The Civic provides clinical training for hundreds of students each year in every field of health care. Clinical training is augmented by an active, very well-attended program of seminars, demonstrations, conferences, and guest speakers.

In collaboration with the Royal College of Physicians and Surgeons, the R.S. McLaughlin Examination and Research Centre, under the directorship of Dr. Ian R. Hart, is becoming a focus for medical training.

In addition to its undergraduate, postgraduate, and continuing education programs, the hospital is also active in patient and public teaching programs, sharing health care knowledge with the communities it serves. Educational activities such as these ensure that the Civic is able to offer its patients a constantly improving level of care.

"Without volunteers, the hospital would be much less personal," says Eleanor Armstrong, director of Volunteer Services. "Our volunteers are cheerful, pleasant, and very caring. Above all, they have time. They humanize the hospital."

The Ottawa Civic Hospital Auxiliary, active for more than 35 years, has devoted much of its time to the hospital's shopping mall, generating more than $500,000 in revenue. The auxiliary has also raised $500,000 for the establishment of an Auxiliary Research Chair, and has committed one million dollars over the next five years toward the research endeavors of the Loeb Institute of Medical Research.

Volunteers also co-ordinate the Pastoral Care Visiting Teams. The volunteers of the May Court Library, which recently celebrated its 60th anniversary, supply books, magazines, and tapes to patients and staff. They recently added a Talking Book Program, the only one of its kind in the health care sector, which supplies patients with books on cassette and music and relaxation tapes.

A small shopping concourse run by the Ottawa Civic Hospital Auxiliary provides a unique service to patients, visitors, and staff while raising funds for the hospital.

Major's Hill Park affords this spectacular twilight vista. Photo by Wayne Eardley/Burke Communications Photography

8

FORTUNE'S SMILE

When the announcement that Queen Victoria had chosen Ottawa to be the capital of Canada was made, the following remarks appeared in *The Ottawa Tribune* on January 30, 1858: "Ottawa is now destined to advance with rapid strides on the road to prosperity. Her natural advantages will be brought prominently before the country, and the time is not far distant when she will rank as one of the first-rate cities of Canada. The goddess of fortune has at last deigned to smile on us benignly."

The prophecy seems to have been made a reality; as one of the major population centres in Canada, an important business centre, and with a rate of growth that has businesspeople cautiously calling the city a "boomtown," Ottawa has come a very, very long way from the rough and ready lumber town it once was.

The "natural" advantages spoken of by the *Tribune* were most probably the city's lovely setting and its proximity to rivers and the man-made Rideau Canal waterway. Today the city's advantages are of a different nature, namely the presence of educational and research facilities that attract and foster a highly trained, well-educated work force, which in turn serves as a stable market for goods and services.

Numerous businesses, as well as the federal and provincial governments, have taken these advantages and helped the city develop to its current prosperous state. What makes Ottawa different from other growing metropolitan areas, however, is that—and this is perhaps a uniquely Canadian tendency—it has approached even the good times with caution, and constantly sought a kind of equilibrium. There is a sense in the city that "bigger" isn't always better.

One of the indications that the city intends to carefully plan its growth was the establishment in 1979 of the Department of Economic Development. That year, of course, the situation required drastic measures; as a result of the government's actions to decentralize its activities, and specifically its moving of hundreds of government employees to a new office complex in Hull, a huge amount of office space was left vacant in Ottawa's downtown core. The City of Ottawa, then under the direction of Mayor Marion Dewar, saw the writing on the empty office walls, and decided that efforts to diversify the local econ-

Stonemasons tend to the stone walls of the Parliament Buildings, which have begun to show the effects of acid rain. Photo by Wayne Eardley/ Burke Communications Photography

omy were not merely desirable, they were mandatory. In 1982 the Department of Economic Development began to actively compete for new business for the city.

In the decade from 1976 to 1986, the federal government's share of the local work force had dropped from 38 percent to 34 percent; the city had wisely stepped in at the right time to encourage other businesses in other sectors of the economy to locate in Ottawa.

The tricky part was, how do you help Ottawa to grow, and still be Ottawa? The commissioner of the Department of Economic Development, James Sevigny, has said that "People here place a high priority on the quality of life in Ottawa. A zeal to promote the economy could affect that, and therefore our goal has been to promote the economy in a very calculated fashion."

Sometimes, Sevigny said with a smile, people complain about the planning process in Ottawa, and one of the department's most visible activities has been to make doing business with City Hall easier. He notes that the extreme example of government laissez-faire is a city like Hong Kong, where there is absolutely no regulation at all of business activities. The result? "It's a free-for-all," Sevigny says. "Of course, it's easy to measure our success in terms of dollars, but really, there's more to Ottawa than that. We're not a Montreal or a Toronto—there are lots of things we *can* do, but what we've done is to define what we *want* to do as a city."

Certainly, the benefits of such a reasoned approach to city planning have been recognized. In their now-classic book, *Man-Made America, Chaos or Control,* authors Christopher Tunnard and Boris Pushkarev wrote that:

Urban regions must be shaped consciously with an end in view, rather than evolving, as they do now, from the haphazard results of thousands of uncoordinated private, corporate, municipal and higher

The Bank of Commerce Building on Sparks Street is an example of the Canadian tradition in bank buildings—strength symbolized by pillars. Photo by William P. McElligott

ABOVE: Two well-known buskers provide music for shoppers in the Byward Market. Photo by Wayne Eardley/ Burke Communications Photography

RIGHT: The detailing on the new provincial courthouse resembles huge boulders. Photo by William P. McElligott

government decisions. Not only is comprehensive planning needed on this new scale so that the decisions can follow a more cooperative pattern, but regional planning must be given a visual, esthetic dimension . . . to this end, designs must be economically and socially based, and, in a democracy, the pleasures and satisfactions of many must always be considered.

Thus, planning in the City of Ottawa and in the region as a whole strives to consider the needs and desires of many people; uppermost, perhaps, is the concept that the city itself is for all people to enjoy, at all times.

As an example, the city has encouraged mixed-use developments for the downtown core. In earlier times, planners all over North America believed in a clear separation of residential and commercial uses, a policy that was a death sentence for the downtown area of many major cities. When the Canlands site, near Parliament Hill in what may well be the "heart" of Ottawa's commercial district, was up for development, the city stipulated that the project must mix uses—to combine a hotel with retail, office, and residential space, so that day or night, people are always there.

There are several basic principles that guide future development in Ottawa. First is the fact that a good deal of the reason the city is so attractive is that while it is a "big city" in terms of commerce, on a human scale it offers the best of a small-town atmosphere. The preservation of the character of Ottawa's many neighbourhoods is a priority, and new development must be sensitive, in both form and scale, to what already exists.

Second is the fact that the city will continue to be the focus of social, economic, and cultural activity for both the nation and the region, into the twenty-first century. While the downtown area will thus be strengthened as a centre of economic activity, employment centres will be encouraged outside the core too, in order to create a balance. The completion of the transitway and the improvement of transportation corridors will create a pattern upon which new development will be based.

The area south of the city is awaiting major development; a new regional shopping

Workers install the copper roof on the new National Museum of Civilization. Photo by William P. McElligott

LEFT: St. Andrew's Presbyterian Church was built in 1872 by Ottawa's Scottish community; the stone is local limestone. Photo by Devries Mikkelsen/ First Light

FAR LEFT: Glittering office towers characterize Ottawa's downtown core. Photo by Wayne Eardley/ Burke Communications Photography

centre and a number of new office centres are among the plans on the drawing board. Although Ottawa is an established city, there are still many opportunities for new ventures.

In fact, new ventures is what the Ottawa Carleton Economic Development Corporation (OCEDO) has set its sights on. The non-profit group represents all 11 municipalities in the Regional Municipality of Ottawa-Carleton, as well as several hundred local corporations and small businesses. Since its formation in 1962, OCEDCO (the acronym is pronounced O-C-edco) has seen many major corporations and public agencies settle in Ottawa, such as the Canadian Red Cross Society, which moved its national headquarters to the Alta Vista area in 1988.

Meanwhile, more than a dozen standing committees pool the talents of local businesspeople for new initiatives in attracting business to the region. Committee members have travelled to the United States, Europe, and Hong Kong, to meet

RIGHT: The York Theatre in the Byward Market is a popular venue for a number of local productions. Photo by Jessie Parker/ First Light

with people who are considering expanding or moving to the capital. Other projects, such as twinning with The Hague, capital city of The Netherlands, have opened the door to new markets.

As more firms choose Ottawa for their head or regional office homes, still others who are suppliers to major companies follow. And there is always the government, now with changing needs that continue to require new expertise and products from the service sector.

Although Ottawa's economy tends to be centred in office developments, the retail sector is very strong too, and as initiatives by both city and regional government to strengthen retail areas become a reality, this area will see even more growth. For example, there is a gathering of

Officeworkers lunch on the Sparks Street Mall under the *trompe d'oeuil* mural. Photo by Wayne Eardley/ Burke Communications Photography

Colorful flowers line the downtown walkways. Photo by Wayne Eardley/ Burke Communications Photography

ABOVE: A film crew takes advantage of the old world charm and scenery in the Byward Market area. Photo by Wayne Eardley/ Burke Communications Photography

RIGHT: A pedestrian makes her way under the bridge over Patterson's Inlet, off the Rideau Canal. Photo by Devries Mikkelsen/ First Light

shops, restaurants, and services along Somerset Street in the City of Ottawa that were begun by members of Ottawa's Vietnamese and Chinese communities. Here people can buy the freshest of produce and the most exotic of herbs and ingredients, from lemon grass for Thai dishes to the transparent noodles fashioned from beans for Chinese cuisine. Now known as Somerset Village, the area has been successfully promoted as a destination for Ottawa shoppers.

Growth will also continue in real estate development, particularly in Ottawa South and in the western portion of the region, near Kanata; older, inner-city industrial areas are slated for redevelopment, as are surplus federal government lands. In the case of the industrial lands, the municipalities are altering zoning by-laws where appropriate, thus removing obstacles to desirable, cohesive development.

Ottawa has already established itself as a leading centre for advanced technol-

ogy; what the future holds is an expansion in the specialty area of biotechnology. Every year sees dramatic new developments in this area—new diagnostic tools that provide scientists with answers in minutes instead of hours or weeks—and Ottawa, with the advantage of research facilities and a trained workforce, naturally has the advantage.

The fashion industry too is budding in Ottawa; already, several local designers have caught the spotlight in Toronto, Montreal, and New York.

Travellers from all over the world are increasingly choosing Ottawa as a destination; 1988 was the biggest and best year ever for tourism, aided in part by the opening of the National Gallery, which was heralded by two world-class exhibitions. As Ottawa's many and varied tourist attractions gain admirers around the globe, tourism will flourish even greater in the capital region.

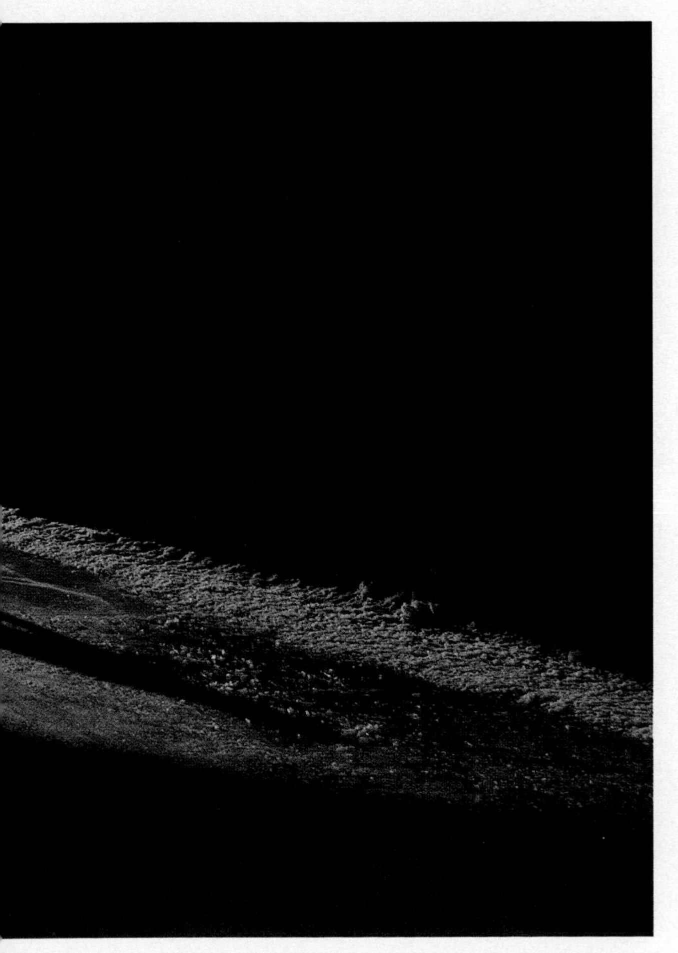

Ottawa's mayor James Durrell has contributed in part to the new awareness of Ottawa as a growing, vital city; although his election in 1985 represented a departure from the former mayors, who were predominantly concerned with social issues—notably Marion Dewar who was among the most progressive mayors in Canada—most citizens have come to recognize the importance of his "Ottawa's open for business" philosophy.

Although the people at the City of Ottawa's Department of Economic Development and OCEDCO have been active—and successful—in promoting a new vision of Ottawa, by fostering the development of existing business sectors and by offering support when and where needed, neither of these groups is in any way an operational arm of local or regional government. Each simply acts as a matchmaker, and who could fail to fall in love with such a city, known for its supportive business community and the hospitality of its citizens?

There is a story about a Japanese businessman, able to speak only a little English, who was met at the Ottawa International Airport by two very friendly Ottawans. They bundled him into a limousine and chauffeured him downtown to his hotel, and saw to it that he had everything he needed. (Of course, the World Figure Skating Association judge, who was of Japanese origin, was a trifle befuddled when he arrived sometime later and found no one to meet him, as he'd been told there would be.)

So it was true that Fortune smiled upon Ottawa in 1858, as she smiles upon the city now; but there is more behind the prosperity and success of Ottawa than luck—there are people who work hard and who also know how to enjoy life.

Photo by Jessie Parker/
First Light.

DAVID INGRAM & ASSOCIATES

Through its representatives and tax and executive office centres across Canada and the United States, David Ingram & Associates provides Canadians with complete and objective financial and tax planning services.

The company strives to take the guesswork out of decision making for its clients—to explain the reality behind every investment option in a way that investors can understand.

"Most of our clients don't have the luxury of being wealthy enough to survive financial mistakes," says Robert Veillette, a partner in the firm's Ottawa office. "For that reason, we emphasize maximum growth—to ensure each customer a secure future."

At each of the firm's centres a client has access to experts in the fields of life and general insurance, investment accounting, mortgages, income tax, retirement planning, debt management, and real estate. Above all though, David Ingram & Associates is known for creating individual pensions for clients that far exceed expectations.

In order to provide each client with security, the company's professionals target five areas and set five objectives. These include increasing a client's financial knowledge, improving net worth, improving cash flow management, reducing exposure to financial risk, and achieving financial independence for retirement. "Every area of a person's financial health has an impact on other areas," Veillette explains. "That's why we work with a client on all five areas—to make sure their money and investments are doing the very best they can."

While helping clients get a clearer picture of their own finances and of investment opportunities, David Ingram & Associates also keeps abreast of changes in the Income Tax Act, government programs, RRSP investment strategies, insurance, and new opportunities for financial self-development. The firm acts as broker for its clients to ensure that the best product is purchased and to make certain that no errors are made in the acquisition of an asset.

Robert Veillette, president and partner in the David Ingram & Associates Ottawa office.

Much of this work is done to reduce a client's financial concerns, to coordinate the existing financial picture with an improved position and a solid plan of action to achieve financial independence as soon as possible.

"There is no way a client can spend the kind of time and effort it takes to keep abreast of changes in the market, new products, and investments," Veillette says. "We take that worry out of the way for them by giving them the information they need and allowing them to rest assured that they have a sensible plan for financial independence."

By giving a client that kind of confidence in his or her finances, David Ingram & Associates has earned its own confidence in its abilities. It is one of the few investment advisory companies in Canada that will waive a counselling fee if a client is unhappy with the advice received.

"This is a sign of our belief in our product," Veillette says. "It's a way of letting the customer know that he can trust us."

Veillette's personal success story in the Ottawa area can also instill confidence in a customer. A partner with David Ingram in the Ottawa operation, Veillette, at just 35 years of age, has made many millions of dollars following the same advice he gives his clients.

His investment acumen is a rare gift and his ability to unravel the intricate financial details of a client's lifetime allows him to work with that client in a beneficial way. He backs that intuition up with strong administrative skills that ensure little can go wrong with investments or products that he offers.

"One of the first things I would say to anyone seeking financial advice is 'look at the person whose ad-

David Ingram & Associates, a complete and objective financial and tax planning service, provides a real estate investment program to create rental pensions for its returning clientele. Shown are just some of the developments available.

vice you're seeking,'" Veillette explains. "Unless that person is financially secure himself, the chances are his advice won't be very useful."

While many people believe that investment and financial planning advice are only for the wealthy, Veillette insists that David Ingram & Associates is dedicated to creating wealthy people, not just serving them. "A sound plan based on achieving financial excellence applies to everyone," Veillette says. "My clients range from those making their very first step to financial security to those who have already made a million and want it to work to its full potential. They all get the same quality of advice, and they are all on their way to real success."

Considering both Veillette's and David Ingram & Associates' records of success, the future looks good for the company's Ottawa office.

"Our advice is sound and our record is solid," Veillette concludes. "When people deal with us, they know we'll be here to take care of every aspect of their financial needs. They know that's our commitment."

COOPERS & LYBRAND

Partners in the Ottawa office of Coopers & Lybrand (seated, from left) are Glenn Ross, John Herzog, Allan Lumsden, Dan Belanger, and John Lisowski. Standing (from left) are Alan Freed, Dave Schijns, Ken Parent, Rich Vickers, Pat Lafferty, and Ron Jackson.

Like the city in which it does business, the Ottawa office of Coopers & Lybrand chartered accountants and the Coopers & Lybrand Consulting Group have enjoyed remarkable prosperity during the past quarter-century.

The rapid ascent of the high-technology industry in the region, coupled with the growing participation of the government of Canada in economic, social, and cultural affairs, has meant an ever greater need for professional accounting and consulting services in the nation's capital.

Coopers & Lybrand has a heritage dating back to the very beginnings of Canada. In 1867 John McDonald opened an accounting practice in Montreal. In 1910 his son George commenced practice and was joined shortly thereafter by George Currie, thus laying the foundation for a firm that for more than 60 years practised in Canada as McDonald, Currie & Co. and today has a staff of more than 2,300 professional people in 21 cities from coast to coast. As one of Canada's largest public accounting firms, Coopers & Lybrand has a full range of auditing, accounting, tax advisory, and business advisory services. In Ottawa, the professional staff consists of 11 partners and 70 professional staff.

The Coopers & Lybrand Consulting Group is the management consulting division of Coopers & Lybrand, and one of the leading management consulting firms in Canada. Its practice is more than 30 years old and services clients from nine offices located in principal cities, including Ottawa. Its 35 consultants offer services in a wide variety of areas—information technology, business and organizational planning, operations improvement, program evaluation, market research, and financial analysis. In addition, the firm's national public-sector practice is based in the Ottawa office. As part of Coopers & Lybrand (International) it offers clients direct and effective access to a network of financial and management consulting expertise worldwide.

The Ottawa office of Coopers & Lybrand is a vastly different place than it was in 1936, when Wainwright Cleary joined the firm, yet continuity has remained its theme. When Cleary died in 1963, he was succeeded by Denis Ross, who retired in 1987. Ross was succeeded by the current managing partner, Allan Lumsden, only the third person to occupy the position in the history of the Ottawa office.

"We have a group of highly trained, dedicated professionals providing services to the community, its businesses, and to the three levels of government," says Allan Lumsden. "We are proud to be associated with companies such as Kinburn Corporation, JWI Ltd., Haley Industries Limited, and Digital Equipment of Canada Ltd. Like Coopers & Lybrand they have a strong local and international presence."

During its early years in Ottawa, Coopers & Lybrand handled a limited amount of government business; however, as the abilities of Wainwright Cleary and his successors became known and respected by federal civil servants, the doors of opportunity began to open.

Today the firm's public and private-sector clients engage its services in a wide range of situations. Federal clients request the preparation of strategic plans and technology forecasts for systems development, evaluation of the effectiveness of government programs and the efficiency of their delivery, and provision of policy advice on issues ranging from accounting to high technology.

Ottawa businesses employ Coopers & Lybrand's assistance to conduct market surveys and to assess the economic impact of introducing new products or services. They continuously rely on the firm's business and tax advice and on its accounting and auditing services.

HULSE AND PLAYFAIR FUNERAL HOMES

The people of Hulse and Playfair Limited are proud of the tradition they represent. It is a tradition of "caring and sharing" that dates back to the company's founding in 1925, when Charles Hulse moved to Ottawa, proudly willing to become "funeral director to paupers and prime ministers."

Since that time Hulse and Playfair has lived up to Charles Hulse and Keith Playfair's promise carrying on the legacy of offering compassionate and caring service—to families and to the community as a whole.

Brian McGarry, president.

Just two years after Hulse founded the firm he was called upon to direct his first state funeral. Charles Lindbergh was visiting Ottawa in the *Spirit of St. Louis* when the pilot of one of his escort aircraft, Thad Johnson, was killed in a collision with another airplane. Mackenzie King, prime minister of the day, called upon Hulse, who was at the scene with the company's new Dodge ambulance, to direct services.

Hulse and Playfair was later called upon to direct services for Prime Ministers Mackenzie King, Lester Pearson, and John Diefenbaker, as well as Governors-General Georges Vanier, Vincent Massey, and Jules Leger. Throughout, the firm has been available to all families, and since the 1960s has maintained a close association with the Memorial Society to serve not only traditional needs but also those desiring nontraditional services.

The Hulse and Playfair tradition has meant active community involvement. Hulse served on the Ottawa School Board for 31 years and served a term as vice-president of Kiwanis International. Several senior directors followed his example, including the current president, Brian McGarry, elected school board trustee in 1985. McGarry has held the office of lieutenant governor in Kiwanis International and is a past president of both the Ontario Funeral Service Association and the Funeral Service Association of Canada.

Community commitment is also seen in the informational assistance Hulse and Playfair offers by promoting programs such as Let's Talk About It series on talking with children about death and helps families by putting them in touch with groups such as the Bereaved Families of Ontario.

For a period of 64 years Hulse and Playfair Limited has been family controlled. Today the McGarry family retains majority ownership; Doug Kennedy, a senior employee, holds a significant interest along with the Trillium Funeral Service Corporation, a Canadian Company. Hulse and Playfair's association with Trillium allows for better service across Canada and internationally.

The Central Chapel, at 315 McLeod Street, where the firm was originally established, has since been joined by the West Chapel, the St. Laurent Chapel, and a special Memorial Services facility in providing Hulse and Playfair Limited's services to all areas of Ottawa-Carleton.

Doug Kennedy, vice-president.

Hulse and Playfair's Central Chapel, at 315 McLeod Street, where the firm was originally established.

BRADLEY/FIRST AIR

Bradley Air Services was founded in 1946 by the late Russell Bradley. Operating originally as a flight school, with some small charter work providing a financial backbone, the company moved in 1950 from the Ottawa International Airport to its present site at the Carp Airport on the west side of the capital region. Since then the firm has become both a successful charter operator and the largest independently owned regional carrier in Canada.

Company president John Jamieson sees Bradley/First Air's growth as an extension of the role it has played in opening up the Arctic for both travellers and businesses. "We've made the entire eastern Arctic accessible from Ottawa," he says. "Towns in the North that couldn't get a reliable source of fresh produce a few years ago are now being supplied, through us, by area businesses."

Jamieson joined the company in 1955, working in the high Arctic at Cambridge Bay fuelling and warming aircraft. It was then that Bradley Air underwent its first major expansion, engaging four new Cessna 180s for charter and aerial survey work on the DEW-Line.

In 1958 the firm began regular operations in the high Arctic islands and engineered the special tundra wheel, which makes it possible for aircraft to land on Arctic tundra. This development accelerated the continuing expansion of northern operations, with numerous government and scientific agencies calling on the company's services.

In 1968 the federal government contracted Bradley Air to provide airborne service to the Polar Continental Shelf Project. This project required extensive air support throughout the Arctic, from Greenland to Point Barrow, Alaska.

Three years later the company opened the world's northernmost commercial air service at Eureka on Ellesmere Island, 600 miles from the North Pole. The following year two DC-3s were put into service to meet the increasing demands of mineral, oil, and scientific exploration in the Arctic islands. In 1973 Bradley opened a major base at Resolute Bay that has become the main staging point for the extensive charter operations now carried out in the high Arctic.

Scheduled passenger services were launched that same year under the trademark name First Air. The original route between Ottawa and North Bay has since been expanded to 22 communities in Ontario, Quebec, the Northwest Territories, Labrador, Greenland, and the

First Air has provided passenger service to 22 communities in Ontario, Quebec, the Northwest Territories, Labrador, Greenland, and the United States, including New York and Boston.

Shown here are two 727s at Bradley Air's Iqaluit, Northwest Territories, maintenance base.

United States, including Boston and New York.

First Air expects to carry approximately 350,000 passengers and 70 million pounds of freight and mail in 1989. Its services are computerized through an agreement with Air Canada, providing worldwide access to travel agents and other airlines. First Air passengers also earn points in Air Canada's frequent flyer Aeroplan program.

While the organization's scheduled airline division has succeeded and grown, so too has the Bradley charter division. Each accounts for about 50 percent of the company's operations.

The reputation earned as the foremost Arctic carrier in the world has also led to work outside the region. In 1974 Bradley was selected to provide airborne support for the Ross Ice Shelf Project in Antarctica. Administered by the United States Navy, this was the first commercial air operation on the Antarctic continent. To this day Bradley provides seasonal air support in Antarctica to a variety of international clients.

Bradley Air was also selected by the United States Air Force to perform the daily logistical support of two Dye sites at 8,000 feet above sea level on the Greenland Ice Cap. The firm currently has the contract for all lateral support of the DEW-Line, resupplying stations from Alaska to Greenland.

As well as providing this charter service to government and business, Bradley also maintains a small fleet of deHavilland Beavers for sportsmen's charters in the upper Ottawa Valley.

Since its inception Bradley has followed a policy of developing in-house technical support in order to be as self-sufficient as possible. This technical support service is also available to others.

The maintenance base is in Ottawa, with hangar and shop facilities at both the Ottawa and Carp airports, and subbases in Iqaluit, Hall Beach, and Resolute Bay. The facility at Ottawa International consists of a 40,000-square-foot hangar and a large cargo warehouse handling all types of goods, including perishable and frozen.

Ambitious expansion plans for the Carp airport—possibly to include a light industrial park—are currently under way. Bradley's present facilities there include a 20,000-square-foot hangar and 7,000 square feet of shops, used for both in-house and client work. Experienced engineering staff provide engine overhaul and maintenance, as well as the testing and repair of avionics, instruments, and airframe.

Bradley has provided major modification and installation services for the United Nations, Bell Telephone, and a number of airborne survey companies.

From the small craft the firm started with in 1946, the fleet has grown to include 4 Boeing 727s, 10 HS 748s, 2 Douglas DC-3s, 7 deHavilland Twin Otters, and 2 deHavilland Beavers. There are plans to add further aircraft and new services.

Six hundred employees and an eagerness to continue "making the North more accessible," fuel Bradley/First Air's determination to maintain its record as the foremost Arctic carrier in the world.

A Bradley Air Services Twin Otter on skiis.

PRICE WATERHOUSE

Audit manager Carol McDonald meets with Michael Stott, executive vice-president/ Corporate Development, Canadian Astronautics Limited.

Price Waterhouse, a Canadian partnership, was founded in 1908. Its Ottawa office, opened in 1949, has established itself as a leader within both the business community and the public sector. The firm's Ottawa office is headed by 10 resident partners and a complement of 70 professional staff. Services offered through this office are supported by a network of associated firms in more than 100 countries, operating under the Price Waterhouse name.

Although Price Waterhouse is auditor of more corporate members of the *Financial Post* 500 than any other firm, this distinction represents only one side of Price Waterhouse, as the firm has established itself as a leader in advising emerging businesses.

"We're big on entrepreneurs and ought to be known as much for our small clients as our large," says Bernard Wilson, managing partner of the Ottawa office. "We've been with many of our clients since start-up, and we've contributed to their success . . . We understand the needs of emerging businesses."

To that end, Price Waterhouse is a founding sponsor of the Canada Opportunities Investment Network (COIN), a computerized venture capital network that matches entrepreneurs in need of capital or strategic partnering with investors.

The firm offers advice and services to businesses in a number of areas, from tax minimization strategies and debt/equity sourcing, to business plans, personnel recruiting, and software selection. Personal financial planning services are also offered.

Its consulting practice advises federal and provincial governments and Crown corporations in numerous areas, including policy evaluation, cost-saving reviews, and assessing government and Crown corporations' efficiency and effectiveness. The Ottawa office is recognized, in particular, for its work in studying and recommending improvements in national, provincial, and local health care delivery systems. In acknowledgement of their expertise in the area of public spending, several Price Waterhouse partners serve on the Independent Advisory Committee to the Auditor-General of Canada.

Public Sector partner David L. Webber and staff accountant Nicole Dufresne-Baker on the site of the new National Museum of Civilization.

TOUCHE ROSS

Touche Ross was founded in Montreal in 1858, making it the oldest firm of chartered accountants in Canada. The firm's Ottawa office has provided service to business, not-for-profit, para-public, government, and individual clients since 1950, when accountant Charles Gale merged his small operation with the growing P.S. Ross & Sons. A subsequent merger in 1958 with George A. Touche & Co. ensured the company's continuing growth and gave it a national presence. In 1984 the firm merged with the practices started by Pierre Séguin and Gérald Préfontaine in Ottawa and Lucien Massé and Donat Vien in Hull, doubling the size of Touche Ross in the region. Today the national capital region practice is backed by a strong national presence through more than 47 Touche Ross offices across Canada.

The firm has the ability to offer all services in both official languages to clients in the region. Today, with one of the largest groups of skilled professionals and support staff, Touche Ross provides services in the capital region to its clients from offices in Ottawa, Hull, Cornwall, Hawkesbury, and Gatineau.

The firm offers a full range of accounting, auditing, management consulting, tax, insolvency, business valuations, and business advisory services—carrying on the high standard of excellence that has become the Touche Ross hallmark.

Touche Ross Management Consultants have been serving the capital for 25 years. The management consulting practice began in 1964, when the Royal Commission on Government Organization created an upsurge in the demand for consulting services in the federal government. Today Touche Ross Management Consultants is a significant local consulting presence and employs the largest number of Certified Management Consultants in the capital region.

These people offer their expertise to hospitals, educational institutions, national associations, business, and all three levels of government. In support of its clients' needs, Touche Ross provides assistance in business strategy, organization and human resource management, financial management operations, and marketing and information systems.

Touche Ross professionals make a major commitment not only to their clients but also to their profession and the community. They are active in many community groups and professional associations, often taking leadership roles.

Touche Ross offices in the region, as well as all offices in Touche Ross Canada, are international in scope, through Touche Ross International. Uniting 53 national firms in 88 countries, more than 30,000 Touche Ross people in 490-plus offices worldwide serve the local, national, and global needs of individuals, businesses, and governments.

CANADA POST CORPORATION

A Canada Post Mail Centre in Domaine Laurentien.

Canada Post is a corporation in transition. Regarded primarily as an essential service for much of its 200-year history, the corporation is currently building an image as a solid member of Canada's business community. From a simple but effective system, it continues to develop into a vast and complex network.

Canada Post Corporation handles a daily volume of more than 30 million letters, collected at more than 140,000 collection points. Each piece of mail is processed first through one of 29 highly automated processing plants and then delivered to one of more than 7,800 postal stations for manual sortation. Each piece is ultimately delivered to any one of more than 10 million Canadian addresses or any address around the world.

Behind this vast network is one of the largest nongovernment work forces in Canada. Canada Post Corporation ranked 43rd in total assets and 13th in operating revenue among the *Financial Post*'s 500 for 1987. This high revenue level is accomplished on average retail sales of less than five dollars per transaction.

Ottawa has been at the centre of Canadian postal service through much of its history. The first post office was opened in the city in 1829, and 36 years later the headquarters of postal administration for the British Province of Canada was located there. When Ottawa was chosen capital of the new nation of Canada in 1867, the city automatically became the site of the postal service's head office.

In 1981 responsibility for operating a national postal service was removed from government and the Crown Corporation, Canada Post, was created with a specific mandate to become more business oriented. In 1986 a National Control Centre was established in Ottawa to encourage and ensure improvements in the quality of service. This around-the-clock, seven-day-per-week centre identifies problem areas, monitors mail flow, and functions as a communications network to ensure smooth operations.

Canadian postal service has been evolving, adapting, and responding to customer needs for more than 200 years. Although the network is large and the technology both complex and changing, the firm has attempted to maintain its traditional commitment to serve Canadians in a reliable and accessible manner.

As it moves into the 1990s, Canada Post Corporation also wants to be known as a business—a business that will pay its own way.

A new retail postal outlet.

MAIL POSTE

Canada Post Corporation / Société canadienne des postes

ARTHUR ANDERSEN & CO.

Arthur Andersen & Co., one of the world's largest and most respected professional services firms, has been offering accounting, audit, tax, and management information consulting services, through Andersen Consulting, to Ottawa and area businesses, individuals, and government since 1977, when seven individuals transferred to Ottawa to open the office. Over 11 years the office has grown, both internally and, more recently, through the acquisition of Synerlogic Inc. and The ACS Group. Currently its professional staff of 225 provides professional services to numerous production, technology, and service-based industries and government. Professionals in the Ottawa office represent more than 15 different universities and have a broad understanding of numerous industries, including manufacturing, health care, construction, and service organizations. Arthur Andersen & Co. employs more than 1,100 skilled professionals in Canada.

The Arthur Andersen & Co. Worldwide Organization operates through more than 231 offices in 49 countries and has more than 45,000 employees. The firm's major operating philosophy—the one-firm concept—ensures that each client has the benefit of a well-established information network. Arthur Andersen & Co. professionals are able to draw on a wide range of expertise to provide practical assistance to larger multinational corporations and smaller owner-managed businesses.

Above: The professionals at Arthur Andersen & Co. provide a wide range of expertise.

Below: Arthur Andersen & Co. has been offering professional services to the Ottawa area since 1977.

Among the elements that make Arthur Andersen & Co. unique are its centralized school for professional develoment at St. Charles, Illinois, and its emphasis on training, quality control, and innovation. Arthur Andersen & Co. is a leader in implementing computers in auditing, and has invested millions of dollars developing a worldwide network for computer auditing. Andersen Consulting is the leader in the planning, design, and installation of information systems.

In additon to providing services to the federal government and many of the capital region's businesses, Arthur Andersen & Co. professionals are also actively involved in many professional and community activities.

THE ENCON GROUP

The ENCON Group occupies a unique position in the insurance marketplace as the largest insurance management firm in Canada. ENCON develops and administers innovative insurance programs in the specialized markets of professional liability, construction, malpractice, and financial risks insurance. Among its principals are North America's leading insurance and reinsurance companies.

The firm's origins can be traced back to the early 1960s, when ENCON established the first comprehensive professional liability insurance program for architects and engineers in Canada.

ENCON Insurance Managers Inc., headquartered in Ottawa, is the Group's main operating subsidiary, offering professional, construction, and legal and medical liability insurance programs through its three main divisions: the Architects' and Engineers' and Directors' and Officers' Division, the Property/ Casualty Division, and the Special Risks Division.

John Tilley, P.Eng., vice-president engineering, carries out a site inspection.

An aerial view of the Annacis Bridge under construction near Vancouver, British Columbia.

The majority of professional architects and engineers in Canada subscribe to ENCON's professional liability programs. The programs are sponsored by the Royal Architectural Institute of Canada, the Association of Consulting Engineers of Canada, and the Canadian Council of Professional Engineers and have been since their inception.

ENCON's expertise in the professional liability field led to the development of the Directors' and Officers' Program by its in-house Research and Development Department. The expertise of this department has been applied to provide critical coverage for directors and officers of both profit and non-profit corporations.

The Property and Casualty Division evolved naturally from the firm's dealings with Canadian design consultants. Since 1972 this division has offered unique builders' risk coverages, comprehensive general liability coverages written on a wrap-up basis, and a number of general liability coverages for businesses involved in the construction industry.

This division's list of insured projects includes some of the largest and best-known construction projects in Canada over the past 17 years—namely Toronto Skydome, the Canadian Museum of Civiliza-

tion, the National Art Gallery, the Olympic Stadium in Montreal, James Bay hydroelectric project, and the Commonwealth Games Stadium.

The Special Risks Division provides liability coverage for legal and medical professionals and paraprofessionals, bailiffs, doctors, nurses, hospitals, ambulance operators, clinics, and laboratories. This division also offers a variety of miscellaneous errors and omissions insurance to a range of industries.

The Research and Development Department is constantly investigating new risks and evaluating the potential for the establishment of new programs. The Title Insurance Program, offering title insurance to new home owners, is a recent example of the work of the R&D Department.

The ENCON Group's other subsidiaries include ENCON Management Services Inc., based in Ottawa, offering management services in the healthcare, financial, actuarial, and claims management fields; ENCON Underwriting, which underwrites large-scale construction projects in the United States; and ENCON Reinsuance Managers Inc., a reinsurance broker, in Toronto.

The ENCON Group's head office in Ottawa employs 110 people.

Top: The National Gallery under construction in Ottawa.

Bottom: The Eaton's Centre with view of the CN Tower in Toronto, Ontario.

NEWVEN CONSULTING GROUP INC.

Especially appropriate for a world moving into the twenty-first century—an era of consultants and computers—Newven Consulting Group Inc. specializes in all aspects of computerization.

The nationally incorporated and Canadian-owned systems consulting firm provides quality services and products in both official languages to the private and public sectors. Its staff and resources are hired on a short-term (project) basis (from three months to three years) as an outside resource.

Newven Consulting started in November 1984 with a staff of six, five partners and a secretary, in a three-room office. From those humble beginnings the company has evolved to a team of 4 partners, a staff of 85, another 100 on call, and an office that occupies two floors at 81 Metcalfe Street. Newven Consulting, now one of the largest consulting firms in volume of work and personnel in the Ottawa region, is experiencing a second major expansion in Canada and the United States as a result of an increasing capital base.

"Newven Consulting is a rapidly growing enterprise," says president Ronald W. Allen. "We plan to double each division by the early 1990s."

The company's three divisions are consulting, turnkey application systems, and a newly added data-entry service.

The consulting division is its largest, and includes such diverse aspects of computer systems as custom design and development, facilities management and support, and equipment and package evaluation. With 22 full-time employees, more than 35 consultants and associates, plus an additional 100 the company can draw on, the division is responsible for more than $2 million of business each year.

The product development division offers a range of application software for both the IBM System 36 and PC systems. Packages are offered either on a custom-designed or general application "off-the-rack" basis, and Newven integrates hardware and software components.

IBM 36 packages include financial applications, a personal management system, a correspondence monitoring system, a large-scale maintenance-facilities management system, and a process manufacturing system. For microcomputers and IBM-compatible PCs Newven offers a comprehensive Rents Receivable Package for residential property managers, a legal administrative system, a sophisticated graphics package based on a technically state-of-the-art microcomputer configuration, a point-of-sale system, and an educational game package designed for educational institutions.

Newven has also developed a tape-to-diskette/diskette-to-tape conversion system based on microprocessing technologies and a disk-storage management system, both

The secure and modern data-entry production environment.

The market offices of Newven Consulting.

of which are available.

The data entry services division, added to the firm with its acquisition of the Dynakey Corporation in 1986, is one of the largest privately owned "shops" in the region. A million-dollar-per-year operation, it occupies most of one complete floor. The building, elevators, and office doors all have computer access codes, making the operation very secure, essential for its top-security work.

Fifty keystation operators work at the new Speed Keyer 5250 and the Key-Edit 1000, producing more than a half-billion keystrokes per year. The company also provides clients with in-house data-entry and related services.

The three division's clients include Canada Post, the Department of Regional and Industrial Expansion, Health and Welfare Canada, the Canadian Radio-Television Telecommunications Commission, Justice Canada, Public Archives Canada, the Bureau of Management Consulting, Transport Canada, Public Works Canada, Parks Canada, Johnson & Bloy Canada, Statistics Canada, Canada Mortgage and Housing Commission, Correctional Services Canada, the Treasury Board, Energy, Mines and Resources, Agriculture Canada, Canadian Home Builders' Association, Consumer and Corporate Affairs, CANMET, Community Nursing Registry of Canada, the National Research Council, the National Capital Commission, University of Ottawa, and numerous other public- and private-sector organizations.

Newven Consulting Group's four partners are Ronald W. Allen, J. Alan MacMillan, John Marion, and Kenneth C. Whittington.

Allen, the company's president, is responsible for marketing and overall strategy. He has 10 years of marketing experience and a wide range of data-processing experience, focussing on the areas of marketing, project management, analysis, development, and personnel management.

MacMillan, Newven's vice-president/finance, is a Certified General Accountant with 20 years' experience in financial management and accounting in the public and private sectors.

Marion has 10 years of experience in data processing, including management consulting, project management and control, information synthesis, conceptual systems design, hardware and software evaluations and analysis, and design of applications.

Whittington's career has been focussed on project management in packaged software in both evaluation and development. His real expertise is in asset management.

Newven is a company set firmly in the present yet linked directly to the future. There is, now more than ever, greater call for microcomputers; networking expertise to link PCs, minis, and mainframes; and fourth-generation languages.

The trend is for computer consultants to act as fine tuners and educators rather than traditional trainers, and to train company staff to modify actual programs. As well, as business becomes increasingly more productivity oriented, more consultants are needed to optimize and streamline these in-house programs.

Newven Consulting Group Inc. fills an increasingly important niche as the world progresses swiftly into the twenty-first century of high technology, computers, and consultants.

A member of the administrative support team.

COULTER FINANCIAL CORPORATION

Coulter Financial Corporation is a thriving enterprise today because it was founded on solid business practices. Since its beginning in 1975 the firm has been driven by a commitment to its customers to provide an unwavering standard of excellence in service.

For that reason Coulter, Canada's largest independent mortgage adviser, is recognized as the leader in its field. Financing for more than 60,000 capital region home purchases has been arranged through its services.

"We have always been guided by the principle that if you give people what they want out of life, you will never have to worry about the future," company president and founder Glen Coulter explains. "Satisfied clients tell their friends, and referrals and endorsements follow."

Until 1975 Coulter was an officer with a major bank but found that the rigidity in the system did not allow the flexibility necessary to meet the needs of real people. He knew there had to be a better way and decided to establish a service-oriented financial institution. Basing the operation of his mortgage brokerage on his service philosophy, Coulter has never looked back.

"Our achievement is a result of trust, skill, integrity, and dedication," he says. "I am proud of every one of our employees and of our clients, who have grown and succeeded through the assistance we've been able to offer."

What the firm offers primarily is the widest selection of home financing products available. Coulter maintains relationships with more than 40 mortgage lenders, allowing the company to find the right package for each client.

Along with this flexibility has come a high degree of efficiency. Through Coulter, mortgages can now be approved in as little as 15 minutes, 24 hours per day. The firm's six Ottawa offices open very early in the morning and remain open until late in the evening to be accessible to customers. Coulter mortgage brokers work more than bankers' hours.

That accessibility is in keeping with both the Coulter philosophy and the company's recipe for success. In 1987 alone Coulter placed more than $480 million worth of residential mortgages for more than 5,800 customers.

The firm prides itself on being more than a financial institution, though. Coulter brokers and agents are available to guide the home

Glen L. Coulter Financial Services Ltd. began in these quarters at 329 Waverly Street.

In October 1983 the firm moved to its new headquarters at 310 Somerset Street West.

buyer step by step through a purchase and are able to pre-approve financing for many properties and buyers.

The organization's success in the area of residential lending led it to expand into other areas, including its growing investment properties division.

Coulter's experienced investment professionals provide advice free, and then arrange financing for those who are in a position to acquire income-producing real estate. With experience in the acquisition of condominiums, apartments, town houses, duplexes, and retail property, the company is willing to lend money where traditional institutions express apprehension.

The reason for that is simple. Coulter believes in its clients and believes that when the customer profits, so does Coulter Financial Corporation. Its staff, trained to have a keen understanding of principles and their affect on investment, are capable of helping customers make the best investment decision.

Sometimes these investment decisions lead to vehicles other than real estate. To more fully meet the needs of a growing clientele, Coulter has developed services to assist investors in finding the best Guaranteed Investment Certificates (GICs), Term Deposits, and Registered Retirement Savings Plans (RRSPs). The firm's staff performs the task of tracking rates at all financial institutions—something most customers just do not have time for—and locates the best investments.

As well as offering this wide range of products and services to individuals, Coulter Financial Corporation is involved in all types of funding for commercial purposes. No mortgage in this area is too small or too large for the company to consider, with assistance offered at every stage, from the purchase of land to project completion.

The firm handles transactions to more than $20 million, and its experience in commercial lending is vast and varied, ranging from raw land to apartment buildings, industrial condominiums, strip plazas, retirement homes, and golf courses.

Coulter also enables small developers with good ideas to engage in larger deals by participating with them in joint-venture projects. The developer gains not only from the financial assistance, but also from Coulter's years of experience in commercial development.

"We're not just a lender, we're a partner," the company's president explains. "We realize that everyone has to start somewhere so we stay flexible and accessible."

Coulter Financial Corporation employs 130 people in its six Ottawa offices. Its success in the capital region has led it to open offices in London, Peterborough, Kingston, Burlington, Windsor, and Whitby.

Late-evening sunlight reflects from tables at an outdoor dining area on Parliament Hill. Photo by Wayne Eardley/ Burke Communications Photography

EPILOGUE

In the tradition of English literature, the epilogue of a given work is intended to round out the principal themes—to close the circle, as it were. More recently, however, epilogues have come to serve as a sort of apology, in the true sense of that word, an explanation or acknowledgement of the things that have been forgotten.

Writing about Ottawa was a difficult task in one way: it is almost impossible to take a snapshot of something that is moving as quickly as is this city. The best one can hope for is a kind of time-lapse photograph, like those intriguing images of cities at night in which the lights from the traffic appear to be festive ribbons swirling through the streets, and the people impressionistic blurs.

Ottawa is by no means an elder among the cities of the world. There are cities with older, grander buildings; there are cities also whose beauty is as breathtaking. But there are few cities indeed that hold the promise Ottawa does. As Francis Bacon wrote more than three centuries ago, "A man that is young in years may be old in hours, if he hath lost no time."

Ottawa is losing no time.

PATRONS

The following individuals, companies, and organizations have made a valuable commitment to the quality of this publication. Windsor Publications and the Ottawa-Carleton Board of Trade gratefully acknowledge their participation in *Ottawa: More Than a Capital City.*

Alphatext*
Annis, O'Sullivan, Vollebekk Ltd. Ontario Land Surveyors*
Arthur Andersen & Co.*
Aselford-Martin Ltd.*
Thomas C. Assaly Corporation Ltd.*
Atomic Energy of Canada Limited*
BA Banknote*
Bayshore Shopping Centre*
Bell Canada*
BNR*
Bradley/First Air*
Bristol-Myers Pharmaceutical Group*
Campeau Corporation*
Canada Post Corporation*
Central Precast Products (1979) Limited*
CFRA/CFMO-FM, A Division of CHUM Limited*
Children's Hospital of Eastern Ontario*
CJOH-TV*
CKBY-FM/W1310-AM*
Coopers & Lybrand*
Coulter Financial Corporation*
Digital Equipment of Canada Limited*
Dollco Printing*
DY-4 Systems Inc.*
Eastcan Beverages Limited*
The Encon Group*
M. Holitzner Limited*
Hulse and Playfair Funeral Homes*
Iber Developments Inc.*
IBM Canada Ltd.*
Industrial Trade & Consumer Shows Inc.*
David Ingram & Associates*
The JWI Group*
Love Printing*
Lumonics Inc.*
Mitel*
National Capital Commission*
Newven Consulting Group Inc.*
Nordion International Inc.*
Northern Telecom Electronics Limited*
OC Transpo*
Osler, Hoskin and Harcourt*
Ottawa Board of Education*
Ottawa Civic Hospital*
Ottawa Congress Centre*
Ottawa General Hospital*
Ottawa Hydro*
Price Waterhouse*
Prior Data Sciences*
Radisson Hotel Ottawa Centre*
Richcraft Homes*
Ricoh Corporation (Canada) Ltd.*
Scott & Aylen*
Soloway Wright*
STM Systems Corp.*
Touche Ross*
Unisys Canada Inc.*
The University of Ottawa*
Urbandale Realty Corporation Limited

*Participants in *Ottawa: More Than a Capital City.* The stories of these companies and organizations appear throughout the book.

BIBLIOGRAPHY

Algonquin College of Applied Arts and Technology. *Meridian Northern Telecom* 2, no. 1 (January 1988): 3-5.

Baer, Nicole. "Gatineau Park." *Ottawa Citizen* (December 29, 1987): D-1

Bennett, Sheila. *Ottawa: A portrait of the Nations Capital.* Willowdale: Gamer/ Hounslow, 1973

Benzing, Karen. "1987." *Ottawa Citizen* (December 29, 1987): D-1.

Bissonnette, John. "Construction Ahead." *Ottawa Business Life* (October 1987): 15, 39-40, 42-43, 46

Bociurkiw, Michael. "King of the Hill." *Globe and Mail* (November 14, 1987): D-1.

Bond, Courtney. *City of Ottawa.* Public Works, Ottawa: 1965.

------- *Where Rivers Meet: An Illustrated History of Ottawa.* Burlington: Windsor Publications, 1984.

Brault, Lucien. *Ottawa, Old and New.* Ottawa Historical Information Institute, 1946.

"Canada: World Leader in Communications Technology." *First Choice* 4, no. 1 (March 1985): 18-20.

Card, Brian. "A Case of Supply and Demand." *Ottawa Business Life.* (October 1987): 46.

City of Ottawa. "A Vision for Ottawa." *Ottawa Citizen* (October 24, 1987).

------- *Ottawa: An Economic Profile.* Economic Development Department, 1987.

"City of Ottawa: the dynamic other face." *Business and Finance* 4, no. 4: 10-11, 18

Crosby, Louise. "Carleton's Drug Research Centre a Canadian First." *Ottawa Citizen* (November 13, 1987): 1.

Diener, Seymour. "Capital Moves." *Business and Leisure/What's On* 30, no. 6: 6-17.

Eggleston, Wilfrid. *The Queen's Choice.* Ottawa: Queen's Printer, 1961.

Gibb-Carsley, Pamela. "Meeting the Divergent Needs of Maternity Care." *The General.* 1, no. 1: 1988.

Government of Canada. Department of Communications, *Communications Annual Report 1985-1986.* Ottawa: Ministry of Supply and Services Canada, 1986.

Kalman, H., and Roaf, J. *Exploring Ottawa.* University of Toronto Press: 1983.

Knight, David B. *Choosing Canada's Capital.* Toronto: McClelland and Stewart, 1977.

Mika, Nick and Helma. *Bytown. The early days of Ottawa.* Belleville: Mika Publishing Company, 1982.

National Capital Commission. *Bytown: a Guide to Lowertown Ottawa.* Ottawa, 1981

Neal, Christopher. "Ottawa is finally getting its tourism act together." *Ottawa Citizen.* (May 143, 1987): B-7.

"OCEDCO: a going concern." *Business and Finance* 4 No. 4 (April 1986): 36-37.

Ryan, Carolyn. "Patients Get Long Distance Healing." *Ottawa Citizen* (February 24, 1988): B-3.

"St. Paul University." *The Mainstreeter.* (June 1988): 13.

Stewart, Walter P. *The Village of Rockcliffe Park.* Ottawa: Walter Stewart Ltd., Publications Division, 1976.

Taylor, John H. *Ottawa. An Illustrated History.* Toronto: James Lorimer and National Musuem of Canada, 1976.

Uren, Janet. "Canada's Capital." *Business and Leisure* 30, no. 6: 51-55.

Wilson, Jane. "Breaking New Ground." *Ottawa Business Life* (March 1987): 15-19.

INDEX

PROFILE INDEX

GENERAL INDEX

Italicized entries indicate illustrations.